"Blending psychology, empirical analysis, and practical insight, Randall Kiser has long been an astute commentator on how lawyers can improve their thinking. This book explains how lawyers can both enhance their own mental health and remedy systemic injustices by placing greater emphasis on altruism. Read it!"

Jean Sternlight, *author,* Psychology for Lawyers, *Professor, UNLV Boyd School of Law, USA, and Founding Director, Saltman Center for Conflict Resolution*

"I've been a fan of Kiser's work since reading *Soft Skills* in 2017. This book is no exception. Its multidisciplinary exploration of the current state of the US legal system comes from a place of genuine concern and an underlying respect for all who are impacted by lawyers' choices."

Sarah Schendel, *Professor, Suffolk University Law School, USA*

"*Well-Being in the Legal Profession* illustrates how the profession has devalued altruism and the harm done to caring lawyers in the process. As lawyers are infected by the system's perverse incentives, justice for the people who depend on the system remains elusive. Kiser pushes us to grapple with this challenge."

Jonathan Rapping, *author,* Gideon's Promise, *and Professor and Director, Criminal Justice Certificate Program, Atlanta's John Marshall Law School, USA*

WELL-BEING IN THE LEGAL PROFESSION

This book provides a critical psychosocial analysis of legal practice, documenting a mental health crisis among lawyers and judges and linking this crisis to a dysfunctional legal system they continue to control.

Tracing studies of lawyers and judges over 40 years, this book demonstrates that decades of mental distress and social detachment in the legal profession have seriously damaged the legal system. Focusing largely on conditions in the United States but also drawing on studies from the UK, Canada, Germany, and Australia, the book depicts how this system is jeopardized by lawyers' egocentrism, depression, anxiety, suicidal ideation, and substance abuse. To improve the legal system and lawyers' mental health—integrating law, psychology, sociology, and policy making—the book advocates a renewed commitment to justice, compassion, respect, and fairness through an ethic of regenerative altruism.

This book will appeal to legal academics concerned with the sociology of legal practice, as well as those involved in training lawyers; it will also be of interest to practicing lawyers, judges, and others engaged by issues of social justice and legal reform.

Randall Kiser is Principal Analyst at DecisionSet®. He is the author of six books on lawyer and law firm performance. Mr. Kiser has taught professional skills courses for law students, lawyers, mediators, and judges throughout the world and is recognized as a leading scholar of the U.S. legal profession.

WELL-BEING IN THE LEGAL PROFESSION

Altruism, Justice, and Legal Reform

Randall Kiser

Routledge
Taylor & Francis Group
a GlassHouse Book

Designed cover image: cnythzl/Getty Images

First published 2025
by Routledge
4 Park Square, Milton Park, Abingdon, Oxon OX14 4RN

and by Routledge
605 Third Avenue, New York, NY 10158

Routledge is an imprint of the Taylor & Francis Group, an informa business

A GlassHouse book

British Library Cataloguing-in-Publication Data
A catalogue record for this book is available from the British Library

Library of Congress Cataloging-in-Publication Data
Names: Kiser, Randall, author.
Title: Well-being in the legal profession : altruism, justice, and legal reform / Randall Kiser.
Description: Abingdon, Oxon [UK] ; New York, NY : Routledge, 2025. | Includes bibliographical references and index.
Identifiers: LCCN 2024027375 (print) | LCCN 2024027376 (ebook) | ISBN 9781032847580 (hardback) | ISBN 9781032847658 (paperback) | ISBN 9781003514848 (ebook)
Subjects: LCSH: Lawyers—Psychological aspects. | Practice of law—Psychological aspects. | Happiness. | Altruism. | Law reform.
Classification: LCC K346 .K489 2025 (print) | LCC K346 (ebook) | DDC 340/.19—dc23/eng/20240621
LC record available at https://lccn.loc.gov/2024027375
LC ebook record available at https://lccn.loc.gov/2024027376

ISBN: 978-1-032-84758-0 (hbk)
ISBN: 978-1-032-84765-8 (pbk)
ISBN: 978-1-003-51484-8 (ebk)

DOI: 10.4324/9781003514848

Typeset in Sabon
by Apex CoVantage, LLC

CONTENTS

ACKNOWLEDGMENTS

In evaluating and upgrading lawyer and law firm performance for 48 years and writing six books on the subject, I have become indebted to many practitioners, judges, mediators, arbitrators, law school professors, and law firm leaders. Some of them have contributed directly to my research while others have contributed indirectly as models of service, achievement, integrity, and altruism. Their ideas have steadily and indelibly permeated my concepts of professional performance, especially in the domain of judgment and decision making.

Among law school professors, I am particularly grateful for the ingenuity, incisiveness, and scholarship of Sverre Blandhol, Neil Hamilton, William Henderson, Peter Huang, John Lande, the late Richard Nagareda, Jeffrey Rachlinski, Donna Shestowsky, James Stark, and Jean Sternlight. Among practitioners, arbitrators, mediators, and law firm consultants, I have greatly benefited from the sagacity and support of Robert Creo, Laura Kaster, Mark LeHocky, Michael Palmer, Gene Roberts, and Peter Zeughauser.

Jim Sandman, President Emeritus of the Legal Services Corporation and Director of the Future of the Profession Lab, University of Pennsylvania Carey Law School, also has served as an inspiration to me and an archetype of professional ethics and altruism. His dual careers as a law firm leader and public interest advocate demonstrate the enormous impact that a single, determined lawyer can have on thousands of lawyers and millions of citizens.

Since this book is intended for a broader audience than my previous books, I enlarged the circle of early reviewers and sought scrutiny from more editors. Thomas LeBien, a principal at Moon & Co. and the former Executive Editor at Harvard University Press, evaluated the first draft of the book and recommended changes that materially improved its structure, arguments, and narratives. Samantha Cassetta, the editor for all of my books, reviewed later drafts and applied her keen sense of organization, language, and reasoning, derived from decades of experience as an editor, author, and lawyer, to refine the book. Other critics provided valuable suggestions that corrected oversights in my initial analysis and introduced sources and ideas that challenged my preliminary thoughts.

Colin Perrin, a commissioning editor at Routledge, has been a highly effective proponent of the book's themes and correctives. His emphasis on interdisciplinary scholarship, socio-legal studies, and contemporary legal issues has been an ideal fit for this book. I am grateful for the confidence, commitment, and responsiveness he displayed throughout the peer review, contract, and production processes. The three anonymous peer reviews he obtained were particularly insightful and instructive. His editorial assistant, Naomi Round Cahalin, also merits special attention because she is a paradigm of efficiency and courtesy.

In writing all of my books, I have been the fortunate recipient of insightful criticism and continual support from my wife, Denise. Her background in science, technology, business, and education has provided perspectives that tested and ultimately enhanced many of the theories, conclusions, and recommendations in my books. The publication of this book coincides with our 40th anniversary, and I am deeply appreciative of the intellectual rigor and humanitarian values that she has always embodied and inspired others to emulate.

A final tribute is due to the thousands of disillusioned civil litigants, crime victims, criminal defendants, parolees, prisoners, lawyers, and judges I have seen in hundreds of courtrooms. They have struggled to realize justice in a system that is often administratively inefficient, financially destructive, personally demoralizing, and substantively unfair. Underpinning this book's emphasis on altruism are clear memories of their disappointment and chagrin as they left the courtrooms to return to their homes, jobs, jails, prisons, law offices, and chambers. We owe them a better legal system.

Randall Kiser
2024

1
OVERVIEW

This book delves into the mental health and egocentrism of lawyers and judges. It takes the controversial position that decades of mental distress and self-absorption in the legal profession have seriously damaged the civil and criminal legal systems. Americans are left with a legal system ranked next to last among the G10 industrial countries. As federal judge Marvin Aspen succinctly observed, "If you were to design a legal system today from scratch, you would regard the one we have as the worst imaginable."[1]

The mental health and egocentrism crises afflicting legal professionals have fostered a mindless bureaucracy posing as a justice system. This bureaucracy—reflecting the devolution of the courts from an aspiring justice system to a grim legal system—is unresponsive, unpredictable, unaccountable, and inhumane.[2] It lacks empathy, fairness, and respect and barely functions through a series of procedures, practices, and rituals favoring lawyers and affluent parties and substituting routines and formulas for justice. For most Americans who cannot afford lawyers, this system bars access to legal advice and representation, eviscerating their rights and dismissing their expectation of justice. Their disaffection, however, is inconsequential to the lawyers and judges benumbed by egocentrism and rendered insensible by chronic anxiety, depression, boredom, isolation, suicidal ideation, and substance abuse.

1 Mayer, Martin. (2006). *The judges* (p. 149). New York: St. Martin's Press.

2 See Bellin, Jeffrey. (2023). *Mass incarceration nation* (p. 3). New York: Cambridge University Press. ("[T]he criminal justice system was becoming a criminal legal system. Criminal courts were moving away from their core purpose: as a forum where citizens went to obtain justice. Courts were increasingly a place where the government went to enforce the law.")

DOI: 10.4324/9781003514848-1

The psychological health and social responsibilities of the lawyers and judges directing the legal system have evaded public scrutiny. Although attorneys and judges routinely evaluate and disrupt others' lives, the legal profession has largely avoided public accountability for its own members and their duties to society. This lack of accountability extends to lawyers' and judges' mental health, the effects of their mental health on the performance of duties owed to clients and the public, and the impact of their chronic self-absorption on society's willingness and ability to effectuate justice for citizens at all income levels. The public does not know whether attorneys and judges lead happy, healthy, and fulfilling lives, or whether they, like some of the people they represent or preside over, are demoralized participants in an expensive, protracted process that eventually wears them down. Nor does the public know whether lawyers and judges are fulfilling their responsibilities to improve the legal system or whether they have become inured to a system that disappoints its constituencies while protecting its functionaries.

This book gets behind lawyers' and judges' flat composure to assess their mental health and social contributions. It shows how widespread mental distress and egocentrism in the legal profession disserve clients and harm the legal system. It then explains why increased altruism would be the most effective step in simultaneously enhancing individual well-being and upgrading the legal system. Accentuating altruism and correlated traits like courage, compassion, and creativity, the book injects crucial ideas, principles, and findings that can quickly and reliably elevate individual well-being and promote justice. As Rosalie Silberman Abella, a former Supreme Court of Canada justice, urges, "we need to put compassion back in the service of law and law in the service of humanity. We need the rule of justice, not just the rule of law. Otherwise, what's the point of law? Or lawyers?"[3]

This introductory chapter serves as a preview and summary of the book's themes. It describes the mental health challenges confronting attorneys and judges, identifies major deficiencies in the civil and criminal legal systems, and shows how altruistic values and actions can improve individual mental health and the quality of justice. The chapter ends with an overview of the book's organization and the purpose and content of each chapter.

Attorneys' and judges' mental health

The American legal system is dysfunctional, and many attorneys practicing within it are depressed, stressed, anxious, bored, lonely, and suicidal.

3 Abella, Rosalie Silberman. (2023, August 14). In this mean-spirited moral free-for-all, we need to put justice back in charge. *The Washington Post*.

They also exhibit high levels of alcohol and drug abuse. Judges, too, report problematic levels of stress, anxiety, secondary trauma, depression, isolation, boredom, and alcohol use. The dysfunctionality of the legal system and the epidemic of mental illness in the legal profession have been treated as unrelated problems, yet it is impossible for society to provide an accessible, responsive legal system when many of the people who operate and evaluate it are mentally unhealthy. They neither recognize nor remedy the consequences of the legal system that they established, manage, and sustain. They continue to control the legal system, but they do not take responsibility for it.

The legal profession's mental health crisis has been evident, yet largely ignored, for 40 years.[4] As psychologist Andrew Benjamin notes, "a third of the actively practicing lawyers, in any given jurisdiction, are either suffering from depression or dysphoria (a combination of depression, anxiety, hostility, or alcoholism) or both. That data has not changed over the years."[5]

Mental health experts, law professors, lawyers, sociologists, and management consultants have consistently observed high levels of depression, anxiety, and substance abuse among attorneys. They also confirm the serious risks that mental illness poses to clients and society:

- "The legal profession has known for decades that its members suffer from mental illness and addiction in staggering numbers, and firms largely have been unmoved by the moral case for change."[6] (Law professor Jerrod Reich).
- "The United States legal profession is in the midst of a cultural reckoning related to the mental health and well-being of its members. Recent national reports indicate that lawyers suffer from exceedingly high rates of depression, anxiety, and substance misuse. For example, in a large nationwide study of 12,825 licensed, currently practicing attorneys, 28% reported symptoms of depression, 23% indicated having mild to extremely severe stress, and 20.6% engaged in problematic drinking. However, this problem extends beyond the individual lawyer and has the potential to impact not only clients but also the legal system more

4 See Benjamin, G. Andrew H., et al. (1986). The role of legal education in producing psychological distress among law students and lawyers. *American Bar Foundation Research Journal*, *11*(2), 225. Benjamin, G. Andrew H., et al. (1990). The prevalence of depression, alcohol abuse, and cocaine abuse among United States lawyers. *International Journal of Law & Psychiatry*, *13*(3), 233.

5 Benjamin, Andrew. (2020, February 3). Beyond the A, episode 5—Dr. Andrew Benjamin. (podcast). https://beyondthea.co/articles/2020/2/25/episode-5-dr-andrew-benjamin-university-of-washington-clinical-professor-of-psychology-and-affiliate-professor-of-law.

6 Reich, Jarrod F. (2020). Capitalizing on healthy lawyers: The business case for law firms to promote and prioritize lawyer well-being. *Villanova Law Review*, *65*(2), 418.

broadly."[7] (Psychiatry professor Justin Anker and addiction counselor and researcher Patrick Krill).

- "To be a good lawyer, one has to be a healthy lawyer. Sadly, our profession is falling short when it comes to well-being. [Studies] reveal that too many lawyers and law students experience chronic stress and high rates of depression and substance use. These findings are incompatible with a sustainable legal profession, and they raise troubling implications for many lawyers' basic competence. This research suggests that the current state of lawyers' health cannot support a profession dedicated to client service and dependent on the public trust."[8] (American Bar Association National Task Force on Lawyer Well-being).
- "Lawyers drink excessively at higher rates than the general population. In particular, lawyers drink excessively at much higher rates than other groups of highly educated professionals. Moreover, problematic drinking among lawyers has grown considerably worse over the last decade, with today's rates of problematic drinking more than 50% above the rates reported in the mid-2000s. Problematic drinking rates among lawyers are highest among young lawyers and those working at large law firms. Alcohol abuse appears to be a particular problem for lawyers, and one that has recently grown much worse."[9] (Law school professor Yair Listokin and attorney Raymond Noonan).
- "According to the American Bar Association, in 2016, there were 1,335,963 'active resident attorneys' in the United States. This number suggests that between 288,000 and 488,000 lawyers 'qualify as problem drinkers.' And either [as] a subset of this number or independent of this number there are about 379,000 lawyers suffering from depression, 257,000 from anxiety, and 312,000 from stress symptoms."[10] (Attorney John Barkett, Shook, Hardy & Bacon LLP).
- "Since the mid-20th century, scores of studies and reports from around the world have explored the prevalence and damaging consequences of psychological ill-health among law students and lawyers, putting beyond doubt the scope and magnitude of the mental health problem within the

7 Anker, Justin, & Krill, Patrick R. (2021). Stress, drink, leave: An examination of gender-specific risk factors for mental health problems and attrition among licensed attorneys. *PLoS ONE*, *16*(5), e0250563. https://doi.org/10.1371/journal.pone.0250563.

8 American Bar Association National Task Force on Lawyer Well-Being. (2017, August). *The path to lawyer well-being: Practical recommendations for positive change* (p. 1). Chicago: American Bar Association.

9 Listokin, Yair, & Noonan, Raymond. (2021, March). Measuring lawyer well-being systematically: Evidence from the National Health Interview Survey. *Journal of Empirical Legal Studies*, *18*(1), 4, 5.

10 Barkett, John M. (2019). *The ethics of lawyers needing assistance* (p. 3). Miami: Shook, Hardy & Bacon L.L.P.

legal profession globally."[11] (Carly Schrever, Judicial Well-being Advisor, Judicial College of Victoria).

These findings indicate that many lawyers entrusted to exercise sound judgment on behalf of their clients may not be sufficiently healthy to direct their own lives, let alone their clients' lives and the nation's legal system.

Despite the alarming incidence of mental illness among lawyers, state bar associations and law firms generally eschew mandatory mental health assessments and third-party interventions. They accede to lawyers' demands for autonomy and privacy in diagnosing and treating the widespread mental illness in the legal profession. The freedom accorded to lawyers to practice self-care and self-regulation, however, is undeserved because many attorneys lack the self-knowledge, maturity, and expertise necessary to accurately diagnose and treat their own mental illness. Those attorneys are oblivious to their afflictions and resistant to treatment, placing clients, society, and themselves at risk. If self-care and self-regulation had the ameliorative effects espoused by lawyers and the organized bar, the legal profession would not have experienced the mental health crisis extensively documented during the last 40 years.

Judges' mental health appears to be better than lawyers' mental health, but it remains problematic. About one-half of judges report that they experience vicarious trauma (emotional distress caused by exposure to another person's traumatic experiences), and one-fourth of judges in a survey of 1,034 judges "met criteria for stress at a level that could be debilitating."[12] Roughly 20 percent of judges "meet at least one criteria for depressive disorder." They report serious symptoms of depression, including "irritable, short-tempered, sarcastic"; "fatigue and low energy"; "interference with attention and concentration"; "ruminate or worry about cases after they are decided"; "not having the initiative to do things I used to do"; "preoccupation with negative thoughts"; and "can't wait for the day's work to end." Judges' level of problematic alcohol use (10 percent) is considerably lower than attorneys' level (21 percent), but it is notably higher than the general population's level (7 percent). Reflecting their isolation and self-protectiveness, only 37 percent of judges currently ask for peer support in managing their stress, although 83 percent indicate they are "interested in" that possibility.

The effects of stress on judges are pervasive and detrimental. As criminal justice professor Monica Miller explains, "judges are constantly exposed to stress. These stressors can affect individual judges as well as the entire judicial

11 Schrever, Carly, et al. (2021, May). Where stress presides: Predictors and correlates of stress among Australian judges and magistrates. *Psychiatry, Psychology and Law*, 29(2), 290. (citations omitted).

12 Data and quotations in this paragraph appear in Swenson, David, et al. (2020). Stress and resiliency in the U.S. judiciary. *Journal of the Professional Lawyer*, 13, 14.

system. As a result, anyone in the system (defendants, victims, etc.) could be adversely affected by a stressed-out judge."[13]

The aggregate effect of mentally distressed attorneys and judges is catastrophic. The legal system invariably suffers from the manifestations of their mental illnesses—low interest, motivation, and energy; decreased empathy, compassion, and perspective-taking; reluctance to seek out new information and sources to facilitate problem solving; extreme risk aversion and avoidance of novel solutions; deficient analytic thinking, planning, creative insight, and problem solving; and overreliance on habitual brain circuits.[14] Impaired attorneys and judges, in short, exhibit impaired executive function.

The symptoms of attorneys' and judges' mental illnesses permeate the legal system and have prevented intelligent, timely change. That system is as moribund as the attorneys and judges directing it. Our continued neglect of the legal profession's mental health crisis and its harmful effects is a grave disservice to the citizens who rely on the legal system and bear the consequences when it fails them.

The dysfunctional legal system

The United States is unique among industrialized countries in having a robust economy and a weak legal system. Although its economy generates the highest GDP per capita among the G20 countries, its legal system is ranked #8 among those countries and #26 in the world. Its rank in "Rights and Voice"—a measure of access to justice, equal protection, and judicial impartiality—is #51, slightly above Mongolia, Senegal, and Serbia. The United States' ranking has steadily deteriorated for nearly 15 years.[15]

13 Miller, Monica K., et al. (2018, Winter/Fall). Judges and stress: An examination of outcomes predicted by the model of judicial stress. *Judicature*, *102*(3), 60.

14 Bishop, Sonia J., & Gagne, Christopher. (2018). Anxiety, depression, and decision making: A computational perspective. *Annual Review of Neuroscience*, *41*, 371. Lawlor, Victoria M., et al. (2019). Dissecting the impact of depression on decision making. *Psychological Medicine*, *50*(10), 1. Leykin, Yan, et al. (2011). Decision-making and depressive symptomatology. *Cognitive Therapy and Research*, *35*(4), 333. Snyder, Hannah R. (2013). Major depressive disorder is associated with broad impairments on neuropsychological measures of executive function: A meta-analysis and review. *Psychological Bulletin*, *139*(1), 81. On the role of depression in creativity, see Baas, Matthijs. (2019). In the mood for creativity. In Kaufman, James C., & Sternberg, Robert J. (Eds.). *The Cambridge handbook of creativity* (p. 257). New York: Cambridge University Press. Heilman, Kenneth M. (2005). *Creativity and the brain*. New York: Taylor & Francis Group.

15 Data regarding the United States' ranking is from the World Justice Project's 2023 WJP Rule of Law Index. https://worldjusticeproject.org/rule-of-law-index/. Social Progress Imperative. 2024 Social Progress Index. www.socialprogress.org/2024-social-progress-index/. Data regarding changes in the rankings between 2010 and 2023 appear in previous versions of the World Justice Project's reports. See also Figure 5.1, "Ranking of U.S. Legal Systems" in

In the specific categories of criminal justice and civil justice the United States' global rank is #29 and #38, respectively. Its criminal justice scores are especially low in due process of the law; impartiality; timeliness, and effectiveness in adjudication; and effectiveness of the correctional system in reducing illegal behavior. Its civil justice scores are particularly low in timeliness; accessibility and affordability; and freedom from discrimination. These world rankings indicate that nearly every critical element of an effective and just legal system is broken or missing in the United States: the administration of justice is discriminatory; due process is compromised; the prisons are ineffectual; citizens cannot afford legal services and lack access to courts; and court processes and procedures cause costly, unreasonable delays.

Lack of public trust and confidence in the legal system

As indicated by its low global rankings, the U.S. legal system has failed to earn the trust and confidence of its citizens. Only 27 percent of surveyed citizens have "a great deal" or "quite a lot" of confidence in the U.S. Supreme Court.[16] Thirty-seven percent say they have "some" confidence in it, while 34 percent express "very little" confidence in it. Most people (58 percent) say they disapprove of "the way the Supreme Court is handling its job," while a minority (41 percent) approve of its actions. The Gallup organization reports that public confidence in the U.S. Supreme Court has "reached a new low in Gallup's nearly 50-year trend," and the recent "11-point drop in confidence in the Supreme Court is roughly double what it is for most institutions that experienced a decline."

Citizens express low levels of confidence in other courts as well. Only 57 percent of surveyed citizens have confidence in the federal courts, and only 61 percent have confidence in the state courts.[17] When asked whether state courts "provide equal justice to all," 48 percent respond, "not well" or "not at all well." As one survey respondent remarked, "It's just an underlying fact that if you have money, if you have connections . . .[then] you have

Kiser, Randall. (2023). *Professional judgment for lawyers* (p. 129). Cheltenham, UK and Northampton, MA: Edward Elgar Publishing.

16 Survey results in this paragraph appear in Gallup. Supreme Court. https://news.gallup.com/poll/4732/supreme-court.aspx. Jones, Jeffrey M. (2022, June 23). *Confidence in U.S. Supreme Court sinks to historic low.* https://news.gallup.com/poll/394103/confidence-supreme-court-sinks-historic-low.aspx.

17 Data and quotations in this paragraph and the following paragraph, except the Kourlis quotation in fn. 18, appear in GBAO. (2023, December 18). 2023 state of the state courts—national survey analysis. GBAO. (2021, October 29). 2021 state of the state courts—national survey analysis. IAALS. (2020, August 27). Trusting the public's perception of our justice system. Legal Services Corporation. (2022, April). *The justice gap: The unmet legal needs of low-income Americans.* National Center for State Courts. (2021). State of the state courts 2021.

the ability to fight a case and win it." When asked whether state courts are fair and impartial, only 51 percent of citizens respond affirmatively, while 42 percent believe that courts do not meet this basic expectation. The National Center for State Courts reports that "public trust in the courts and other institutions is waning," and its surveys show that "the real threat for the court system is the widespread deterioration in trust we have seen."

The lack of trust in the legal system is acute among ethnic minority and low-income citizens. Only 32 percent of African Americans believe state courts "provide equal justice to all," and only 28 percent of low-income Americans believe that "people like me are treated fairly in the system." A minority of low-income Americans, only about four out of ten, believe that the legal system "can help people like me solve important problems" and "people like me can use the system to protect and enforce rights." The pervasive lack of trust in the legal system reflects what Rebecca Love Kourlis, a former justice of the Colorado Supreme Court, calls a "profound reality: people do not trust the system because the system is not trustworthy."[18]

Even judges acknowledge that the legal system is failing to provide equal justice. When asked, "Do you believe that systemic racism exists in the criminal justice system?" 65 percent of judges responded, "Yes."[19] Research regarding judges' sentencing decisions substantiates their concerns. Federal sentencing data, for example, shows that, after adjustments for crime severity and a defendant's conviction history, "blacks receive sentences that are almost 10 percent longer than those of comparable whites arrested for the same crimes."[20]

Attorneys' negative perceptions of the legal system

Attorneys, like judges, express serious reservations about the legal system. They also have low opinions of each other. Summarizing results from their extensive survey of 7,805 attorneys, law professor Lawrence Krieger and psychologist Kennon Sheldon state, "this large sample of professionals has a positive view of neither the justice in the justice system nor the professional behavior of professionals in the system—a very troubling finding and a call to action for legal educators and bar leaders."[21]

18 Kourlis, Rebecca Love. (2019, September 13). Public trust and confidence in the legal system: The way forward. https://iaals.du.edu/blog/public-trust-and-confidence-legal-system-way-forward.

19 Firth, Anna-Leigh. (2020, July 14). Most judges believe the criminal justice system suffers from racism. *Judicial Edge Today*.

20 Starr, Sonja B. (2014). Racial disparity in criminal sentences. *Journal of Political Economy*, *122*(60), 1320. See O'Hear, Michael, & Wheelock, Darren. (2021, June). Life "with" or "without"? An empirical study of homicide sentencing. *Journal of Empirical Legal Studies*, *18*(2), 409.

21 Krieger, Lawrence S., & Sheldon, Kennon M. (2015). What makes lawyers happy?: A data-driven prescription to redefine professional success. *The George Washington Law Review*, *83*, 554, 612.

Other surveys indicate that law firm partners think that associate attorneys are not meeting their basic fiduciary duty to put their clients' needs and interests above their own. Thirty-six percent of surveyed partners agree with the statement, "The younger lawyers in my firm put their own needs and interests ahead of those of the firm and our clients."[22] Only 28 percent of partners *dis*agree with that statement. Male Millennial generation partners have an even lower opinion of associate attorneys' professionalism; 41 percent of those partners believe that associates take care of their own needs and interests first.

Associate attorneys, for their part, contend that law firms are discriminatory and exploitative—and their leaders are ineffective has-beens. Associates have little or no confidence in law firms' business model or their leadership, as shown by these results from large surveys of Gen Z and Millennial generation attorneys[23]:

- 54 percent believe that "the law firm business model is fundamentally broken."
- 56 percent agree that "the current generation of law firm leadership has outstayed their effectiveness."
- 72 percent believe that the COVID-19 pandemic "has revealed how law firm leverage models favor partners at the expense of associates."
- 70 percent concur that "law firm culture is inherently biased against women." (84 percent of female attorneys believe this bias exists.)
- 65 percent report that "law firm culture is inherently biased against racially diverse lawyers."

In yet another sign of associates' disaffection and partners' disengagement, less than one-half of Gen Z associates believe that "the partners at my firm genuinely care about associate professional development."

22 Cartusciello, Yolanda, et al. (2020, March). *Multiple generations in law firms* (p. 93). Washington, DC: NALP and PP&C Consulting.

23 Data in this paragraph appears in Fivel, Michelle, & Bhatt, Ru. (2019). *2019 millennial attorney survey: New expectations, evolving beliefs and shifting career goals*. Washington, DC: Major, Lindsey & Africa. Major, Lindsey & Africa. (2021). *Making their mark: How millennial lawyers could reshape the industry*. Washington, DC: Major, Lindsey & Africa. Major, Lindsey & Africa. (2023). *Searching for balance: Millennial lawyers' perspectives on the legal industry*. Washington, DC: Major, Lindsey & Africa. Major, Lindsey & Africa. (2023). *Gen-Z: Now influencing today's law firm culture*. Washington, DC: Major, Lindsey & Africa.

Public distrust of attorneys

Attorneys generally have a low opinion of other attorneys; partners and associates have serious misgivings about each other; and, it turns out, the public doesn't like them much either. Most U.S. residents know someone who is a lawyer; and when asked to think of people they trust and then specify how many of them are lawyers, most residents designate "0."[24]

Only 16 percent of the public has a high opinion of lawyers' honesty and ethical standards.[25] The public's opinions of lawyers' honesty and ethics are distressingly below their opinions of two other professions—doctors (67 percent high opinion) and accountants (42 percent high opinion). These results are replicated in Australian surveys. Only 26 percent of Australians rate the legal profession as being "high" or "very high" in ethics and honesty, while 82 percent and 38 percent rate doctors and accountants, respectively, as being high or very high in ethics and honesty.[26] Attorneys' comparatively low ratings stem from public perceptions that lawyers are "greedy," "make too much money," and "use the legal system to protect the powerful and get rich."[27] As one attorney notes, "Just as people are not born bigots, the public was not born hating lawyers—we earned that distinction."[28]

Public perceptions of attorneys have plummeted while attorneys' preoccupation with money has soared. Federal judge Laurence Silberman finds that, as lawyers' status in society has declined, "they have been driven to acquire more property."[29] This is a decades-long shift, as he recalls: "When I entered Harvard Law School in 1958, Dean Griswold told the entire assembled class that if we wished to earn a great deal of money we should go across the river to the business school. Oh, we would certainly do all right, but a lawyer's satisfaction came largely from the value of the service he or she performed to

24 These survey results are reported by NORC University of Chicago in The General Social Survey (gssdataexplorer.norc.org). The survey questions are "Do you know a woman or a man who is a lawyer?"; "How many are lawyers?"; and "Now I'm going to ask you some questions about people that you trust . . . How many are lawyers?".

25 Brenan, Megan, & Jones, Jeffrey M. (2024, January 22). *Ethics ratings of nearly all professions down in U.S.* https://news.gallup.com/poll/608903/ethics-ratings-nearly-professions-down.aspx.

26 Roy Morgan. (2021, April 27). Roy Morgan image of professions survey 2021 (Article No. 8691). https://www.roymorgan.com/findings/roy-morgan-image-of-professions-survey-2021-in-a-year-dominated-by-covid-19-health-professionals-including-nurses-doctors-and-pharmacists-are-the-most-highly-regarded-but-almost-all-professions-d.

27 See Galanter, March. (1998, Spring). The faces of mistrust: The image of lawyers in public opinion, jokes, and political discourse. *University of Cincinnati Law Review*, 66, 805.

28 Weiss, Debra Cassens. (2007, December 13). Lawyer depression comes out of the closet. *ABA Journal* (Attorney comments).

29 Silberman, Laurence H. (1998, Spring). Will lawyering strangle democratic capitalism?: A retrospective. *Harvard Journal of Law & Public Policy*, *21*(2), 615.

society as a whole."[30] The contemporary version of this story might depict the dean of the business school advising students to transfer to law school if money was the driver in their lives. Median salaries of new Harvard Law School graduates exceed those of new Harvard Business School graduates, and large law firms like Milbank and Davis Polk pay higher salaries for new graduates than major consulting firms like McKinsey & Company and Bain & Company pay for new MBA graduates.[31]

Outcomes of civil and criminal justice systems

Perceptions of the legal system are distressingly negative, and the outcomes of that system are consistently baneful. On the civil side, "most of the civil justice problems that Americans experience receive no legal attention of any kind, ever. They never make it to court. They never receive consideration from any kind of legal professional such as a lawyer."[32] Low-income citizens, in particular, have scant access to legal assistance; 93 percent of low-income citizens who experience a legal problem receive no or inadequate legal help.[33] The Institute for the Advancement of the American Legal System estimates that 120 million legal problems are *not* resolved fairly each year.[34] Even when citizens are able to access legal processes to resolve disputes, only 48 percent report that the problem "is done and fully resolved."[35]

On the criminal law side, the United States is best known for mass incarceration, the ghoulish outcome of a system sometimes characterized as "point-and-convict adjudication."[36] The focus on mass incarceration, how-

30 Oral History Project, Historical Society of the District of Columbia. (2019). *Honorable Lawrence H. Silberman* (p. 213). https://dcchs.org/sb_pdf/complete-oral-history-laurence-silberman/.

31 See Lake, Sydney. (2022, June 24). Harvard Law School vs. Harvard Business School—here's a look at their paychecks. *Fortune*. Randazzo, Sara. (2021, June 12). Entry-level lawyers are now making $200,000 a year. *The Wall Street Journal*.

32 Sandefur, Rebecca L. (2019, Winter). Access to what? *Daedelus*, *148*(1), 49.

33 Legal Services Corporation, *supra* note 17. See Poggio, Marco. (2023, November 30). Gap in access to legal assistance remains wide, ABA finds. *Law 360*. ("On average, there are about 2.8 paid legal aid lawyers for every 10,000 U.S. residents living on or below the federal poverty threshold.") Reynolds, Matt. (2023, November 30). 2023 "Profile of the legal profession" report spotlights the scarcity of legal aid lawyers. *ABA Journal*. ("But some sobering news is that of the 1.3 million lawyers in the United States, only around 10,000—that's barely three-quarters of 1%—are full-time legal aid lawyers.").

34 Institute for the Advancement of the American Legal System. (2021). *Justice in a changing world: 2021 annual report*. https://iaals.du.edu/sites/default/files/documents/annual-reports/iaals_2021_annual_report.pdf.

35 World Justice Project. (2019). *Global insights on access to justice*. https://worldjusticeproject.org/sites/default/files/documents/WJP-A2J-2019.pdf.

36 The term "point-and-convict adjudication" appears in Neily, Clark, (2020, June 7). *America's criminal justice system is rotten to the core*. www.cato.org/blog/americas-criminal-justice-system-rotten-core. Neily is the senior vice president for legal studies at the Cato Institute.

ever, obscures the insidious reach of the criminal legal system. Although nearly two million citizens are incarcerated in jails or prisons, four million other citizens are on parole and probation. The increase in citizens subjected to "community supervision" mirrors the increase in incarcerated citizens: "From 1980 to 2020, the incarceration rate grew by 251% (from 146 to 367 people per 100,000), whereas the community supervision rate grew 238% (from 179 to 426 people per 100,000)." The expansion of community supervision has been an abject failure. After examining data from all 50 states, Vincent Schiraldi, the former commissioner of the New York City Departments of Probation and Correction, determined that it "has failed to achieve its two primary goals: reducing incarceration and improving public safety. In fact, we found that these practices *increase* incarceration with so many imprisoned for technical violations and that states with more parolees actually had more, not less, crime."

Mass incarceration

The United States usually has the highest jail and prison population and the highest incarceration rate of any country in the world.[37] Although it has only five percent of the world's population, the United States confines about 25 percent of the world's prisoners.[38] Its incarceration rate is five times more per capita than it was 40 years ago. Black Americans, moreover, are "incarcerated at a rate (600 per 100,000) more than three times the rate for whites (184 per 100,000)."[39] To sustain these incarceration rates, millions of Americans would have to be arrested annually. One in ten Americans, accordingly, have been arrested for a non-traffic violation by age 15, and one in three Americans have been arrested for a non-traffic violation by age 23.[40] If all

---

The data and other quotations in this paragraph are from Lopoo, Evangeline, et al. (2023). How little supervision can we have? *Annual Review of Criminology*, 6, 23. Schiraldi, Vincent. (2023, October 16). Parole and probation don't work. *The Washington Post.*

37 Gramlich, John. (2021, August 16). American's incarceration rate falls to lowest level since 1995. *Pew Research Center.* In some recent periods, the incarceration rate and the total number of incarcerated individuals in the United States have declined due to COVID-19 related releases, legal reforms, and court slowdowns. During these periods, China had the highest number of incarcerated individuals, and El Salvador, Cuba, Rwanda, and Turkmenistan had higher incarceration rates than the United States' rates. See Bellin, Jeffrey. (2023, February 3). We can ensure public safety and still reduce incarceration. *Law 360.* Institute for Crime & Justice Policy Research. World prison brief. www.prisonstudies.org.

38 Collier, Lorna. (2014, October). Incarceration nation. *Monitor on Psychology*, *45*(9).

39 Zhen, Zeng, & Minton, Todd D. (2021, March). *Jail inmates in 2019.* U.S. Department of Justice. https://bjs.ojp.gov/content/pub/pdf/ji19.pdf.

40 Data in this sentence and the next sentence appears in Friedman, Matthew. (2015, November 17). Just facts: As many Americans have criminal records as college diplomas. *Brennan Center for Justice.* Smith, James P. (2018). The long term economic impact of

arrested Americans congregated as a nation, it would be the 18th largest nation in the world—larger than France.

Nearly 500,000 Americans are imprisoned awaiting trial.[41] They have not been convicted of a crime but are held in pre-trial detention despite the oft-cited presumption of innocence. Only 29 percent of the individuals confined in local jails are serving a sentence or awaiting sentencing following a conviction; the other 71 percent have not been convicted of a crime and are awaiting court action. The number of ostensibly innocent citizens in pre-trial detention now exceeds the total number of citizens incarcerated in 1980.

Mass incarceration owes its deplorable success, in part, to lengthy sentences. Fifty-seven percent of incarcerated Americans are serving a sentence of ten or more years, and 15 percent are serving a life sentence.[42] American citizens serve sentences that are five to ten times longer than sentences imposed on French citizens for similar crimes and three to twelve times longer than the sentences typically imposed on German and Dutch citizens.[43] These severe prison sentences generally serve no legitimate purpose because long sentences do not deter crime or reduce recidivism and have been correlated with higher crime and recidivism.[44]

---

criminalization in American childhoods. *Crime & Delinquency*, *65*(3), 422. See Weidner, Justin. (2018). 1 in 3 Americans arrested by age 25 [chart]. *DB Global Markets Research*.

41 Data in this paragraph is reported in U.S. Department of Justice, Office of Justice Programs. (2022, December 20). *U.S. jail population increased while prison population decreased in 2021* [Press release]. https://www.ojp.gov/files/archives/pressreleases/2022/us-jail-population-increased-while-prison-population-decreased-2021.

42 Vera Institute of Justice. (2023, February). A new paradigm for sentencing in the United States. https://www.vera.org/publications/a-new-paradigm-for-sentencing-in-the-united-states.

43 American Civil Liberties Union, & The Sentencing Project. (2022). *Racial disparities in sentencing in the United States* (p. 1). Bellin, *supra* note 2 at 129. Vera Institute of Justice. (2013). *Sentencing and prison practices in Germany and the Netherlands: Implications for the United States*. https://www.vera.org/publications/sentencing-and-prison-practices-in-germany-and-the-netherlands-implications-for-the-united-states.

44 For studies of sentencing severity effects on crime and recidivism rates see Blumstein, Alfred. (2002). Youth, guns, and violent crime. *The Future of Children*, *12*(2), 38. Doob, Anthony N., & Webster, Cheryl Marie (2003). Sentence severity and crime: Accepting the null hypothesis. *Crime & Justice*, *30*, 143. Green, Donald P., & Winik, Daniel. (2010). Using random judge assignments to estimate the effects of incarceration and probation on recidivism among drug offenders. *Criminology*, *48*(2), 357. Grogger, Jeffrey T. (2000). An economic model of recent trends in violence. In Blumstein, Alfred, & Wallman, Joel (Eds.). *The crime drop in America* (p. 266). New York: Cambridge University Press. Harding, David J., et al. (2017). Short-and long-term effects of imprisonment on future felony convictions and prison admissions. *Proceedings of the National Academy of Sciences*, *114*(42), 11103. Hawken, Angel, & Kleiman, Mark. (2009). *Managing drug involved probationers with swift and certain sanctions: Evaluating Hawaii's HOPE (Document No. 229023)*. Washington, DC: National Institute of Justice. Loeffler, Charles E., & Nagin, Daniel S. (2022). The impact of incarceration on recidivism. *Annual Review of Criminology*, *5*, 133. Loughran, Thomas A., et al. (2009).

Although the likelihood of apprehension has a deterrent effect on crime, increasing the severity of punishment is not an effective deterrent. People contemplating unlawful actions "know little about the sanctions for specific crimes" and do not engage in prospective cost-benefit analyses based on judges' sentencing guidelines.[45] As criminologists Anthony Doob, Cheryl Marie Webster, and Rosemary Gartner explain, "we know of no reputable criminologist who has looked carefully at the overall body of research literature on 'deterrence through sentencing' who believes that crime rates will be reduced, through deterrence, by raising the severity of sentences handed down in criminal courts."[46] Long prison sentences, ironically, sometimes increase crime: "inmates learn more effective crime strategies from each other, and time spent in prison may desensitize many to the threat of future imprisonment."[47]

Attorneys deflect responsibility for mass incarceration by claiming that they are only enforcing laws enacted by the legislature. This argument is misleading because prosecutors have been actively involved in lobbying for more criminal laws and harsher punishments. In California, for instance, prosecutors have lobbied "for a preferred legislative outcome for

---

Estimating a dose-response relationship between length of stay and future recidivism in serious juvenile offenders. *Criminology*, *47*(3), 699. Mears, Daniel P., et al. (2016). Recidivism and time served in prison. *The Journal of Criminal Law & Criminology*, *106*(1), 81. Nagin, Daniel. (2013). Deterrence in the twenty-first century: A review of the evidence. *Crime and Justice*, *42*, 199. Pryzybylski, Roger, et al. (2022, November). *The impact of long sentences on public safety: A complex relationship*. Washington, DC: Council on Criminal Justice. Ramirez, Juan R., & Crano, William D. (2003). Deterrence and incapacitation: An interrupted time-series analysis of California's three-strikes law. *Journal of Applied Social Psychology*, *33*(1), 110. Rhodes, William, et al. (2018). Relationship between prison length of stay and recidivism: A study using regression discontinuity and instrumental variables with multiple break points. *Criminology & Public Policy*, *17*(3), 731. Smith, Paula, et al. (2002). *The effects of prison sentences and intermediate sanctions on recidivism: General effects and individual differences*. Ottawa: Solicitor General of Canada. Tonry, Michael. (2008). Learning from the limitations of deterrence research. *Crime & Justice*, *37*(1), 279. U.S. Department of Justice, National Institute of Justice. (2016, May). *Five things about deterrence.* https://nij.ojp.gov/topics/articles/five-things-about-deterrence. Vera Institute of Justice (2023), *supra* note 42. Webster, Cheryl Marie, & Doob, Anthony N. (2012). Searching for Sasquatch: Deterrence of crime through sentence severity. In Petersilia, Joan, & Reitz, Kevin R. (Eds.). *The Oxford handbook of sentencing and corrections* (p. 173). New York: Oxford University Press.

45 U.S. Department of Justice, National Institute of Justice (2016), *supra* note 44.

46 Doob, Anthony, et al. (2014, February 14). *Issues related to harsh sentences and mandatory minimum sentences: General deterrence and incapacitation* (p. A-3). Toronto: Centre for Criminology & Sociolegal Studies, University of Toronto.

47 U.S. Department of Justice, National Institute of Justice (2016), *supra* note 44. See Nagin, Daniel S., et al. (2009). Imprisonment and reoffending. *Crime and Justice*, *38*(1), 115. ("Compared with noncustodial sanctions, incarceration appears to have a null or mildly criminogenic effect on future criminal behavior.")

approximately 56% of the criminal justice bills introduced in the state's legislature."[48] Throughout the nation, "prosecutors were nearly twice as likely to lobby in favor of a law that created a new crime or otherwise increased the scope of criminal law than a law that would create a defense, decriminalize conduct, or otherwise narrow the scope of criminal law. And when state prosecutors lobbied in favor of a bill, it was more than twice as likely to pass than an average bill."

Prosecutors also are individually responsible for charging decisions. They exercise discretion in determining the charges brought against a defendant, personally directing the fate of individual defendants. Each prosecutor wields tremendous power, as former federal prosecutor Miriam Krinsky explains:

> With the stroke of a pen, they can eliminate the death penalty. With the stroke of a pen, they can decide whether young people are going to be pushed into the adult system or treated commensurate with their brain development. With the stroke of a pen, they decide whether "three strikes" penalties will be sought. With the stroke of a pen, creating policies, they'll decide whether there will be a post-conviction justice unit in their office to look back at past convictions and past excessive sentences.[49]

The individual prosecutor's power is extraordinary, as U.S. District Court Judge Jed Rakoff affirms: "what really puts the prosecutor in the driver's seat is the fact that the prosecutor—because of mandatory minimums, sentencing guidelines, and simply his ability to shape whatever charges are brought—can effectively dictate the sentence by how he drafts the indictment."[50] Charging defendants under higher-penalty statutes, for instance, can increase the odds of a disposition favorable to the prosecution by 60 percent.[51]

The practice of overcharging to obtain advantages in plea bargaining—described in an American Bar Association report as the use of "impermissibly coercive incentives"—increases prosecutors' negotiation leverage and

48 Quotations in this paragraph appear in University of North Carolina School of Law. (2021). *Prosecutor lobbying in the States, 2015–2018* (pp. 4, 35). https://law.unc.edu/wp-content/uploads/2021/06/Prosecutor-Lobbying-in-the-States-2015-2018.pdf.

49 Keckley, Andrea. (2022, October 28). Miriam Krinsky on the work of reform-minded prosecutors. *Law 360*.

50 Rakoff, Jed S. (2021). *Why the innocent plead guilty and the guilty go free* (p. 25). New York: Farrar, Straus and Giroux.

51 Judge, Shana M., & Dole, Jenna L. (2022). Charging sex traffickers under federal law: What dispositions should we expect when applying theories on prosecutorial decision-making? *Journal of Empirical Legal Studies*, *19*, 677.

pressures defendants to plead guilty to lower-level offenses.[52] As Judge Rakoff observes, "it is the prosecutor, not the judge, who effectively exercises the sentencing power, albeit cloaked as a charging decision." And the plea bargaining that follows the charging decision may be tainted by racism; White defendants are 25 percent more likely than Black defendants to have their most serious charge dropped or reduced, according to law professor Lucian Dervan.

Judges, too, are complicit in promoting mass incarceration. Aligning themselves with populist "tough on crime" exhortations to punish and imprison, many judges impose excessive sentences or stretch statutes to facilitate convictions and justify prison sentences. In *People v. Valencia*, for example, the defendant had removed a bathroom window screen from a house but did not open the window itself.[53] He was arrested shortly after driving away from the house and charged with burglary. The burglary statute, California Penal Code Section 459, required proof that the defendant had *entered* the house: "Every person who enters a house . . . with intent to commit grand or petit larceny or any felony is guilty of burglary." The California Court of Appeal ruled that entry of a building had occurred, within the meaning of the statute, although the window remained closed and was never penetrated. (A dissenting opinion drily notes that a person "enters" a building by going inside it; and when a person "remains outside the closed window because he cannot open it," he has not "entered" the building.)

Judges' selective interpretations of laws, their frequent imposition of prison sentences, and their casual treatment of the constitutional protection against cruel and unusual punishment have transformed the criminal justice system into an administrative behemoth. Nine percent of all males will be imprisoned at some time in their lives, and the lifetime risk of imprisonment for Black males and American Indian/Alaska Native males is 16 and 50 percent, respectively.[54] Most of these incarcerated individuals are parents; about 3 million minor children, roughly one in every 28 children, have a parent locked away in a jail cell following a judge's sentencing. As law professor Jeffrey Bellin pointedly notes, "courts were not neutral observers to the rise

52 The American Bar Association's characterization and Professor Lucian Dervan's comment appear in Karp, Jack. (2023, February 22). Use of plea bargains undermining justice, ABA report says. *Law 360*.

53 This description of *People v. Valencia* appears in Bellin, *supra* note 2 at 131–132. For a summary of excessive prison sentences imposed by New York trial judges, see Poggio, Marco. (2024, April 5). Study shines light on excessive NY prison sentences. *Law 360*.

54 Data and quotes in this paragraph are derived from Bellin, *supra* note 2 at 140. Jay, Meg. (2019). *Supernormal* (p. 204). New York: Twelve. Roehrkasse, Alexander F., & Wildeman, Christopher. (2022, December 2). Lifetime risk of imprisonment in the United States remains high and starkly unequal. *Science Advances*, *8*(48), eabo3395.

of Mass Incarceration. They chose a side. And more often than not, that side was incarceration."

Mentally impaired inmates

Mass incarceration has a particularly heinous impact on the mentally ill. Imprisonment is the most likely disposition for mentally ill citizens, as associate administrative judge Steven Leifman and political scientist Norm Ornstein explain:

> People with mental illnesses in the United States are 10 times more likely to be incarcerated than they are to be hospitalized. Those who don't end up in prison are likely to cycle repeatedly through patchy psychiatric care, spells of homelessness, and emergency rooms. And every year, about 2 million arrests are made of people with serious mental illnesses.
>
> As a result, the makeup of our prison population tells its own tale: More than 70 percent of people in American jails and prisons have at least one diagnosed mental illness or substance-use disorder, or both. Up to a third of those incarcerated have serious mental illnesses, a much higher rate than is found at large. On any given day, approximately 380,000 people with mental illnesses are in jail or prison across the United States, and another 574,000 are under some form of correctional supervision.[55]

About one in two mentally ill citizens will be arrested during their lifetimes. The mentally ill are involved in about 25 percent of the fatal police shootings, and when they are imprisoned they are more likely to receive longer sentences, be committed to solitary confinement, and commit suicide.[56] Roughly one-half of the recently executed criminal defendants had been diagnosed with a mental illness.[57] Although most industrialized countries prohibit the execution of

55 Ornstein, Norm, & Leifman, Steve. (2022, May 30). Locking people up is no way to treat mental illness. *The Atlantic*. See U.S. Department of Justice, Office of Justice Programs. (2017, June). Indicators of mental health problems reported by prisoners and jail inmates, 2011–2012. ("The percentage of jail inmates who met the threshold for SPD [serious psychological distress] (26%) was five times higher than the percentage of adults who met the threshold for SPD in the total standardized general U.S. population (5%) or those in the standardized general population with no criminal involvement in the past year (4%).")

56 Roth, Alisa. (2018). *Insane* (pp. 3–4). New York: Basic Books. See Stanford Justice Advocacy Project. (2017). The prevalence and severity of mental illness among California prisoners on the rise. ("Over 30 percent of California prisoners currently receive treatment for a 'serious mental disorder,' an increase of 150 percent since 2000. . . . Furthermore, there is evidence that CDCR's projections underestimate the current number of prisoners with mental illness.")

57 Baumgartner, Frank, & Neill, Betsy. (2017, April 3). Does the death penalty target people who are mentally ill? We checked. *The Washington Post*. Office of the State Public Defender. (2021). *California's broken death penalty: It's time to stop tinkering with the machinery*

mentally ill defendants—and the American Bar Association and the American Psychiatric Association support a ban on the death penalty for seriously mentally ill defendants—the federal and state governments continue to impose and methodically effectuate death penalty sentences on them.

Most incarcerated individuals exhibit traumatic brain injury (TBI), a frequently disabling injury that disrupts normal brain functions and is caused by an external force.[58] The prevalence of TBI among incarcerated individuals ranges from 51 to 60 percent; the incidence of TBI in the general population is 12 percent. A meta-analysis of 64 studies involving 52,540 participants subjected to incarceration, probation, parole, and supervised hospitalization found that 46 percent had sustained mild, moderate, or severe TBI. The actual incidence of TBI, the researchers note, is higher because individuals subjected to the criminal justice system are more likely to have sustained a head injury but less likely to have sought and obtained medical care resulting in a patient medical record confirming TBI.

Jail and prison conditions

Conditions in many U.S. jails and prisons are abysmal. About 50,000–80,000 incarcerated individuals are locked in solitary confinement, typically a 6′ x 9′ cell. "No window. No mirror. No clock. No concept of time," recalls Pamela Winn, a registered nurse who served five years in prison.[59] The number of inmates in solitary confinement in U.S. jails and prisons approximates the *total* number of inmates in the United Kingdom. The former United Nations Special Rapporteur on Torture, Juan E. Méndez, condemns solitary confinement, citing scientific evidence that it causes some permanent mental damage within a few days. "Considering the severe mental pain or suffering solitary confinement may cause," he warns, "it can amount to torture or cruel, inhuman or degrading treatment or punishment when used as a punishment, during pre-trial detention, indefinitely or for a prolonged period, for persons

---

of death. https://www.ospd.ca.gov/wp-content/uploads/2024/02/White-Paper.pdf. Poggio, Marco. (2023, November 27). They are mentally ill; Some states want them off death row. *Law 360*.

58 Data in this paragraph is derived from Hunter, Shelby, et al. (2023). The prevalence of traumatic brain injury (TBI) among people impacted by the criminal legal system: An updated meta-analysis and subgroup analyses. *Law and Human Behavior*, *47*(5), 539.

59 Ridderbusch, Katja. (2021, October 4). COVID precautions put more prisoners in isolation. It can mean long-term health woes. *NPR News*. www.npr.org/sections/health-shots/2021/10/04/1043058599/rising-amid-covid-solitary-confinement-inflicts-lasting-harm-to-prisoner-health. See Poggio, Marco. (2024, February 16). Inmate suicides linked to Federal Prison Bureau's failures. *Law 360*. ("More than half of the 344 people who died in federal custody during an eight-year period beginning in fiscal year 2014 killed themselves. Homicide was the second-highest cause of death.")

with mental disabilities or juveniles."[60] He also notes that the absence of witnesses facilitates the torture of individuals locked in solitary confinement.[61]

The risk of rape in many jails and prisons is continual, as economics professor Tyler Cowen explains:

> [I]t is widely accepted that rape is commonplace in American prisons. Precise numbers are hard to come by, but estimates are that between 2 percent and 21 percent of prisoners have been victims. Note that in prison even apparently voluntary interactions can have a strongly coercive element, such as when a prisoner trades sexual favors for protection or privileges. So it is not just the number of rapes. It is the broader system under which the very notion of voluntary interaction is often meaningless.
>
> Even if a prisoner is never raped, that threat can be hanging over their heads for their entire stay.[62]

Cowen describes the penal system "as an unconstitutional moral horror" and implores Americans "to realize they have been creating and sanctioning a moral horror and to treat it as a major political issue." As Cowen observes, the entire criminal justice system is a travesty, and the courts "have ceased to be venues for the accurate, factual examination of innocence and guilt. Instead, they are dominated by a series of procedural kludges designed mostly to keep the process orderly but certainly not fair."

A first step in bringing the penal system up to international standards would be for state and federal officials to allow inspections by the United Nations Special Rapporteur on Torture and Other Cruel, Inhuman or Degrading Treatment or Punishment. The refusal to allow those inspections has relegated the U.S. to a band of rogue nations like Syria, Pakistan, and Russia generally associated with authoritarian governments and exceptionally cruel treatment of people in prison.

60 (2011, October 18). Solitary confinement should be banned in most cases. *United Nations UN News*. https://news.un.org/en/story/2011/10/392012.

61 An individual in solitary confinement describes his treatment: "[Officers] locked me in solitary confinement for 10 days handcuffed and shackled to a metal bed. During that time they would extinguish their cigarette butts on my body and flip hot ashes in my face and eyes and place meal trays just out of reach. Once I yelled for water to drink. The officer rammed the nozzle of a chemical fire extinguisher into my rectum and flooded my insides with liquid and chemicals that caused me to scream with agony." American Friends Service Committee. (2014). Survivors speak: Prison testimonies of torture in United States prisons and jails. https://afsc.org/sites/default/files/documents/Survivors%20Speak%20-%20AFSC%20CAT%20Shadow%20Report%202014.pdf.

62 Cowen, Tyler. (2018, December 28). The moral horror of America's prisons. *Bloomberg*.

The promise of altruism

If we had to select a single attribute with the highest potential to simultaneously reform the legal system *and* upgrade attorney well-being, that attribute would be altruism. Altruism and correlated qualities like empathy, courage, generosity, fairness, morality, industry, and reliability are the most promising correctives to the legal system's dysfunctions and the legal profession's extensive mental health disorders. Altruism underpins prosocial behavior, supporting systems and institutions that elevate the overall standard of living, and it promotes mental well-being, generating positive emotions from the act of helping others. One study of 46,336 employees, for instance, found that volunteering and charitable work, including pro bono professional work, was the only intervention that reliably improved well-being. The other 90 interventions tested in the study, e.g., relaxation methods and coaching, showed neutral or negative effects.[63]

In a country whose legal system is ranked second-to-last among the G10 nations and whose attorneys are 8.5 times more likely to contemplate suicide than the general population, a dramatically new approach is imperative. That new approach has to be sufficiently simple to be implemented quickly, sufficiently comprehensive to address fundamental problems, and sufficiently powerful to effectuate durable solutions. Altruism meets these criteria. It enables the public to experience the legal system they deserve, and it instills in attorneys the sense of well-being they need to thrive and serve clients. It also realigns judges' values, motives, and interests to overcome the stress, frustration, boredom, anxiety, and depression that can impair their public service.

Public interest drift

Aspiring lawyers enter law school with a strong desire to help other people. About one-third of undergraduate students planning to attend law school cite "opportunities to be helpful to others or useful to society/giving back" and "advocate for social change" as one of their three main motivations.[64] Twenty-three percent of first year law students intend to practice public interest law, and 44 percent of lawyers strongly agree that their main motivation for attending law school was "you believed a law degree would allow you

63 Fleming, William J. (2024). Employee well-being outcomes from individual-level mental health interventions: Cross-sectional evidence from the United Kingdom. *Industrial Relations Journal*, *55*(2), 162.

64 Association of American Law Schools, et al. (2018). *Beyond the Bachelor's: Undergraduate perspectives on graduate and professional degrees* (p. 42). Washington, DC: Association of American Law Schools.

to help others/contribute to society."[65] Despite these initially strong altruistic motivations, only 6 to 8 percent of graduating law students are employed by public interest organizations.[66] For the students who drift away from their altruistic goals, the major source of disappointment in law practice is that they "feel that they are not contributing to the public good."[67]

What happened to the law students who started with altruistic aspirations and ended up in conventional law practices, usually representing private parties in ethically neutral and morally inconsequential disputes? The standard explanation is that they incurred substantial student indebtedness and felt obligated to obtain high-paying, private sector jobs. Survey data compiled by the State Bar of California, for instance, shows a strong relationship between student indebtedness and the switch away from public interest work: "the majority of law students who drifted from public interest cited debt as a major reason for their decision."[68] The State Bar's analysis of debt data corroborates the students' attributions, finding that "students who drifted from their initial plans to practice in a public interest area had a median law school loan debt 40 percent higher than their peers who stayed committed to public interest careers." Other studies, however, find that debt has "a significant but small negative relationship to first job and current job in a public interest setting," and students are attracted to private firms' high salaries "regardless of their debt burden."[69]

65 Gallup & AccessLex Institute. (2018). *Examining value, measuring engagement* (p. 10). Washington, DC: Gallup. State Bar of California. (2019). *Public interest drift: Findings from the 2019 California law student survey* (p. 3). https://www.calbar.ca.gov/Portals/0/documents/accessJustice/California-Law-Student-Survey.pdf. See Long, Brittany L. (2024, March 8). More law students into public interest but firms win. *Bloomberg Law*. ("One in four law students aspire to practice in the public interest, according to data from Bloomberg Law's most recent Law School Preparedness Survey.")

66 See NALP. (2022). *Jobs and JD's: Employment for the class of 2021*. NALP. (2018). *Class of 2017 national summary report*. NALP. (2013). *Law school class of 2012 finds more jobs, starting salaries rise—But large class size hurts overall employment rate.*

67 Levit, Nancy, & Linder, Douglas O. (2010). *The happy lawyer* (p. 106). New York: Oxford University Press.

68 State Bar of California, *supra* note 65 at 6.

69 Albiston, Catherine, et al. (2021). Making public interest lawyers in a time of crisis: An evidence-based approach. *Georgetown Journal of Legal Ethics*, *34*, 223. McGill, Christa. (2006, Summer). Educational debt and law student failure to enter public service careers: Bringing empirical data to bear. *Law & Social Inquiry*, *31*(3), 677. See Bliss, John. From idealists to hired guns? An empirical analysis of "public interest drift" in law school. *U.C. Davis Law Review*, *51*, 1973. Boutcher, Steven A., et al. (2023, January). A Faustian bargain? Rethinking the role of debt in law students' career choices. *Journal of Empirical Legal Studies*, 189. ("Across all of our analyses, we find no evidence that student debt is a barrier to a graduate's decision to take a GPI [government and public interest] position at career launch or a factor in a graduate's longer-term career aspirations.")

Since debt is a disputed factor in public interest drift, other factors may exert a stronger influence on career choices. Law professor Catherine Albiston identifies the socialization of law students as a critical factor:

> Research further suggests that law students' conception of what it means to be a lawyer tends to coalesce around the norm of private practice, marginalizing their prior public interest role models. During law school, students express growing skepticism about law's capacity to effect social change or even to help individual clients, reframing their own ethical commitment from doing good to not inflicting harm. In addition, students come to see corporate practice as both more demanding and more significant than representing the poor because of the much greater amounts of money at stake—making money rather than social value the measure of significance.[70]

The meandering nature of law students' values is historical. Writing *The Death of Ivan Ilyich* in 1882, Leo Tolstoy describes the moral evolution of a dying judge: "In law school he had committed acts which had formerly seemed to him of great vileness and had inspired a feeling of self-loathing in him at the time he committed them; but subsequently, seeing that such acts were also committed by highly placed people and were not considered bad, he, without really thinking them good, forgot all about them and was not troubled in the least by the memory of them."[71]

Benefits of altruism

If lawyers could recover the altruistic motivations that initially attracted them to law school, they would experience greater well-being and could reform the legal system. Extensive research demonstrates that altruism improves self-esteem, positive affect, and well-being and reduces anxiety, fear, anger, stress, despair, sleep difficulties, and depressive symptoms.[72] It also enhances

70 Albiston, Catherine, *supra* note 69.

71 Tolstoy, Leo. (2009). *The death of Ivan Ilyich and other stories* (p. 48). New York: Alfred A. Knopf. See Beard, Mary. (2013, November 5). Facing death with Tolstoy. *The New Yorker*.

72 For effects of altruism, see Feng, Yi, et al. (2020). When altruists cannot help: The influence of altruism on the mental health of university students during the COVID-19 pandemic. *Global Health*, *16*(1), 61. Kahana, Eva, et al. (2013, February). Altruism, helping and volunteering: Pathways to well-being in late life. *Journal of Aging and Health*, *24*(1), 159. Post, Stephen G. (2005). Altruism, happiness, and health: It's good to be good. *International Journal of Behavioral Medicine*, *12*(2), 66. Schwartz, Carol, et al. (2003). Altruistic social interest behaviors are associated with better mental health. *Psychosomatic Medicine*, *65*, 778. Tolonen, Iina, et al. (2023). High compassion predicts fewer sleep difficulties: A general population study with an 11-year follow-up. *Brain and Behavior*, *13*, e3165. Valk, Sofie L., et al. (2017). Structural

purposefulness and meaningfulness and increases perceptions of self-efficacy and competence. Altruists feel stronger, calmer, and more energetic; report less physical pain and fewer illnesses; exhibit lower rates of telomere attrition and DNA damage; and live longer, sometimes up to ten years longer, than people preoccupied with negative emotions.

Altruistic individuals think differently and are more effective problem-solvers—exactly what is required to reform the legal system. Their thinking is "more creative, integrative, flexible, and open to information."[73] They have a wider scope of attention, and they display what psychologists call a "broader thought-action repertoire"; that is, they engage in more "big picture" creative thinking.[74] Their thoughts tend to be novel, independent, and accurate in separating practical solutions from "internal and external realities they are powerless to change."[75] Since altruists incorporate more information into their decisions and are highly adaptable, realistic, empathic, and purposeful, altruism can "empower them to effect meaningful change."[76]

Perhaps most importantly, altruism is an essential element of morality. Altruism enables people to understand others' interests, perspectives, needs, and rights and to recognize how short-sighted, egocentric behavior can harm others. As comparative religion scholar Joseph Campbell observes, "When we quit thinking primarily about ourselves and our own self-preservation, we undergo a truly heroic transformation of consciousness."[77] In this transformation, altruism becomes the motivational core of moral character and behavior.[78] This transformation is considerably more than an aspiration because our brains are structured to facilitate altruistic, moral decision making while performing other higher-order, deliberative functions. Altruistic, moral decision making is integrated with complex, prosocial executive functions performed by the medial prefrontal cortex (mPFC), a part of the frontal lobe. mPFC functions include social cognition; the ability to assess

---

plasticity of the brain: Differential change after socio-affective and cognitive mental training. *Science Advances*, 3(10), e1700489. Wang, Yilu, et al. (2020, January 14). Altruistic behaviors relieve physical pain. *Proceedings of the National Academy of Sciences*, *117*(2), 950.

73 Post, *supra* note 72 at 66.

74 Fredrickson, Barbara L., & Branigan, Christine. (2005). Positive emotions broaden the scope of attention and thought-action repertoires. *Cognition & Emotion*, *19*(3), 313. Post, *supra* note 72 at 66.

75 Schwartz, *supra* note 72 at 778.

76 Ibid.

77 Campbell, Joseph, & Moyers, Bill. (1998). *The power of myth* (p. 126). New York: Broadway Books.

78 See Cohen, Taya R., & Morse, Lily. (2014). Moral character: What it is and what it does. *Research in Organizational Behavior*, *34*, 43. Rachel, James. (2000). Naturalism. In LaFollette, Hugh (Ed.). *The Blackwell Guide to Ethical Theory* (p. 74). Oxford: Blackwell Publishing. Underwood, Bill, & Moore, Bert. (1982). Perspective-taking and altruism. *Psychological Bulletin*, *91*(1), 143.

others' perceptions, beliefs, and emotions; self-monitoring; self-control of emotions and actions; being responsible for one's actions; risk evaluations; moral and legal blame attributions; and "moral decision-making based on empathy or altruism."[79]

When people allow egocentrism to eclipse altruism, they produce conditions similar to the disorders and dysfunctions that now afflict many lawyers and the legal system. A fixation on self-interest and extrinsic rewards like income is correlated with lower levels of well-being; decreased helping behavior; disrupted professional development; reduced enjoyment of leisure activities; diminished community involvement; less consideration of consequences and outcomes for other people; declining tolerance of others' beliefs and opinions; and minimal compassion.[80] Egocentrism also is correlated with increased cheating, dishonesty, competitiveness, and risk-taking behavior. At an organizational level, groups that consistently overemphasize income generation, like many law firms, devolve into self-interested work units distinguished by their resistance to change and their substitution of career protection strategies for career development practices.[81]

Altruism and professionalism

Law is one of the few occupations where altruism is mandatory. Although attorneys may regard altruism as an optional personal characteristic unrelated to their law practices, it is the essence of professionalism and the central feature of their fiduciary duties. Professionals, by definition, are an altruistic moral community. They perform a public service; occupy a special relation of trust with society and the individuals they serve; embrace and display a service orientation; and are "altruistic and motivated by universalistic values."[82]

79 Jones, Owen D., et al. (2024). *Brain science for lawyers, judges, and policymakers* (p. 37). New York: Oxford University Press.

80 The disadvantages of egocentrism and extrinsic rewards are explained more fully in Chapter 6 and the research cited in that chapter. See also Allan, Scott M., et al. (2019). The fearful and anxious professional: Partner experiences of working in the financialized professional services firm. *Work, Employment & Society*, *33*(1), 112. Grant, Adam. (2013). *Give and take*. New York: Penguin Books. Keltner, Dacher. (2009). *Born to be good*. New York: W.W. Norton & Company. Keltner, Dacher. (2016). *The power paradox*. New York: Penguin Press. Kiser, Randall. (2017). *Soft skills for the effective lawyer* (pp. 82–87). New York: Cambridge University Press. Leana, Carrie R., & Meuris, Jirs. (2015). Living to work and working to live: Income as a driver of organizational behavior. *The Academy of Management Annals*, *9*(1), 55. Pink, Daniel H. (2009). *Drive*. New York: Riverhead Books.

81 Grant, Adam, & Patil, Shefali. (2012). Challenging the norm of self-interest: Minority influence and transitions to helping norms in work units. *Academy of Management Review*, *37*(4), 547. Allan, *supra* note 80.

82 Evetts, Julia, et al. (2006). Professionalization, scientific expertise, and elitism: A sociological perspective. In Ericsson, K. Anders, et al. (Eds.). *The Cambridge handbook of expertise and*

To satisfy the requirements of professionalism and their fiduciary duties, they are required to subordinate their own needs to those of the greater society and place others' interests above their own. The American Bar Association, for instance, specifically implores attorneys to "seek improvement of the law, access to the legal system, the administration of justice and the quality of service rendered by the legal profession."[83]

The overarching issue for attorneys and society is not whether altruism is essential but how so many attorneys could so thoroughly neglect the necessity of altruism for so many years. In a profession bound by fiduciary duties to clients and moral responsibilities to society, it is remarkable that the most enduring legacies of many attorneys will be a profession-wide mental health crisis; an inaccessible, prohibitively expensive civil justice system; a barbaric criminal justice system; and a personal, knowing contribution to extreme income inequality.

Organization of this book

To understand the extent of mental distress in the legal profession, its effects on attorneys, clients, and society, and the imperative of altruism, this book is organized into nine distinct yet imbricated chapters:

Overview (Chapter 1)—summarizes the nature, history, and extent of mental illness in the legal profession; identifies egocentrism and a lack of altruism as traits common to many attorneys; highlights failures in the civil and criminal legal systems; and describes the singular role of altruism in improving well-being and reforming the legal system.

Damaged Lawyers (Chapter 2)—examines the types, prevalence, and predictors of mental distress in the legal profession; reviews international studies and surveys of lawyer well-being; reveals the extent and effects of law firms' efforts to stigmatize and ignore mental illness; and shows how law firm size and practice areas impact well-being.

Causes and Effects of Lawyers' Mental Distress (Chapter 3)—identifies and analyzes the sources, causes, risks, and effects of lawyers' mental impairments and demonstrates the relative harm of specific factors like billable hour requirements, gender bias, bullying, sexual harassment, lack of control over work assignments, toxic partners, boring, meaningless work, moral injury, and ineffective law firm leadership.

---

expert performance (pp. 107–108). New York: Cambridge University Press. See Gardner, Howard, & Shulman, Lee S. (2005, Summer). The professions in America today: Crucial but fragile. *Daedalus*, *134*(3), 14. (A defining characteristic of all professions is "a primary orientation to community interest rather than personal interest.")

83 A.B.A. Model Rules of Prof'l Conduct, Preamble and Scope.

Stressed Judges (Chapter 4)—surveys the stresses, conditions, and self-imposed limitations that impair judges' performance and social value; describes the effects of judges' isolation, vicarious trauma, and tendency to ignore or minimize symptoms of mental illness; and questions judges' role in protecting attorneys' prerogatives instead of advancing ordinary citizens' interests.

Elements of Well-being (Chapter 5)—specifies and explains the factors and qualities that promote well-being, reduce mental illness among lawyers, and increase attorneys' sense of social responsibility, including autonomy, meaning, engagement, interpersonal relationships, self-efficacy, and intrinsic motivation.

Altruism (Chapter 6)—discusses the types, elements and benefits of altruism; illuminates beliefs, traits, and actions correlated with altruism; considers altruists' motivations; specifies methods of increasing altruistic behavior; and introduces the concept of regenerative altruism to improve lawyer well-being and repair the legal system.

Altruism in Practice (Chapter 7)—identifies public interest programs, law practice areas, and pro bono work associated with well-being and altruism; describes the challenges and achievements of public defenders, Legal Aid lawyers, MacArthur Fellows, Skadden Fellows, death penalty lawyers, public interest law organizations, and private practice lawyers providing pro bono services to indigent clients; studies the motivations of attorneys in altruistic practices; and highlights judges who have initiated altruistic programs and have taken altruistic positions on sentencing.

Accelerating Well-being, Altruism, and Reform (Chapter 8)—shows how altruism and the legal system should be advanced by bar associations, law firms, judges, district attorneys, public defenders, and law schools; proposes specific changes like the elimination of billable hour requirements, the establishment of mandatory pro bono legal services, a requirement for periodic mental health assessments of judges, and the diversion of mentally ill defendants from the criminal legal system; and shows how law schools and the legal profession are decades behind medical schools and the medical profession in fostering altruism.

Conclusion (Chapter 9)—discusses the values, attitudes, and incentives in the legal profession that elevate self-interest and threaten altruism; depicts the corrosive effects of cynicism, passivity, and amorality and the ameliorative effects of altruism, engagement, and principle; and portrays a model life of altruism.

Lawyers and judges will need personal courage to improve their mental health and moral courage to repair the legal system. This book serves to evoke and extol that courage—and to question whether lawyers and judges merit their exclusive privileges if they will not demonstrate it.

2

DAMAGED LAWYERS

Lee Mark Smolen was a partner at Sidley Austin, a 1,700-attorney law firm when he resigned in 2012.[1] He was the co-global coordinator of the firm's real estate practice group and a member of the firm's executive committee. He usually worked 12–15 hours per day, excluding work at home and on weekends, and slept three to four hours per night. In some years, he billed 3,332–3,576 hours, and in his last year at Sidley, he was paid $3.5 million. Although Smolen was among the most highly compensated lawyers at Sidley, some of his partners recall him seeking additional compensation "with intensity" and conveying the impression that he was "a little underwhelmed by his compensation."

Between 2007 and 2011, Smolen submitted more than 800 receipts for taxi cab expense reimbursements. Sidley paid him about $70,000 for those expenses. Smolen, however, did not take those cab rides. When Sidley's general counsel, William Conlon, asked Smolen about the cab expenses in September 2012, he acknowledged that he had not taken the rides but was entitled to the money "because he came in early, stayed late and did a lot of practice development." Smolen also claimed that he used the cab ride reimbursement funds for other client development expenses he paid by cash.

1 The descriptions of Lee Mark Smolen and his disciplinary action are derived from the Report and Recommendation of the Hearing Board, In the Matter of: Lee Mark Smolen, Attorney-Respondent, No. 6191003, Commission No. 2013PR00060, Before the Hearing Board of the Illinois Attorney Registration and Disciplinary Commission, January 7, 2015, and the order of the Supreme Court of the State of Illinois approving the report and recommendation on March 12, 2015. These documents are available at www.iardc.org.

DOI: 10.4324/9781003514848-2

The Illinois Attorney Registration and Disciplinary Commission filed a complaint against Smolen in June 2013. The hearing board, after considering testimonial and documentary evidence, issued its report in early 2015. The board determined that Smolen prepared "false receipts by covering existing dates and amounts on old receipts and writing new dates and amounts on top of them. He then photocopied the falsified receipts and gave the copies to his secretary." Sidley paid the reimbursement claims by direct deposit into Smolen's bank account. In response to Smolen's assertion that he "simply acted without thinking," the hearing board stated, "We do not find credible Respondent's assertion that he did not realize he was doing anything wrong. An attorney of any level of experience should recognize the wrongfulness of fabricating expenses."

In mitigation, Smolen called two psychiatrists, Stafford Henry, M.D., and Neal Spira, M.D., as witnesses at the hearing. Dr. Henry diagnoses were "generalized anxiety disorder, major depressive disorder, moderate, in partial remission and obsessive-compulsive personality disorder." In Dr. Henry's opinion, a "loose association" existed between Smolen's personality disorder and his misbehavior because Smolen "was excessively devoted to work as a result of his obsessive-compulsive disorder." Dr. Spira testified that Smolen "had been suffering from severe mental distress for a long period of time" and "had features of anxiety and depression while he was working at Sidley." In Dr. Spira's opinion, these disorders "were connected to his fabrication of the cab receipts," and Smolen "had no idea he was doing something wrong because he felt he was a great employee and did not intend to steal anything."

The hearing board recommended that Smolen be suspended from the practice of law for one year, and the Supreme Court of Illinois approved and confirmed the board's report and recommendation.

The stigma of mental health impairments

It would be easy to dismiss the Smolen disciplinary matter as a one-off, an idiosyncratic reaction by an overworked partner resulting in what Dr. Spira described as a "tremendous impairment of judgment." But surveys and studies consistently demonstrate that the legal profession is distinguished by high levels of psychological distress. About one-third of the nation's lawyers might be too anxious, depressed, bored, tired, disengaged, or impaired by alcohol or drugs to serve their clients effectively. A recent survey conducted by *The American Lawyer*, for instance, indicates that 69 percent of lawyers feel anxious, and 36 percent feel depressed.[2] Fifteen percent of the surveyed attorneys

2 Choudhury, Rashmita. (2024, May 17). Mental health by the numbers: The 2024 survey infographic. *The American Lawyer*. See Fredlund, Chelsey. (2023, May 18). Mental health by the numbers: An infographic mapping the legal industry's well-being. *The American Lawyer*.

had contemplated suicide at some time in their careers, and 17 percent knew someone in the legal profession who had committed suicide within the last two years.

A *Bloomberg Law* survey corroborates these findings, reporting that 65 percent of attorneys in law firms and legal departments experienced anxiety within the last six months, and 28 percent experienced depression.[3] Sixty-eight percent of those attorneys also experienced disrupted sleep; 44 percent experienced difficulties in focusing on work tasks; and 17 percent acknowledged an increase in their alcohol usage or drug abuse. The attorneys said that they felt burned out in their work "48% of the time."[4]

The impairments reported in these surveys are compounded by attorneys' reluctance to seek and obtain professional help. As behavioral health expert Patrick Krill notes, "discussing substance abuse and mental health issues has often been considered taboo in the legal industry."[5] The legal profession enforces the taboo of mental illness by stigmatizing attorneys who exhibit mental health problems. Eighty-one percent of law firm leaders believe that suffering from depression is a stigma in the legal profession, and 75 percent believe that the profession stigmatizes anxiety.[6] More than 90 percent of law firm leaders report that having an alcohol or drug addiction is stigmatized in the profession.

Lawyers' perfectionism and drive to project invulnerability intensify the stigma of mental illness and discourage lawyers from seeking mental health care. The widow of Gabe MacConaill, a 42-year-old partner at Sidley Austin who committed suicide by shooting himself in the parking garage of the firm's Los Angeles office, attributes his death, in part, to the "Big Law" culture. In that culture, she writes, "it's shameful to ask for help, shameful to be vulnerable, and shameful not be perfect."[7] Laura Mahr, a lawyer and mental health consultant, voices similar concerns: "Historically, there has been a stigma in the field of law around getting mental health support. Many of us have come to believe that we will be seen as inferior, the weak link on the team, if we admit we need help, so we protect ourselves by pretending nothing is wrong."[8]

3 Bloomberg Law. (2023, December). *Bloomberg Law* attorney workload and hours, 2023 Q1 and Q2. (Survey conducted August 2–25, 2023).

4 Ibid.

5 Krill, Patrick. (2018, September 14). ALM survey on mental health and substance abuse: Big Law's pervasive problem. *The American Lawyer*.

6 Krill, Patrick. (2018, September 24). Big law leaders say stigma comes with addiction and mental health problems. *The American Lawyer*.

7 Litt, Joanna. (2018, November). 'Big Law killed my husband': An open letter from a Sidley partner's widow. *Law.com*.

8 Roe, Dan. (2023, May 18). There's a lot of backlog to address: Why mental health in the legal profession is getting worse. *The American Lawyer*.

By stigmatizing addiction and mental illness, the legal profession pressures attorneys to ignore their mental health, minimize signs of mental illness, and avoid treatment. The taboo of mental illness also enables law firms to overlook their attorneys' behavior until their billable hours plummet and their compensation cannot be justified. "Unfortunately, the help really begins to emerge," Krill observes, "when the performance falls off."[9] For many attorneys, this intervention comes too late. A few days before he committed suicide, MacConaill was exhausted from overwork and told his wife that "his body was failing him."[10] When she encouraged him to quit his job, he said he could not quit in the middle of a major bankruptcy case. "The irony is not lost on me," she reflects, "that he found it easier to kill himself."

The stigmatization of addiction and mental illness would suggest that these disorders are anomalies among attorneys, and the stigmas are invoked to inhibit occasionally aberrational behavior in an otherwise healthy profession. The disturbing reality in law firms, however, is that mental health problems are chronic. When asked whether alcohol abuse occurs in their firms, 90 percent of law firm leaders responded affirmatively.[11] When asked about the occurrence of other mental health problems within their firms, 93 percent of law firm leaders acknowledged anxiety, 86 percent acknowledged depression, and 48 percent acknowledged drug abuse.

An objective observer, unfamiliar with law firms and the legal profession, might wonder why law firms don't make more of an effort to facilitate counseling or treatment, including on-site therapists and psychologists. Many law firm leaders, however, resist this idea, claiming it "would send the wrong message."[12] Although some firms provide an on-site psychologist, others view this as a reputational risk and competitive disadvantage. "Our competitors will say we have crazy lawyers," remarked an AmLaw 50 law firm chairperson.[13]

Studies of attorneys' mental health impairments

Although research has documented serious mental health problems among attorneys and law students for 40 years, many attorneys and law professors continue to disregard these findings, minimize their significance, and criticize their methodologies. A vocal segment of the legal profession is determined to believe that, despite extensive and generally consistent studies signaling a mental health crisis in the legal profession, attorneys are actually mentally

9 Randazzo, Sara. (2017, May 22). Law firms tackle a taboo. *The Wall Street Journal.*
10 This quotation and the following quotation appear in Randazzo, *supra* note 9.
11 Krill (2018, September 24), *supra* note 6.
12 Randazzo, *supra* note 9.
13 Ibid.

healthy professionals living fulfilled lives in somewhat stressful jobs. The assertion or implication that attorneys might have abnormally high levels of anxiety, depression, and alcoholism is anathema to a large body of successful, dedicated professionals.

This section summarizes a few recent studies of attorneys' mental health. Additional studies—involving attorneys in Australia, Canada, England, France, Germany, Guernsey, Isle of Man, Jersey, New Zealand, Republic of Ireland, the United States, and Wales—are analyzed in Appendix A. Although some of the studies in this chapter and Appendix A have been criticized justifiably for errors in sampling and shortcomings in statistical analysis, they convey in aggregate an alarmingly consistent message: attorneys suffer from mental health problems at rates higher than the general population.

Even if the incidence of mental health problems among attorneys is typical of the general population in the United States, as some critics assert, it is an unacceptably high rate for American lawyers in fiduciary relationships with clients. Adults in the United States have the highest rates of depression and anxiety relative to 11 other high-income countries. The United States also has the highest suicide rate and second-highest substance abuse death rate.[14] If the general population of the United States exhibits the highest levels of mental disorders, why should those levels function as the standard for American lawyers dutybound to serve their clients as fiduciaries?

National Health Interview Survey (NHIS) and National Survey on Drug Use and Health (NSDUH) analysis

Analyzing the largest comparative surveys regarding lawyers' mental health, law professors Benjamin Pyle and Clifford Rosky found that lawyers "experience serious psychological distress significantly more often than people with a BA, people with a graduate degree, and doctors." They also found that about 20 percent of lawyers have a mental illness, an incidence considerably higher than the general public and medical professionals. Nine percent of lawyers, moreover, experience alcohol abuse and dependence, and one in four lawyers report driving while intoxicated within the last year.[15]

14 For data regarding depression, anxiety, suicide, and death rates from substance use in high-income countries, see Tikkanen, Roosa, et al. (2020, May). Mental health conditions and substance use: Comparing U.S. needs and treatment capacity with those in other high-income countries. *The Commonwealth Fund*.

15 Pyle, Benjamin, & Rosky, Clifford. (2023, December 22). *Measuring lawyer mental illness: Evidence from two national surveys*. [Preliminary paper presentation. American Association of Law Schools Annual Meeting. Empirical Study of Legal Education and the Legal Profession Section Works-In-Progress Incubator, January 5, 2024, Washington, DC].

The American Lawyer survey

About 2,500 lawyers responded to the most recent Mental Health Survey of the Legal Profession, conducted by ALM Intelligence and Law.com.[16] Seventy-seven percent of those lawyers reported that the legal profession has had a negative effect on their mental health; 67 percent believe that their personal relationships have suffered as a result of "being a member of the legal profession"; and 49 percent state that "mental health problems and substance abuse are at a crisis level in the legal industry."

The average survey results, based on lawyers' responses during the last four years, depict a mentally unhealthy profession:

- 36 percent of lawyers feel depressed.
- 70 percent are anxious.
- 17 percent have contemplated suicide.
- 10 percent acknowledge an alcohol problem.
- 28 percent state that they have increased their use of drugs and/or alcohol as a result of their work or work environment.

Other survey findings reflect a struggling, deeply troubled profession. A majority of lawyers are experiencing "physical and mental overwhelm and fatigue"; trouble concentrating; decreased satisfaction and sense of accomplishment; a loss of motivation; exhaustion; and an increasingly cynical and negative outlook. Nearly one in four lawyers report that they "hate" their jobs.

Bloomberg Law survey

Seventy-eight percent of the 1,129 *Bloomberg Law* survey respondents work in law firms, and the remaining 22 percent are employed in in-house legal departments.[17] As explained earlier, 68 percent of all respondents report disrupted

16 Data in this section appears in Choudhury, *supra* note 2, Fredlund, *supra* note 2 and Roe, *supra* note 8. In the 2022 *American Lawyer* survey, female lawyers reported slightly higher levels of anxiety and depression than male lawyers. The highest levels of depression were exhibited by Hispanic lawyers (45 percent) and Black lawyers (38 percent). About 20 percent of the surveyed lawyers had contemplated suicide. Female lawyers reported the lowest incidence of suicidal ideation, and Asian lawyers reported the highest incidence of suicidal thoughts. Nineteen percent of Black lawyers said they had contemplated suicide, a large decline from a previous survey of different lawyers showing that 31 percent of Black lawyers had considered suicide. Eighty-two percent of Black attorneys said "their firm had contributed to their mental health issue, the highest of any group, and 80% of Asian lawyers said the same." Roe, Dan. (2022, June 21). Mental health improves for women and minority lawyers, but disparities persist. *The American Lawyer*.

17 Bloomberg Law (2023, December), *supra* note 3. The differences in survey responses between female lawyers and male lawyers are described in Blaemire, Jessica R. (2023, October 2). Analysis: Female lawyers report more stress, burnout than males. *Bloomberg Law*.

sleep during the last six months, 65 percent experienced anxiety, and 28 percent experienced depression. Forty percent said their overall well-being had declined during the last six months, and 25 percent experienced "new or increased health issues." Only 21 percent said that their overall well-being had improved. Six in ten lawyers reported an "inability to disconnect from work" and three in ten lawyers said that work-related issues had adversely affected their personal relationships. Fifteen percent reported increased alcohol usage, and 5 percent acknowledged "thoughts of self-harm."

Female lawyers experienced higher levels of mental distress relative to male lawyers. Among lawyers who have minor children, female lawyers "felt burnout" in their jobs 59 percent of the time while male lawyers felt burnout 47 percent of the time. Among lawyers who do not have minor children, female lawyers felt burnout 53 percent of the time while male lawyers felt burnout 38 percent of the time. In seven of the eight categories of mental distress measured by *Bloomberg Law* (disrupted sleep, anxiety, physical health issues, personal relationship issues, depression, increased alcohol usage, self-harm thoughts, and increased drug abuse) female lawyers reported higher incidence rates than male lawyers. In a single category (self-harm thoughts) the reported incidence was identical for both female and male lawyers.

In a related *Bloomberg Law* survey, in-house counsel exhibited higher levels of psychological distress than law firm lawyers. Forty-six percent of in-house lawyers said that their well-being had worsened in the last six months, compared with 39 percent of law firm lawyers reporting a decline in their well-being.[18] "The survey responses indicate that in-house attorneys are working longer and have worse well-being than their law firm counterparts," concludes *Bloomberg Law* reporter Jessica Blaemire, "shattering the long-held belief in the legal profession that working in-house is not as draining as law firm work."

International Bar Association report on mental well-being

The International Bar Association received survey responses from 3,256 member attorneys. Their average mental well-being score was 51 percent, a clinical indicator "for a health professional to screen for depression, and suggests a more formal assessment of mental health problems is warranted."[19] Roughly consistent with the results in *The American Lawyer* and *Bloomberg Law* surveys, the IBA survey results show that 55 percent of the attorneys recently experienced anxiety, and 41 percent experienced depression.

18 The data and quotation in this paragraph appear in Blaemire, Jessica R. (2023, November 30). Analysis: In-house counsel say they work more than firm lawyers. *Bloomberg Law*.

19 International Bar Association. (2021, October). *Mental wellbeing in the legal profession: A global study*. London: International Bar Association.

Attorneys practicing in civil law jurisdictions displayed higher levels of well-being than attorneys in common law jurisdictions like the United States and the United Kingdom, indicating "that the more adversarial forms of legal practice commonly associated with common law jurisdictions are potentially detrimental to wellbeing."[20] Attorneys in the North American Regional Forum (United States, Canada, Mexico, and Puerto Rico) "posted the worst negative impact scores, with 46 per cent of respondents saying that their work negatively affected their wellbeing."[21]

Younger attorneys, associate attorneys, female attorneys, ethnic minority attorneys, and disabled attorneys were more likely to report work and health-related problems resulting from poor mental wellbeing. Nearly 20 percent of disabled lawyers "reported experiencing suicidal thoughts as a result of work-related mental wellbeing issues and one in eight had self-harmed."[22]

Suicidal ideation, depression, drug abuse, and working hours study

This intensive study of 654 legal professionals in two states in the western United States found that lawyers "were significantly more likely to report suicidal ideation 'several days' and 'more than half the days' as compared with the general working population."[23] The lawyers were more depressed than the general population at all levels of depression: mild, moderate, and severe. Eighteen percent of the lawyers "were experiencing symptoms equivalent to a diagnosis of a major depressive disorder." In two related studies of lawyers, researchers discovered that drug abuse and working more than 50 hours per week were correlated with major depressive disorder; and lawyers who experienced burnout were more likely to use illegal drugs.[24]

20 Ibid at 30.

21 Ibid at 32. The report also states at p. 40, "In terms of regions, it was respondents in the North American Regional Forum who experienced the most [health] issues across the board."

22 Ibid at 40.

23 Thiese, Matthew S., et al. (2021). Depressive symptoms and suicidal ideation among lawyers and other law professionals. *Journal of Occupational and Environmental Medicine, 63*(5), 381.

24 Lee, Hyejung, & Thiese, Matthew S. (2021). Association between major depressive disorder and work and personal factors among Utah lawyers. Ogbonnaya, Uchenna, & Thiese, Matthew S. (2021). Assessing a relationship between burnout and drug use disorder among lawyers. Abstracts for both of these studies appear in The University of Utah Virtual NORA Symposium. *Utah NORA Abstract Booklet 2021.* https://rmcoeh.com/images/NORA%20Symposium%20Booklets/2021-Utah-NORA-Virtual-Symposium-Abstract-Booklet-compressed.pdf. See also Ogbonnaya, Uchenna, et al. (2022, June). Burnout and engagement's relationships to drug abuse in lawyers and law professionals. *Journal of Occupational and Environmental Medicine*, 64(7), 621.

California and Washington, D.C. attorneys survey

The researchers in this study obtained survey responses from 2,863 lawyers randomly sampled from the California State Bar and Washington, D.C. Bar. Fifty-one percent of the lawyers screened positive for risky drinking, and 30 percent screened positive for high-risk/hazardous drinking.[25] Female attorneys were more likely than male attorneys to engage in risky drinking and high-risk/hazardous drinking.

About one-half of the lawyers reported mild-severe depression and anxiety symptoms, and 58 percent reported moderate-severe stress. Female attorneys reported higher levels of anxiety, depression, and stress than male attorneys. Female attorneys also were more likely than men (24 percent vs. 17 percent) to contemplate leaving the profession "due to mental health problems, burnout, or stress."[26]

In related surveys, 8.5 percent of attorneys reported suicidal ideation, a rate double that of the general population.[27] Attorneys who reported high levels of stress were 22 times more likely to contemplate suicide than attorneys reporting low stress. Thirty-one percent of attorneys stated that the legal profession had been detrimental to their mental health, and 40 percent reported a prior diagnosis of a mental health disorder.[28] The overall mental and physical health of the attorneys, the researchers concluded, "falls below the general population."

Canadian lawyers survey

An extensive survey of 6,364 lawyers in Canada found that 57 percent were experiencing "very high" or "high" levels of psychological distress; 28

25 Anker, Justin, & Krill, Patrick R. (2021). Stress, drink, leave: An examination of gender-specific risk factors for mental health problems and attrition among licensed attorneys. *PLoS ONE, 16*(5) e0250563. https://doi.org/10.1371/journal.pone.0250563. Despite the attorneys' high incidence of risky and hazardous drinking, only two percent of them had ever received an Alcohol Use Disorder diagnosis. This gap between lawyers' actual alcohol consumption and their medical diagnoses "suggests an extreme level of underdiagnosis and treatment for a widespread problem, possibly owing to pervasive denial, stigma, and a professional culture that normalizes heavy drinking." (at 12). Lawyers evidently are rarely diagnosed with alcohol use disorders because they rarely seek diagnosis and treatment.

26 Ibid at 4. The disparities between female lawyers and male lawyers, the researchers assert, "is an undesirable outcome for a profession long bedeviled by its inability to retain female attorneys and raises the question of whether improving workplace factors that influence poor mental health might be an important missing ingredient in those efforts." (at 13).

27 Krill, Patrick, et al. (2023). Stressed, lonely, and overcommitted: Predictors of lawyer suicide risk. *Healthcare, 11*, 536.

28 Krill, Patrick R., et al. (2022). People, professionals, and profit centers: The connection between lawyer well-being and employer values. *Behavioral Sciences, 12*, 177.

percent reported moderate to severe depressive symptoms; and 36 percent reported anxiety symptoms.[29] Most lawyers (56 percent) showed moderate to severe levels of burnout. The incidence of major depressive disorders among legal professionals was twice that of the general population, and the incidence of generalized anxiety disorders among legal professionals was nearly three times that of the general population.

When asked "Since you began practicing professionally, have you ever had suicidal thoughts?" one in four lawyers responded affirmatively. The age group with the highest proportion of legal professionals contemplating suicide is 36–40 years old, followed by 46–50 years old.

High billable hours targets were correlated with high levels of mental distress. The incidence of burnout is 17 percent higher for legal professionals in firms with >1,800 annual billable hour targets than for those working in firms with 1,200–1,800 annual billable hour targets. Higher annual billable hour targets also were correlated with lower levels of commitment to the legal profession and higher scores on intention to leave the profession.

Attorneys' stories

Studies and surveys may not adequately convey the stress, frustration, anger, and despair that attorneys experience in their practices. Those feelings are best expressed by attorneys themselves. To complement the studies summarized above and convey the personal side of attorneys' mental distress, this section presents attorneys' opinions about three subjects critical to their well-being: the distinct, stress-inducing features of law practice; the mental effects of law practice; and the changes necessary to restore their emotional health.

Distinct features of law practice

The practice of law in adversarial legal systems is invariably intense, competitive, and consequential. A leading trial lawyer describes the adversarial context as being like "a surgical suite where one surgeon tries to save the life of a patient while another surgeon, similarly trained and equally competent, tries to wrest the scalpel from his hand."[30] That adversarial setting is aggravated by law firm economics and cultures that prize overwork and de-emphasize

29 Data reported in this section appears in Cadieux, Nathalie, et al. (2022). *Research report (preliminary version): Towards a healthy and sustainable practice of law in Canada*. National Study on the Psychological Health Determinants of Legal Professionals in Canada, Phase I (2020–2022). Sherbrooke, QC: Université de Sherbrooke, Business School.

30 Kiser, Randall. (2011). *How leading lawyers think* (p. 29). Heidelberg and New York: Springer.

well-being. These lawyers' comments depict some of the distinct, difficult features of law practice:

- "The legal profession combines long hours, high stress, isolation, a trained need to never show vulnerability, and work that by its very definition is antagonistic and conflict-laden, and that makes for a toxic environment conducive to addiction and mental health issues. Legal work combines all the elements that contribute to substance abuse and other disorders into one toxic pot."[31]
- "Lawyers must constantly scan the horizon, trying to predict the next threat or catastrophe. They constantly ask the question, 'What's the worst thing that could happen?' As a result, lawyers are in permanent 'fight or flight' mode, constantly on guard. Also, lawyers have nothing to sell but their time and advice. They're not cranking out widgets. They can't make more time. As their workload grows, something has to give. First, it's vacations. Then weekends. Then evenings. Then family and friends."[32]
- "Lawyers play a . . . game—I'll call it the 'My-Life-Sucks-More-Than-Yours-A-Thon.' This is a competitive race to the bottom in which lawyers trade tales about how little sleep they've gotten, the number of vacations they have not enjoyed, the number of births of their children they've missed, and so on. Many of us have competed in this challenge, or at least have witnessed a few rounds. At the same time, we watch many talented colleagues drop out of the practice of law after the 'My-Life-Sucks' game loses its luster."[33]

The stress of law practice is often aggravated in large law firms. "The economics drive a hierarchical structure that is and will always be opposed to any genuine culture of caring or well-being," states a senior litigation attorney in a large law firm. "Those who make it to the top by virtue of having withstood this for decades will not really be able to have empathy for those below. It's just not part of what happens."[34]

Law practice effects

Most surveyed lawyers believe that the legal profession and its "always on call/can't disconnect" mindsets have harmed their mental well-being.[35] As a

31 Port, Dina Roth. (2018, May 11). Lawyers weigh in: Why is there a depression epidemic in the profession? *ABA Journal* (Your voice).

32 Ibid.

33 Brafford, Anne M. (2014, January). Remodeling the "unhappiest job in America". *Orange County Lawyer*.

34 Zaretsky, Staci. (2024, May 22). Young BigLaw associates are struggling in their 'toxic' workplaces. *Above the Law*.

35 Choudhury, *supra* note 2.

former large law firm lawyer explains, "Lawyers aren't just encouraged but expected to work to the point of exhaustion and continue to push for months and years after they've experienced burnout."[36] He ruefully recalls his first week out of law school when his supervising partner told him, "Bring a sleeping bag—the carpet is not as soft as it looks." Other lawyers describe the negative impact of law practice on their lives:

- "As a practicing litigation attorney and a former enlisted Marine, the pressure, stress and mental toll of practicing law compares to my combat experience. This is a very intellectually and, at times, physically demanding job. I was once told litigation is not for everyone, and that's definitely true. As a solo practitioner in one of the most stressful areas of law, I can see why depression, anxiety and substance abuse would be so prevalent, just like they may be among combat veterans."[37]
- "I didn't want to be a lawyer when I was growing up, but I always figured I would be one. My dad was a solo [practitioner]; respected by his peers; but he wasn't happy. Like my father, I have done everything except railroad reorganizations, and it has had its moments. Most of these moments have been morsels of bitter irony and farce. Not the stuff of 'happiness.' The practice of law is not an antidote for depression. On the contrary, there are some who think it is a contributing factor. . . . [F]or the sad students digging a debt hole to get that J.D. [Juris Doctor], don't expect the happiness to follow. . . ."[38]
- "I think of burnout as a gateway process because it can invite in other physical, mental and emotional issues, and for me, it was chronic anxiety. Burnout resurrected the panic attacks that I thought I had successfully eradicated years earlier. . . . In addition, the high levels of stress caused such severe stomach aches that I ended up in the emergency room twice. I saw more than half a dozen doctors during this time. . . . I was at a point where if someone had asked me how I was doing, I literally would have burst into tears, revealing the truth I had been keeping a secret because I didn't want to seem like the odd lawyer at work who couldn't hack it. As a result, I ended up diagnosing my own burnout, which I could only do after I left my job and reflected back on what happened."[39]

36 Albrecht, Eli. (2024, March 15). I left the Big Law work-life balance trap and found integration. *Bloomberg Law*.
37 Port, *supra* note 31.
38 Comment posted to Neil, Martha. (2008, January 22). Which lawyers love their jobs? *ABA Journal*.
39 Davis, Paula. (2018, May 17). I fought the law and the law won: My burnout story. *Forbes*.

Necessary changes to law practice

Forty-two percent of lawyers report that clients "always" or "often" have unreasonable demands.[40] When asked whether their law firms push back on unreasonable client demands, 70 percent of lawyers respond, "No." Most lawyers also report that billable hour pressures have a negative effect on their stress level and general mental well-being. And about one-half of lawyers feel isolated and believe that they lack the appropriate resources to perform their work. The lawyers' comments below depict—and show what steps are necessary to counter—clients' unreasonable demands, law firms' acquiescence to those demands, and the corrosive effects of billable hour requirements and incentives:

- "Lawyers need to be willing to tell clients with unreasonable demands that their demands are unreasonable. It is routine for senior lawyers to dump work on junior lawyers with the statement 'I know this sucks, but this client refers a lot of work to us and we can't push back on any of their requests.' You can. If you can't make a practice work without making people miserable, you don't deserve a legal practice."[41]
- "No more billable hours and eliminate [client] origination credits—these two things cause extreme competition within firms and are basically the sole factors that determine compensation; billable hours cause clients to be untrustworthy of bills; it causes unethical billing; it favors men; and it has no bearing on the quality of an attorney's work. Clients would be appalled to know how firms compensate their attorneys, if they don't know it already. . . . [E]liminate as much as possible the antiquated white male fraternity system."
- "We need to become a profession again, where the mission is great, ethical work for clients for which we serve as true counselors. We are managing to profits, rather than to developing people who will be innovators with [a] deep commitment to and enjoyment of the work and their workplace. . . . Firms need to recognize that work-life balance is critical to the profession's progress on inclusion and attracting people with full lives, who can engage with clients as counselors."

The changes necessary to promote and maintain mental health in law firms would challenge long-established policies, practices, and priorities. "You

40 Data cited in this paragraph appears in Choudhury, *supra* note 2.

41 All quotations in this section, except the quotation cited in fn 42, appear in Henderson, Lauren, & Henderson, Bill. (2020, June 21). What needs to change to improve mental health in the legal profession? *Legal Evolution*. www.legalevolution.org/2020/06/what-needs-to-change-to-improve-mental-health-in-the-legal-profession-171/.

would have to postulate a business model that defies social norms and measures success in something other than money," a lawyer in a 1,000+ attorney law firm muses. "Not likely, I'm thinking."

Many law firm partners dismiss attorneys' mental distress as chronic whining. "People need to suck it up and just do their jobs," asserts a male partner. "Quit complaining and always making excuses for poor work or non-performance!" Another male partner dismisses attorneys' complaints as self-indulgent: "When my parents and my generation were coming along, we were too busy focusing on how to be successful to have time to indulge in micro-analysis of our behaviors. If you think I'm not sympathetic to all of this, you are right!" Partners' responses like these contribute to attorneys' sense of despair and their conviction that fundamental changes to law firms' values and business models are unlikely. "It will never change, ever," observes an allied professional in a +1,000 attorney law firm. "The basic personality of a lawyer is highly intelligent, highly skeptical with extremely low emotional intelligence."

Clients, for their part, may be even less sympathetic to attorneys' stories of stress, overwork, and despondency. "You guys charge us hourly rates that are absurd," writes a client. "And in exchange for us paying those giant bills which support all of you, we expect no whining, no excuses, and an attitude that recognizes we are the client. If you are looking for sympathy, go cry to your spouses. If you want a friend, go buy a dog."[42]

Practice setting effects

It seems logical that lawyers working in small law firms or legal aid organizations with low-income clients would be more distressed than their highly paid colleagues working in large law firms with affluent individuals and well-capitalized businesses as clients. Lawyers, however, are an exception to the general finding that relatively high incomes and status are associated with relatively high levels of happiness and health. Despite profits per equity partner of nearly $3 million in Am Law 100 firms, studies show that attorneys in large law firms display lower levels of satisfaction and happiness and higher levels of depression, anxiety, and substance abuse than their less affluent counterparts in small law firms, public interest practices and government legal departments. This phenomenon—higher income and prestige and worse health and well-being—is known as a "status-health paradox."[43]

42 Slater, Dan. (2008, March 26). Best of the law blog. *The Wall Street Journal*, p. B8.
43 Koltai, Jonathan, et al. (2018). The status-health paradox: Organizational context, stress exposure, and well-being in the legal profession. *Journal of Health and Social Behavior*, *59*(1), 20.

Studies conducted during the last 20 years indicate that government and nonprofit/public interest lawyers tend to be more satisfied with their careers than private practice lawyers, despite significantly lower compensation in government and nonprofit/public interest jobs. Lawyers in smaller firms also tend to be more satisfied than lawyers in large and midsize firms. These studies are summarized below and in Appendix B. Illustrative findings include:

National Survey of College Graduates (NSCG). The NSCG survey is conducted by the U.S. Bureau of the Census for the National Science Foundation. It includes 12,848 graduates whose highest degree is a Juris Doctor. The results of six surveys completed between 2003 and 2019 show that lawyers working in private law firms are the least satisfied: "Relative to those employed by a private for-profit firm, those who are self-employed, employed by a not-for- profit, or employed by state or local government have job satisfaction that is higher by about 8–12 percentage points."[44]

U.S. News & World Report's law firm ratings. The "U.S. News Best Companies to Work For: Law Firms" ranks 344 law firms in six categories: quality of pay and benefits; work/life balance and flexibility; job and company stability; physical and psychological comfort; belongingness and esteem; and career opportunities and professional development.[45] The 50 largest law firms (average firm size of 1,196 lawyers) achieve higher scores on quality of pay and benefits, job and company stability, belongingness and esteem, and professional development than the 50 smallest law firms (average firm size of 39 lawyers). But the smallest firms score higher than the largest firms on work/life balance and flexibility and physical and psychological comfort. As shown by Figure 2.1, lawyers in the largest law firms obtain an incremental increase in compensation while sustaining an appreciable decrease in work/life balance and flexibility.

U.S. and Canada large law firms study. In this study of lawyers and law firms in the United States and Canada, researchers discovered that "the larger the firm and the more lucrative the role, the more likely a lawyer was

44 Hersch, Joni. (2023). Gender, race, and job satisfaction of law graduates: Intersectional evidence from the National Survey of College Graduates. *Journal of Empirical Legal Studies, 20*, 368.

45 "2024 U.S. News best companies to work for: Law firms." https://money.usnews.com/careers/companies/rankings/best-companies/law-firms. The largest law firms' high scores on job and company stability and belongingness and esteem are consistent with an earlier survey of large law firm lawyers showing that they scored higher than a comparison group of professionals and managers on "security." A high score on security indicates that an individual "values certainty, predictability, and risk free environments; interested in structure, order, and planning for the future." Foster, Jeff, et al. (2010). *Understanding lawyers: Why we do the things we do*. Washington, DC: Hildebrandt Baker Robbins.

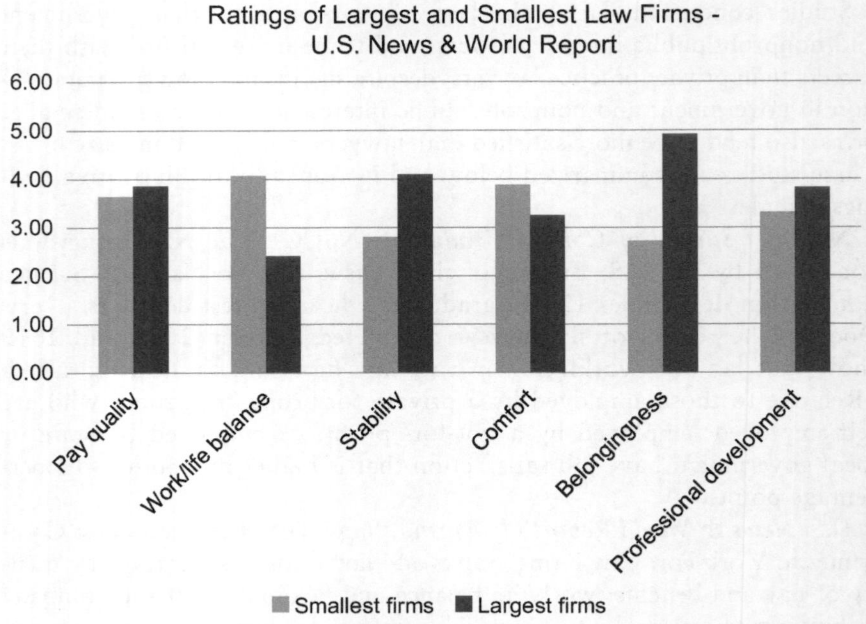

FIGURE 2.1 Ratings of Largest and Smallest Law Firms

Source: *U.S. News Best Companies to Work For: Law Firms*

to experience depressive symptoms."[46] Lawyers in larger firms reported more depression than public sector lawyers; and lawyers in U.S. large firms displayed "a lower probability of good health and a higher probability of poor health relative to those in the public sector *and* those in solo practices and small firms."[47]

Clio midsize and small firms report. Clio, a prominent legal technology company, surveyed 1,134 legal professionals in midsize and small law firms.[48] The survey results revealed that billing rates, billable hours, and annual revenue growth were higher in midsize firms, but lawyers in small firms "reported higher states of well-being than those in mid-sized firms." The small firm lawyers were more satisfied with their professional lives at all

46 McQuigge, Michelle. (2017, October 22). Successful lawyers more likely to experience mental health problems, study finds. *Toronto Star*.

47 Koltai, *supra* note 43.

48 Clio. (2023). Legal trends for mid-sized law firms. https://clio.drift.click/mm-ltr-2023. Clio. (2023, July 27). Clio's 2023 legal trends for mid-sized law firms report reveals increased business growth, lower lawyer satisfaction rates [Press release]. https://www.clio.com/about/press/2023-legal-trends-for-mid-sized-law-firms/.

levels of well-being: relationships with clients; relationships with colleagues; time management; professional life; personal earnings; and emotional and mental wellness.

National Health Interview Survey. Law professor Yair Listokin and law student Raymond Noonan reviewed data regarding 1,000 lawyers, compiled by the Center for Disease Control in its National Health Interview Survey (NHIS).[49] The data shows that "alcohol abuse in the legal profession has been getting worse—increasing dramatically over the last 15 years." The rate of problematic drinking at private law firms is 50 percent greater than the rate among government lawyers. Problematic drinking rates, Listokin and Noonan conclude, "are highest among young lawyers and those working at large law firms."

Texas lawyers survey. Law professor Milan Markovic and psychology professor Gabriele Plickert analyzed survey results from 11,000 State Bar of Texas members.[50] They found that the median annual income of private practitioners in Texas is $125,000, considerably higher than the median government attorney income ($88,000) and median nonprofit/public interest lawyer ($60,000). Sixty-five percent of private practitioners report that they are satisfied with their careers, but higher career satisfaction rates are reported by government lawyers (68 percent) and nonprofit/public interest lawyers (74 percent). Markovic and Plickert's statistical analysis shows that private practice employment "increases a lawyer's odds of career *dis*satisfaction by 38.8% compared to employment in government and 67.9% compared to employment in a non-profit/public interest setting."[51]

Four-state lawyer survey. Law professor Lawrence Krieger and psychology professor Kennon Sheldon obtained survey results from 7,805 members of four state bar associations. The survey results demonstrated that lawyers in "prestige" practices (e.g., 100+ attorney firms) had higher income, law school grades, and law review participation than "service" lawyers (e.g., public defender, criminal prosecutor, and nonprofit legal services). Service lawyers, however, "reported greater well-being than the more 'elite,' highly paid, 'prestige' lawyers, despite substantially lower earnings. 'Prestige' lawyers also reported more alcohol use."[52] Although the prestige lawyers had

49 Listokin, Yair, & Noonan, Raymond. (2021, March). Measuring lawyer well-being systematically: Evidence from the National Health Interview Survey. *Journal of Empirical Legal Studies*, *18*(1), 6, 32.

50 Markovic, Milan, & Plickert, Gabriele. (2018, April). Attorneys' career dissatisfaction in the new normal. *International Journal of the Legal Profession*, 1.

51 Ibid at 13. (Markovic & Plickert also find that "firm size does not affect lawyers' career dissatisfaction," although they acknowledge that previous empirical research "suggested that firm size is negatively correlated with career satisfaction.")

52 Krieger, Lawrence S., & Sheldon, Kennon M. (2015). What makes lawyers happy?: A data-driven prescription to redefine professional success. *The George Washington Law Review*, *83*, 554, 591.

the highest grades and income of all groups in this survey, they "were not as happy as 'service lawyers,' the group with the lowest pay and law school grades."[53]

ABA and NALP study of attorneys admitted in 2000. The American Bar Association (ABA) and the National Association for Law Placement (NALP) have tracked the careers of 5,000 lawyers who were admitted to law practice in 2000. In their third longitudinal study of this nationally representative cohort, they find that "the highest satisfaction with job substance is in the nonprofit and education sectors. As in the previous reports, the lowest job setting satisfaction was expressed by respondents in the large law firms, led by firms of 101–250 lawyers, followed closely by respondents in the largest law firms."[54] Government and public interest attorneys also reported higher satisfaction with the substance of their work and their job settings than attorneys practicing in all three categories of large law firms (21–100, 101–250, and 251+ attorneys).

University of Michigan Law School alumni surveys. About 13,000 graduates of the University of Michigan Law School have participated in its annual alumni surveys.[55] These surveys yield at least two critical findings about the effect of practice setting on attorney satisfaction. First, among private practitioners, attorneys working in small firms were more satisfied with their careers than attorneys working in large firms. Second, among all attorneys, those working in private law firms were the least satisfied with their careers: "fewer of the graduates working in private law firms [59 percent] or as corporate counsel or businesspersons [63 percent] were quite positive than were those working in government, public interest organizations, legal services, public defenders, and education [71 percent]. They were also less satisfied overall than 'everyone else,' a group that is composed of persons neither practicing law nor working in business, but rather working in unions or nonprofit organizations or in any of the wide range of other occupations in which law-school graduates end up in (including, for example, painters, poets, and physicians)."

Attorneys practicing in the legal services/public interest context reported markedly higher levels of satisfaction with the value of their work to society. Among the 15- and 25-year graduates, for instance, only 24 percent of attorneys in very large firms were "quite positive" about the value of their work to society, in comparison with "86 percent of those in legal services/

53 Ibid at 618.
54 Dinovitzer, R., et al. (2014). *After the JD III: Third results from a national study of legal careers* (p. 53). Chicago: American Bar Foundation and NALP Foundation for Law Career Research and Education.
55 Chambers, David L. (2013). *Satisfaction in the practice of law: Findings from a long-term study of attorneys' careers*. U. of Mich. Public Law Research Paper No. 330.

public interest [who] were quite positive about the value of their work to society." Attorneys' perceptions of the value of their work to society were largely determinative of their overall career satisfaction. For 90 percent of the surveyed attorneys, the two factors most strongly correlated with overall career satisfaction were "their satisfaction with the quality of their relationships with co-workers and superiors at their place of work and their satisfaction with the value of their work to society."

Criticisms of mental health studies

Studies of attorneys' mental health provoke derision, criticism, and denial. They are frequently perceived as attacks on attorney competence instead of constructive alerts. Since the possibility of widespread mental illness is often seen as an insult and a threat to the legal profession, the profession is divided attitudinally between attorneys who ignore or minimize mental impairments and those who recognize and intend to ameliorate mental distress. Some attorneys have become so complacent about surveys documenting extensive mental illness that they routinely dismiss them, as evidenced by this survey response from a senior male partner in a 1,000+ attorney law firm: "Stop putting together obviously biased surveys like this. What a joke!. . . I can see it now: Law Firm Stress at Crisis Levels, yadayadayada."[56]

The division in the legal profession is replicated in academic research. As law professor John Monahan and psychiatry professor Jeffrey Swanson write, "There are two literatures on lawyer satisfaction and their findings differ so starkly that one might wonder whether they are studying the same phenomenon."[57] In the first literature—described by Monahan and Swanson as "much better known both to lawyers and nonlawyers alike"—attorneys are shown to be more depressed, anxious, addicted, and suicidal than the general population.[58] In the second literature, "only a small portion of attorneys hold negative views overall about their jobs or careers."[59]

The disparities described by Monahan and Swanson can be reconciled. As law professor David Chambers explains, "Even if disproportionate numbers of attorneys suffer from alcoholism or depression, it could still be the case that

56 Henderson & Henderson, *supra* note 41.

57 Monahan, John, & Swanson, Jeffrey. (2009). Lawyers at mid-career: A 20-year longitudinal study of job and life satisfaction. *Journal of Empirical Legal Studies*, 6(3), 452.

58 Ibid at 452–453.

59 Monahan, John, & Swanson, Jeffrey. (2019). Lawyers at the peak of their careers: A 30-year longitudinal study of job and life satisfaction. *Journal of Empirical Legal Studies*, 16(1), 6. See Hersch, *supra* note 44 at 367. ("To summarize, even with extensive controls for individual characteristics, work setting, and family background, Black women report satisfaction about 20 percentage points lower and Asian women about 14 percentage points lower than White men.")

two-thirds or three-fourths of all attorneys are well satisfied with their current jobs and their careers." A survey of Utah attorneys substantiates Chambers' argument.[60] In that survey, attorneys simultaneously reported high levels of depression, anxiety, and suicidal ideation—and high levels of job and career satisfaction. Although these findings may strike academics as inconsistent, we have no reason to doubt the attorneys' sincerity in describing their emotional states. The possibility that many attorneys are mentally impaired, as measured by objective standards, and quite satisfied with themselves and their careers, as reported by subjective standards, simply means that attorney well-being is a more complex and intractable problem than we previously recognized.

Four other studies, discussed below, suggest that attorneys can be objectively impaired and subjectively satisfied. In a *Bloomberg Law* survey, attorneys were asked to rate their job satisfaction on a 0–10 scale.[61] The attorneys who rated their job satisfaction in the 7–10 range were categorized as "Satisfied Attorneys," and the attorneys with lower ratings were categorized as "Unsatisfied Attorneys." Both categories of attorneys were asked about symptoms of work-related mental and physical impairments. Although the Satisfied Attorneys reported fewer symptoms than the Unsatisfied Attorneys, the Satisfied Attorneys exhibited abnormally high levels of mental and physical impairments:

- *Disrupted sleep*. Seventy-one percent of Satisfied Attorneys reported disrupted sleep due to work-related issues.
- *Anxiety*. Sixty-four percent of Satisfied Attorneys were experiencing work-related anxiety.
- *Physical problems*. Twenty percent of Satisfied Attorneys identified work-related physical health issues.
- *Depression*. Nineteen percent of Satisfied Attorneys felt depressed.[62]

Only 15 percent of the Satisfied Attorneys were *not* experiencing a work-related mental impairment or physical health issue.

Although the Satisfied Attorneys reported relatively high levels of subjective job satisfaction, their mental and physical health, by any objective standard, was at risk. They were comparatively, but not objectively, healthy.

60 Thiese, Matthew S. (2020, March/April). The Utah lawyer well-being study: Preliminary results show Utah lawyers at risk. *Utah Bar Journal*, pp. 29–30. See Appendix A and Utah Community Builders & Salt Lake Chamber. (2022, April). *Living Well in Law*.

61 Ouyang, Linda. (2021, March 17). Analysis: Survey data exposes roots of attorney dissatisfaction. *Bloomberg Law*.

62 Thirty-nine percent of Satisfied Attorneys reported "a reduction in work-life balance;" twenty-nine percent said their work had caused problems in their personal relationships; and twenty-eight percent "feel burnt out a majority of the time."

Many of them could be regarded as "morbidly satisfied"—satisfied with their jobs while experiencing unhealthy, work-related mental and physical impairments that tend to cause further harm.

The *Bloomberg Law* survey results are consistent with a second survey, conducted by Law360 Pulse, in which 68 percent of the lawyers said they were "satisfied or very satisfied with their overall job."[63] Seventy-one percent said they "would not switch careers if given a chance for a do-over." But 83 percent of the surveyed lawyers were "stressed at least some of the time," and 46 percent of the female lawyers "felt stress all or most of the time." One-third of the female lawyers reported that "their work-life balance had gotten worse in the past year," and nearly one-half of the female lawyers also had "personally encountered gender discrimination on the job." Most of the surveyed lawyers worked 51–60+ hours per week, and one in five expected their total annual vacation time to be one week or less.

A third study, based on University of Michigan Law School alumni surveys, also indicates that attorneys can be subjectively satisfied and objectively impaired. In those surveys, the attorneys who were more stressed and more compulsive than their classmates reported higher levels of subjective well-being:

> The graduates who were quite positive about their careers despite high stress tended to be those who also characterized themselves as comparatively compulsive about work: among those who reported high stress, a much higher proportion of those who saw themselves as above average in compulsivity about work were quite positive about their careers than among those who saw themselves as below average in compulsivity.[64]

The fact that stressed, compulsive attorneys were more satisfied with their careers is not evidence of sound mental health. Instead, it connotes emotional numbing, lack of self-awareness, and a law firm culture that may equate value with intense pressure, constant work, and extreme profitableness. As law professor Jonathan Todres reflects on his previous career in private practice and the legal profession's work culture, "Another week, I billed 129 hours, including all-nighters on Friday and Saturday nights. Arriving at the office on Monday morning, I was greeted with praise. At the time, it felt good. Today, I see those moments as indicative of how quickly I lost any expectation that self-care and life beyond work mattered."[65]

63 Weiss, Debra Cassens. (2023, April 11). Lawyers report high level of satisfaction with their jobs, but stress remains an issue, survey finds. *ABA Journal Daily News*.

64 Chambers, David L. (2013). *Satisfaction in the practice of law: Findings from a long-term study of attorneys' careers*. U. of Mich. Public Law Research Paper No. 330, p. 24.

65 Todres, Jonathan. (2022, March 15). A healthier legal profession starts with law schools. *Bloomberg Law*.

A fourth study also highlights the gap between objective findings and attorneys' subjective reactions. In that study, 481 attorneys were asked to identify a pending case and confirm in writing their minimum goal for the outcome of that case.[66] After the cases were resolved, the researchers contacted the attorneys to determine whether they had met their minimum goal (objective standard) and how they felt about the case outcome (subjective reaction). The attorneys' objective performance had little or no bearing on their subjective satisfaction: "Fewer than one fifth of the lawyers (18%) were very disappointed or somewhat disappointed with the case outcome, although more than twice as many (43%) actually failed to achieve their stated minimum goal. Of the group of lawyers who did not achieve their minimum goal . . . two thirds reported that they were somewhat pleased or very pleased with the actual outcome."

Attorneys' subjective evaluations of their own condition and conduct seem to be self-protective, self-serving, and self-denying. Their tendency to report high levels of subjective satisfaction in the face of objective evidence warranting lower levels may indicate a serious lack of introspection, self-knowledge, and self-awareness. In the case of compulsive attorneys, this tendency may reflect the inaccurate perceptions, unrealistic assessments, and destructive drives that characterize the disorder itself.

Researchers who challenge the high rates of mental illness shown in some studies and contend that attorneys are generally satisfied with their careers may be overlooking their own biases. Chambers identifies three possible biases displayed by critics and apologists:

> first, that many of those [lawyers] who put themselves above midpoints on satisfaction scales are barely more positive than negative about their careers and might well speak of their careers in the same sort of beleaguered tones reported in the negative literature; second, that surveys conducted at a single point in time convey an incomplete impression of the satisfaction of work in any given setting (such as a law firm) because they necessarily fail to include the views of those who previously worked in that setting but have now gone elsewhere; and third, that few studies address the problem of bias that may be caused by lower rates of response from the least satisfied persons in the population sampled.[67]

"Survivorship bias" may be the most pernicious bias in surveys showing average or above-average levels of job and career satisfaction among attorneys working in large law firms. About four out of five associate attorneys

66 Goodman-Delahunty, Jane, et al. (2010). Insightful or wishful: Lawyers' ability to predict case outcomes. *Psychology, Public Policy, and Law*, *15*(2), 133.

67 Chambers, David L. (2014, Spring). Overstating the satisfaction of lawyers. *Law & Social Inquiry*, *39*(2), 313.

leave their large law firm jobs within five years, citing "lack of control over my work schedule," "lack of control over my assignments," "number of hours," and "lack of diversity of my colleagues" as factors they most dislike.[68] If surveys of attorney job and career satisfaction are limited to the people who stay and flourish in these environments, deserted by thousands of attorneys who initially encountered them, we should question whether the survivor samples are representative of the general attorney population.

A remaining criticism of recent attorney survey results is that they are skewed pessimistically by the Covid-19 pandemic. This criticism is weakened by four factors: (1) the data reported in some recent surveys was compiled before the onset of the Covid-19 pandemic; (2) some survey results have been analyzed to identify, assess, and adjust for Covid-19 anomalies; (3) some surveys indicate that attorneys' mental well-being, especially among female and ethnic minority lawyers, was worse before law firms allowed them to work remotely during the pandemic; and (4) workers generally reported higher levels of stress, anger, disengagement, and dissatisfaction in 2023 than in the earlier 2020–2022 period when companies were adhering to stricter pandemic protocols. Although the Covid-19 pandemic may have affected some survey results, multiple reports during the last 25 years "indicate that lawyers suffer from exceedingly high rates of depression, anxiety, and substance misuse."[69]

If the surveys suffer from a single, major deficiency, it most likely is the failure to include clients' perspectives. Clients' legal interests may not be adequately protected by impaired lawyers, and clients are directly and sometimes permanently harmed by the indifference, inattention, inefficiency, extreme risk aversion, lack of problem-solving skills, and flawed strategies resulting from their attorneys' mental distress. Aarash Darroodi, General Counsel for Fender Musical Instruments Corporation, crystallizes the client's perspective when he probes, "Would a law firm feel comfortable working with a client organization [where] perhaps maybe greater than 60 percent of the individuals are either depressed, alcoholic, or suicidal? Of course not. They would have some serious, grave concerns about that. We have some serious, grave concerns about that as well." Darroodi elaborates, "I don't think that the environment of firms is really taking a look at mental health. It is absolutely critical. We want our lawyers that we work with on the outside to be healthy, happy individuals that want to work."[70]

68 Cartusciello, Yolanda, et al. (2020, March). *Multiple generations in law firms* (p. 27). Washington, DC: NALP and PP&C Consulting.

69 Anker & Krill, *supra* note 25 at 1.

70 Thomson Reuters Institute. (2023, February 21). *2023 State of the Legal Market webinar.* (Remarks by Aarash Darroodi, General Counsel, Executive Vice President and Corporate Secretary, Fender Musical Instruments Corporation, webinar recording starting at 32:16).

3

CAUSES AND EFFECTS OF LAWYERS' MENTAL DISTRESS

The causes of attorneys' mental distress are embedded deeply in law firm cultures, practices, and economics. Although the stigma of mental illness presumes that individual traits and weaknesses cause mental impairments, the consistency, pervasiveness, severity, and distribution of lawyers' mental illness indicate that its causes are more likely to be structural and systemic. The probability of structural and systemic causes is heightened by studies showing that lawyers exhibit average mental health before they enter law school, and their mental health deteriorates during law school and law firm employment.[1] If lawyers' distress was idiosyncratic—caused by the vagaries of individual personalities—we would be witnessing a most peculiar type of mental illness that remains latent in early adulthood and evades detection until being triggered by law school enrollment and the start of a legal career. And large law firms would necessarily have developed a unique skill in identifying, recruiting, and retaining lawyers who will eventually exhibit levels of mental distress and alcohol abuse not evident in government and nonprofit/public interest lawyers.

The longstanding effort to treat mental illness among lawyers as idiosyncratic is both suspect and irresponsible. It persists because it deflects scrutiny of

1 See Daicoff, Susan Swaim. (2004). *Lawyer, know thyself.* Washington, DC: American Psychological Association. Iijima, Ann L. (1998). Lessons learned: Legal education and law student dysfunction. *Journal of Legal Education*, *48*, 524. Jackson, Janet Thompson. (2022, January). Work, wellness, and meaning: Reimagining legal education and the first 10 years of law practice. *NALP Professional Development Quarterly*. Kern, Margaret L., & Bowling, Daniel S. (2014). Character strengths and academic performance in law students. *Journal of Research in Personality*, *55*, 29. Krieger, Lawrence S., & Sheldon, Kennon M. (2015). What makes lawyers happy?: A data-driven prescription to redefine professional success. *The George Washington Law Review*, *83*, 554, 596.

DOI: 10.4324/9781003514848-3

internal practices, retards reform, and, ultimately, preserves a business model dependent on ever-increasing revenue generated by ever-increasing hours billed at ever-increasing rates.[2] As sociology professor Diane Vaughan found in her analysis of the Challenger space shuttle disaster, adverse outcomes in organizations are generally not traceable to aberrations in individual behavior but instead are "socially organized and systematically produced by social structures."[3] Those social structures, Vaughan relates, have three purposes: the production of culture, the perpetuation of a culture of production, and the legitimation of organizational secrecy. These three purposes coalesce in an organizational dysfunction that Vaughan calls "normalization of deviance." Rooted in organizational structures, routines, and incentives, normalization of deviance, she explains, became "a way of seeing that was simultaneously a way of not seeing."[4]

Major causes of lawyers' mental distress

When asked to identify the major factors negatively affecting their well-being, attorneys focus on billable hour pressures, long hours, unrealistic time pressures, poor work/life balance, high stress working environments, lack of sleep, no workload control, unreasonable client demands, and inability to disconnect from work.[5] Seventy-nine percent of attorneys state that their

2 See Thomson Reuters Institute, & Georgetown Law Center on the Legal Profession. (2022). *2022 report on the state of the legal market.* https://www.thomsonreuters.com/en-us/posts/wp-content/uploads/sites/20/2022/01/State-of-Legal-Market-Report_Final.pdf. Thomson Reuters Institute, & Georgetown Law Center on the Legal Profession. (2021). *2021 report on the state of the legal market.* https://legal.thomsonreuters.com/content/dam/ewpm/documents/legal/en/pdf/reports/2021_sotlm_web_v2.pdf.

3 Vaughan, Diane. (1996). *The Challenger launch decision* (p. 394). Chicago: The University of Chicago Press. For an analysis of organizational failures in the health care context, see Elliott, Carl. (2024). *The occasional human sacrifice.* New York: W.W. Norton & Company.

4 Ibid.

5 See ALM Intelligence. (2021, May). *Mental health and substance abuse.* New York: ALM. Cartusciello, Yolanda, et al. (2020, March). *Multiple generations in law firms* (p. 27). Washington, DC: NALP and PP&C Consulting. Choudhury, Rashmita. (2024, May 17). Mental health by the numbers: The 2024 survey infographic. *The American Lawyer.* International Bar Association. (2021, October). *Mental wellbeing in the legal profession: A global study.* London: International Bar Association. Henderson, Lauren, & Henderson, Bill. (2020, June 21). What needs to change to improve mental health in the legal profession? *Legal Evolution.* www.legalevolution.org/2020/06/what-needs-to-change-to-improve-mental-health-in-the-legal-profession-171/. Krill, Patrick R., et al. (2022). People, professionals, and profit centers: The connection between lawyer well-being and employer values. *Behavioral Sciences, 12,* 177. Major, Lindsey & Africa. (2021). *Making their mark: How millennial lawyers could reshape the industry.* Hanover, MD: Major, Lindsey & Africa. Major, Lindsey & Africa. (2023). *Searching for balance: Millennial lawyers' perspectives on the legal industry.* Hanover, MD: Major, Lindsey & Africa. Major, Lindsey & Africa. (2023). *Gen-Z: Now influencing today's law firm culture.* Hanover, MD: Major, Lindsey & Africa.

work environment contributes to their mental health problems; and only 31 percent of attorneys report that their law firms "push back on unreasonable client demands."[6]

If lawyers had discovered a different industry reliably correlated with mental illnesses that workers attribute to workplace conditions, they might have recommended that those workers initiate class actions. The concept of law firm liability for undermining lawyers' well-being, in fact, may not be as remote as it seems. A harbinger of possible legal action against law firms is the Solicitors Regulation Authority's investigation of 24 cases involving alleged bullying, harassment, and pressure within U.K. law firms. In those cases, senior law firm leaders "who repeatedly fail to address toxic behaviour could face prosecution. Law firms themselves can be fined up to £25,000 [about 32,000 USD] if they fail to protect employee wellbeing."[7]

Negative workplace conditions compel associate attorneys to leave law firms at an extraordinary rate. The average annual attrition rate ranges from 18 to 26 percent; and annual turnover in large law firms ranges from 17 percent to 74 percent.[8] The attrition rate for attorneys of color is 24–34 percent, "an ongoing higher attrition rate for associates of color than their peers."[9] Most associate attorneys believe that their law firms "aren't actively trying to keep them."[10] The current attrition rates, according to a Thomson Reuters report, are "one of the higher levels that we have seen in the past decade."[11] These turnover rates are estimated to be about ten times higher than those in well-run corporations.[12]

6 Choudhury, *supra* note 5.

7 Mawardi, Adam. (2024, March 14). Law firms facing two dozen toxic workplace investigations amid burnout crisis. *The Telegraph*.

8 Johnson, Julia Brunette. (2023, April 19). Law firm hiring cools down from 2021, NALP Foundation study finds. *The National Jurist*. Kiser, Randall. (2019). *American law firms in transition: Trends, threats and strategies* (p. 67). Chicago: American Bar Association. Konnath, Hailey. (2022, April 26). Associate attorney hiring, attrition up sharply in '21'. *Law 360*. NALP Foundation. (2022, April 26). *Update on associate attrition*. NALP Foundation. (2024, April 10). *Update on associate attrition*.

9 Rubino, Kathryn. (2022, May 2). Associates left law firms in droves last year. Why'd they go? *Above the Law*. NALP Foundation (2024), *supra* note 8.

10 Robert, Amanda. (2023, October 11). Most BigLaw associates think their law firms aren't trying to keep them, new survey shows. *ABA Journal Daily News*.

11 Maloney, Andrew. (2023, June 22). 'A huge concern': Big Law leaders grappling with attorney disengagement. *The American Lawyer*.

12 Krill (2022), *supra* note 5, citing Steinbaum, Carly. Law firm musical chairs: Hidden reasons behind associate attrition rates and what firms can do about it. *ABA Journal*. https://www.americanbar.org/careercenter/blog/law-firm-musical-chairs/.

In the survey comments that follow, lawyers convey some of their concerns about the workplace and show why law practice is now ranked as the "single most stressful occupation":[13]

- "The constant stress and pressure of deadlines and pressure to bill hours do not stop at the end of the work day. I struggle to shut off the work part of my brain. The stress is always there in the background."
- "I have a busy practice and a heavy workload, leading to feelings of overwhelming stress about half the time. It invades my home life, my dreams."
- "The ability to disconnect is non-existent, so much client pressure and internal pressure in Big Law. I'm on track to bill 2,150 hours this year and I have a 19-month old baby. This setup is not sustainable and completely unhealthy."
- "We are in internal competition and external competition, and we exacerbate it by reporting annual [financial performance] numbers to things like the AmLaw100. . . If a firm slips in the standings, they 'can't recruit.' It's a treadmill with one button: 'Faster'. . . . No one should be surprised that the tradeoff is mental health and stability."
- "From what I've observed in other industries it appears corporations value mental health of employees more because they are focused on the long term. . . . [Law firm partners] prioritize short term profitability over employee well-being, employee retention, and adapting to new technologies and changing business models."
- "I didn't even realize I was feeling burnt out until I was burnt out. . . . I think the maximum I billed one year was 3,500 or 3,600 hours. I just taught myself how to get by on an hour or an hour and 45 minutes of sleep a night. And to do that day in and day out over years and years and years, you begin to have a real disassociation from what I would consider to be real life."

A partner in a 1,000+ attorney firm pleads, "Destigmatize mental illness and addiction." She describes how her firm responds to impaired attorneys: "No one in my firm, including my direct supervisors and HR [Human

13 The "most stressful occupation" rating is based on four Bureau of Labor Statistics American Time Use surveys conducted between 2010 and 2021. Van Dam, Andrew. (2023, January 6). The happiest, least stressful, most meaningful jobs in America. *The Washington Post*. The first two bulleted quotations appear in International Bar Association (2021), *supra* note 5. The next three bulleted quotations and the quotation in the last paragraph of this section appear in Henderson & Henderson, *supra* note 5. The last bulleted quotation appears in Bloomberg Law. (2022, November). The billable hour: Why Big Law just can't quit it. www.youtube.com/watch?v=n_TQOzsTiJo.

Resources], has ever expressed any support at all for people who are suffering mentally, aside from providing health benefits and an EAP [Employee Assistance Program] pamphlet. The assumption is that an addicted or mentally ill lawyer can't do the job, so no one talks about it."

Specific factors and their effects

Structural and systemic factors contributing to attorneys' mental distress include long hours; billable hour requirements; lack of control over workload and assignments; being ignored or treated as a profit center; boring, meaningless work; gender bias; sexual harassment; bullying; poor relationships with other attorneys; and inadequate firm leadership. These factors and their effects on lawyer performance are discussed below.

Long hours/billable hour requirements

When asked, "What do you dislike the most about your job?" associate attorneys rank "lack of control over my work schedule" as the worst aspect.[14] The runner-up is "number of hours." When asked, "Thinking about lawyers with whom you started who have left the firm, why do you think they went elsewhere?" associate attorneys identify the three leading reasons as "they wanted a different work/life balance"; "they found better opportunities elsewhere"; and "the workload was too heavy." Nearly one-half of law firm partners state that the main reason associates leave their firms is because "they wanted a different work/life balance."

Although associate attorneys deplore onerous workloads, the top priority for most surveyed law firm leaders is "motivating the lawyers to work harder."[15] The persistent pressure imposed by billable hours is evident in an internal memo sent by an AmLaw 100 law firm's managing partner to the entire firm: "As we look across the partnership, we see that success typically means an 'all in' commitment on your part (for those who work full time) in the range of 2,400 hours per year."[16] He elaborates, "Many of our partners regularly surpass this range, however, and most partners in leadership roles exceed it by necessity. Ideally, a significant proportion of the expected annual hours commitment will be on client chargeable work because that remains the best way to build our brand and drive profitability."

14 Data reported in this paragraph appears in Cartusciello, *supra* note 5 at 90, 120, and 122.
15 McKenna, Patrick J., & Rynowecer, Michael B. (2024, January 30). The 2024 'burning issues' confronting firm leaders. *Business of Law Digest*.
16 Walker, Hannah. (2022, May 16). Hogan Lovells sets out hours 'requirements' to become a partner at the firm. *The American Lawyer*.

Success in law firms, as that managing partner declares, requires an "all in" commitment. That commitment increases with the size of the law firm.[17] Attorneys in 701+ attorney firms, for example, work 11 percent more hours per year than attorneys in 101–250 attorney firms. Billable hour requirements also display a linear relationship with firm size, increasing with each category of firm size: < 101 attorneys (baseline); 101–250 attorneys (2 percent increase over baseline firm); 251–500 attorneys (1 percent increase over 101–250 firm); 501–700 attorneys (1 percent increase over 251–500 firm); and 700+ attorneys (2 percent increase over 501–700 firm). Billable hours requirements have "the strongest negative relationship with well-being" and are correlated with increased alcohol use.[18] As law professor Lawrence Krieger and psychology professor Kennon Sheldon report, "each increase in billable hours brings moderately greater income and slightly less happiness."[19]

Law firms' fixation on billable hours leads to overwork, and overwork is strongly correlated with depression, anxiety, burnout, alcoholism, drug abuse, chronic physical pain, cognitive impairment, learned helplessness, impulsivity, insensitivity, unethical behavior, decision-making errors, and cardiovascular disease.[20] Sleep deprivation, a concomitant of overwork, impedes learning, creativity, communication, memory consolidation, flexibility, and empathy, and it increases forgetfulness, emotional reactivity, negativity, paranoia, aggression, and the attractiveness of financial rewards. Although overwork serves as a proxy for commitment in many law firms, its actual effects are often the antithesis of professional service.

17 Data reported in this paragraph is derived from NALP. (2016). Update on associate hours worked. *NALP Bulletin*.

18 Krieger & Sheldon (2015), *supra* note 1 at 596, 615.

19 Ibid.

20 For research regarding the effects of overwork and sleep deprivation, see Bishop, Sonia J., & Gagne, Christopher. (2018). Anxiety, depression, and decision making: A computational perspective. *Annual Review of Neuroscience*, *41*, 371. Chlap, Nora, & Brown, Rhonda. (2022). Relationships between workplace characteristics, psychological stress, affective distress, burnout and empathy in lawyers. *International Journal of the Legal Profession*, *29*(2), 159. Cote, Kimberly, et al. (2014). Impact of total sleep deprivation on behavioural neural processing of emotionally expressive faces. *Experimental Brain Research*, *232*(5), 1429. Harrison, Yvonne, & Horne, James A. (2000). The impact of sleep deprivation on decision making: A review. *Journal of Experimental Psychology: Applied*, *6*, 236. Lawlor, Victoria M., et al. (2019). Dissecting the impact of depression on decision making. *Psychological Medicine*, *50*(10), 1. Lewis, Penelope A. (2013). *The secret world of sleep*. New York: Palgrave Macmillan. Leykin, Yan, et al. (2011). Decision-making and depressive symptomatology. *Cognitive Therapy and Research*, *35*(4), 333. Li, Wei, et al. (2017, March). REM sleep prunes and maintains new synapses in development and learning. *Nature Neuroscience*, *20*(3), 427. Simon, Eti Ben, et al. (2022). Sleep loss leads to the withdrawal of human helping across individuals, groups, and large-scale societies. *PLOS Biology*, *20*(8), e3001733. Walker, Matthew. (2017). *Why we sleep*. New York: Scribner.

The damage inflicted by excessive work ultimately harms both law firms and clients:

> [W]hen lawyers experience ill-health, they are presumptively delivering lower quality work and doing so less efficiently, even while meeting their billable hour obligations. After all, when people are sick, they are distracted by their ailments and have trouble concentrating. This may ultimately result in client dissatisfaction with work product and loss of future business opportunities for the employer. Furthermore, some research has shown that costs associated with a lack of productivity among unhealthy employees were even higher than the direct medical claims costs associated with sick workers.
>
> Stress and decreased well-being can also result in diminished cognitive function in lawyers, which presents other risks such as an increased likelihood of costly mistakes, problems which are on the rise even as many law firms are reporting record profits. In fact, payouts for legal malpractice claims reached an all-time high in 2020. Additionally, legal employers with an unhealthy workforce are more likely to experience significant costs associated with high attrition.[21]

Law firms would experience a 10–20 percent decline in profitability if annual median billable hours were reduced to 1,800—a seemingly small cost to reduce malpractice claims and improve efficiency, quality, attention, and well-being.[22]

The stress induced by chronic overwork affects attorneys' judgment and advice in five critical respects.

- *Emotional regulation.* Stress inhibits functions of the prefrontal cortex, shifting control to the amygdala and preventing intelligent, balanced evaluations of problems and solutions. The emotional regulation otherwise conducted by the prefrontal cortex yields to the more reactive amygdala.[23]
- *Risk aversion.* Sustained stress results in a tendency to overemphasize small probabilities and ignore large probabilities. Stressed decision makers

21 Krill (2022), *supra* note 5.

22 Roe, Dan. (2023, July 27). The 1,800 hour year: Pipe dream or essential for lawyers' well-being? *The American Lawyer*. In a different context, estimating the financial effects of AI on law firms, Toby Brown projects that a 5 percent reduction in partner hours and a 20 percent reduction in non-partner hours would result in a 13 percent decline in revenue and a 7 percent decrease in profit margins. Strom, Roy. (2024, May 16). Law firms' AI nightmare is fewer billed hours and lower profits. *Bloomberg Law*.

23 See LeDoux, Joseph. (2002). *The synaptic self*. New York: Penguin Group. Schwartz, Jeffrey M., & Begley, Sharon. (2002). *The mind & the brain*. New York: HarperCollins.

display extreme levels of risk aversion and avoid novel solutions or any other alternatives that are unfamiliar.[24]

- *Empathy*. Stress suppresses empathy and prevents lawyers from understanding and relating to their clients. Stress directly impairs the ability to accurately interpret facial expressions and identify others' moods.[25]
- *Memory*. "Chronic stress inhibits neurogenesis in the hippocampus," as neuroscientist Lisa Genova explains. "So if you're experiencing unrelenting, unmanaged stress, you'll have a smaller hippocampus, which means fewer neurons available to consolidate memories, which means your ability to create new memories will be impaired."[26]
- *Decision making*. Stress causes atrophy of the medial prefrontal cortex and the striatum, preventing accurate evaluations of consequences and fostering a bias toward habitual strategies and dysfunctional decision-making.[27]

Although attorneys regard pessimism as a virtue—"seeing troubles as pervasive and permanent is a component of what the law professions deems prudence"—it might actually be an unhealthy reaction to anxiety and stress.[28] Being in an anxious state, explains physicist Leonard Mlodinow, "leads to a pessimistic cognitive bias; when an anxious brain processes ambiguous information, it tends to choose the more pessimistic from among the likely interpretations. Your brain becomes overactive in perceiving threats and tends to predict dire outcomes when faced with uncertainty."[29]

As the medial prefrontal cortex atrophies under chronic stress, decision makers lose the capacity to evaluate probabilities objectively and respond to problems flexibly. They revert to habitual strategies like pervasive pessimism. Preoccupied with small probabilities, they "develop a selective attention to negative precedents" and discern threats "where none exists."[30] From a neu-

24 Kandasamy, Narayanan, et al. (2014). Cortisol shifts financial risk preferences. *Proceedings of the National Academy of Sciences*, *111*(9), 3608.

25 See Cote, Kimberly A., et al. (2014, May). Impact of total sleep deprivation on behavioural neural processing of emotionally expressive faces. *Experimental Brain Research*, *232*(5), 1429. Martin, Loren J., et al. (2015). Reducing social stress elicits emotional contagion of pain in mouse and human strangers. *Current Biology*, *25*(3), 326. Peterson, Andrea. (2016, September 12). The unexpected ways sleep deprivation makes life tougher. *The Wall Street Journal*.

26 Genova, Lisa. (2021). *Remember* (p. 204). New York: Harmony Books.

27 Dias-Ferreira, Eduardo, et al. (2009, July 31). Chronic stress causes frontostriatal reorganization and affects decision-making. *Science*, *325*, 621.

28 Seligman, Martin E. (2002). *Authentic happiness* (p. 178). New York: Free Press.

29 Mlodinow, Leonard. (2022). *Emotional* (p. 8). New York: Pantheon Books.

30 Kandasamy, *supra* note 24 at 3612. See Wemm, Stephanie E., & Wulfert, Edelgard. (2017, March). Effects of acute stress on decision making. *Applied Psychophysiology and Biofeedback*, *42*(1), 1. ("Compared to controls, participants in the stress condition responded with higher heart rates and skin conductance responses, reported more negative affect, and on the decision-making task made less advantageous choices.")

rological perspective, attorneys' vaunted "issue spotting" and preoccupation with everything that could go wrong could be seen as cognitive impairments resulting from chronic stress rather than attributes typically ascribed to a keen legal mind.

Lack of control over work and assignments

Associate attorneys' lack of control over their work is entangled with work/life balance, time pressures, billable hour requirements, and an inability to disconnect from work. Roughly one-half of Millennial generation attorneys state that they would trade a portion of their compensation for "more time off," "a cut in billable hours," or "a flexible work schedule."[31] When asked to identify the most important reason for being open to a new job opportunity, Millennial generation attorneys most frequently select "work/life balance."[32]

Female associate attorneys are slightly more likely than male associate attorneys to identify "lack of control over my work schedule" and "lack of control over my assignments" as the job factors they most dislike. These comments from female associate attorneys are illustrative[33]:

- "There need to be more options to work less and make less money, without this being like you 'can't stand the heat.' I can stand it, I just don't want to. Surely it would be better for them to allow me to contribute my specialism (sometimes from home) with reasonable targets than just have me leave when I finally crack. I know others feel this way too."
- "There is a culture that the client is king, so we can go without sleep for 3 or 4 nights. . . . No partner in a law firm is ever going to say 'no' to a client, and when you are dealing with 5 or 6 transactions at the same time you are pulled in too many directions. . . . Discrimination is widespread, sexism is very common and there is very little regard for people's well-being and mental health."
- "Trying to go leaner and leaner in a race to the bottom becomes counterproductive at a certain point, not least because it ends up putting so much pressure on associates and staff that their mental health and morale is adversely affected. . . . [S]etting reasonable client expectations . . . will not necessarily result in lost clients. Many clients respect boundaries, and, with appropriate boundaries, attorneys are happier and, consequently, more productive."

31 Major, Lindsey & Africa. *Searching for balance: Millennial lawyers' perspectives on the legal industry*, *supra* note 5 at 13.
32 Ibid at 34.
33 Henderson & Henderson, *supra* note 5.

Although partners acknowledge that law practice is stressful for associate attorneys, nearly one-half of partners deprecate associate attorneys' work ethic and commitment. Forty-seven percent of partners *dis*agree with the statement, "The younger lawyers in my firm work as hard as my classmates did."[34] Forty-one percent of partners believe that "the younger lawyers in my firm are not as ambitious as my classmates were."[35] Male partners are more likely than female partners to be critical of younger lawyers' work ethic and commitment, and Baby Boomer partners are more critical than Millennial partners.

Despite outward expressions of empathy and support for associates, many partners are dismissive of associates' work/life balance complaints. Forty percent of partners believe that "the younger lawyers in my firm expect too much from the firm" and 22 percent believe that "our firm worries too much about what our younger lawyers think."[36] At the core of work/life balance issues is a harsh, possibly irreconcilable conflict between many partners' precepts and priorities and associates' values and expectations.

Being ignored or treated as a profit center

An ambitious study of 1,959 attorneys, randomly selected to complete a survey regarding their well-being, demonstrates a close relationship between a firm's treatment of its lawyers and their mental health.[37] The surveyed attorneys were divided into three groups based on their responses to the question, "What do you feel your employer values most about you?" The three groups and the traits most valued in those groups are as follows:

Professionalism/Individual. ("Everything, they value my inherent worth as a human being." "My overall talent and skill as a lawyer.")
Financial Worth/Availability. ("My productivity or the hours I bill." "My responsiveness and availability.")
No Value/No Feedback. ("Not much—my employer does not make me feel valued." "I don't know—I get very little feedback.")

Most of the attorneys (62 percent) met the criteria for the Professionalism/Individual group, indicating that they felt their employer most valued their professionalism and skills. Twenty-eight percent were in the Financial Worth/Availability group, reflecting their belief that their employers valued them primarily for their revenue generation and work availability. The remaining

34 Cartusciello, *supra* note 5 at 91.
35 Ibid at 92.
36 Ibid at 91.
37 Krill (2022), *supra* note 5.

10 percent were in the No Value/No Feedback group that felt unvalued or lacked sufficient feedback to know what their employers valued about them. Another way of understanding these results is to conclude that roughly 60 percent of the attorneys believed that their employers most valued their professionalism and skills, while 40 percent felt that their employers were primarily interested in their financial contributions or not really interested in them at all.

The mental health of attorneys in the Financial Worth/Availability and No Value/No Feedback groups was considerably worse than that of the Professionalism/Individual group:

> Regarding perceived stress, mental health, and work overcommitment, a discernible trend emerged between our three groups, resulting in what might be described as a health hierarchy. Specifically, lawyers in the Professionalism/Individual group reported better mental health, with lawyers in the Financial Worth/Availability group reporting worse outcomes. The group with the worst health and most limitations are those who either felt unvalued by their employer or did not have enough feedback to know what their employer values most about them (the "No Value/No Feedback" group). Those in the No Value/No Feedback group experienced worrisome levels of perceived stress that would clearly warrant employer intervention due to their likely association with mental health problems among their lawyers.[38]

Although lawyers in the No Value/No Feedback group displayed the worst levels of mental health, all of the attorneys, on average, reported substandard mental and physical health. The lawyers' health, the researchers conclude, "falls below the general population. This is true irrespective of which of our three categories lawyers fall into regarding what their employer values most about them."[39]

The lawyers' substandard health presents another illustration of the status-health paradox discussed in Chapter 2. The finding that lawyers report lower levels of physical and mental health than the general population "takes on significance because lawyers tend to fall higher on the socioeconomic scale, and it is typically people of lower socioeconomic status who are more likely to have worse self-reported health and lower life expectancy and suffer from more chronic conditions when compared with those of higher socioeconomic status."

38 Ibid.

39 This quotation and the remaining quotations in this section appear in Krill (2022), *supra* note 5.

This study also corroborates other studies documenting the specific, negative effects of private law firms in general and large law firms in particular. Lawyers in the Financial Worth/Availability group "were more likely to work in private practice and significantly less likely to work in a government setting compared to the other two groups." Those lawyers also were more likely to report that their time in the legal profession caused their use of alcohol and/or other drugs to increase. When the researchers combined the Financial Worth/Availability group with the No Value/No Feedback group, "we see that the biggest proportion of this group, by a wide margin, is made up of private firm lawyers. This indicates that, as a cohort, private firm lawyers experience the worst mental and physical health." Examining the effects of law firm size, the researchers also found that "the larger the firm, the less likely lawyers are to feel valued for their professional or human worth, and the more likely they are to feel most valued for their financial and productivity contributions and, consequently, report worse health."

Boring, meaningless work

Despite popular depictions of lawyers leading exciting and consequential lives, many lawyers are demoralized by the utter boredom and meaningless nature of their work. "This job is simultaneously extremely demanding and dull," remarks a midlevel corporate associate.[40] When asked to place themselves on a scale in response to the statement, "I am bored with my work," one in three associate attorneys selected the half-way point between "Frequently" and "Never," signaling a level of ambivalence and disengagement that may devolve into inattention, distraction, and apathy.[41] In other studies, 34 percent of lawyers identified "poor quality, repetitious, monotonous work" as the main reason for being unhappy; and 43 percent cited "repetitive tasks rather than complex matters" as the reason their work was not interesting.[42] These reports of boredom are consistent with studies showing that most attorneys are not engaged in their work.[43]

40 Roe, Dan. (2023, August 22). Associates say the darndest things: 2023 edition. *The American Lawyer*.

41 Cartusciello, *supra* note 5 at 121.

42 Debney, Claire, & Sharpe, Emma. (2020). *The Mosaic mood index* (p. 4). London: The Mosaic Collective. Axiom. (2022). *The view from inside: Why are in-house counsel leaving and where are they going*? (p. 7). Chicago: Axiom.

43 Gallup & Access Lex Institute. (2018). *Examining value, measuring engagement* (p. 15). Washington, DC: Gallup. See Axiom, *supra* note 42, reporting that 40 percent of in-house counsel in companies with annual revenue exceeding $25 million state that their work is not challenging or engaging. Cf. NALP. (2024, February 6). Should I stay or should I go? ("The majority of associates reported they were highly engaged. . . .")

The demoralizing nature of many attorneys' work is memorialized by Elizabeth Wurtzel, a graduate of Yale Law School who worked at Boies Schiller Flexner between 2008 and 2012 and wrote the bestseller *Prozac Nation*:

> [M]ost people who think they are practicing law are actually making binders, and my guess is that most people who think they are doing whatever important thing they are doing are making binders. The binders from law firms go to a locker in a warehouse in a parking lot in an office park off an exit of a turnpike off a highway off an interstate in New Jersey, never to be looked at again. No one ever read them in the first place. But some client was billed for the hourly work.[44]

Wurtzel's observations, however dismaying, emerge from an experience that many attorneys would regard as a dream job—working with firm founder, David Boies. As she writes, "It has been a singular privilege to work for David and to get to know him as well as I have. It's enough to make me believe in luck. He is the smartest person I have ever met, and it is a steep fall to second place."[45] Boies has represented an elite set of clients including the U.S. Justice Department, former vice-president Al Gore, Oracle, CBS, and the National Football League.

The demoralizing effects of boring work are compounded by a sense of alienation. Only 22 percent of associate attorneys believe that their personal values are closely aligned with their *clients'* business values.[46] This percentage drops to 11 percent for Black associate attorneys. When asked whether their personal values are aligned with their *law firms'* values, only 38 percent see those values as being closely aligned. This percentage again drops to 11 percent for Black associates. The extent of associate attorneys' alienation is reflected in their response to the question, "At your firm, are you aware of partners whose careers and lives you would like to emulate? In other words, do you see viable role models?" Twenty-seven percent of associate attorneys respond, "No." For those attorneys, the firm has no live model of their future.

When attorneys do not share or actually disagree with client and firm values, they may experience "moral injury," the dissonance and distress resulting

44 Wurtzel, Elizabeth. (2013, January 6). Elizabeth Wurtzel confronts her one-night stand of a life. *New York*.

45 Ibid.

46 The data cited in this paragraph and the following paragraph are reported in Cartusciello, *supra* note 5 at 113, 114. See Major, Lindsey & Africa. (2023). *Gen Z: Now influencing today's law firm culture* (p. 8). Hanover, MD: Major, Lindsey & Africa. (The third most common response to the question, "What would make you leave your law firm job?" is that "the practice was not aligned with their values.")

from events that conflict with a person's moral or ethical code. Legal representation invariably presents some tensions between an attorney's personal values and the professional duties of competence and diligence, as litigator Jordan Rothman describes:

> [N]umerous times in my career, I have represented clients that were accused of pretty heinous claims, and in all likelihood, had at least some level of culpability in the acts complained of in the litigation. In certain instances, the faults of my clients possibly resulted in deaths or serious injuries to others. . . . In some instances, I would get cases dismissed on procedural grounds with the understanding that this would greatly reduce or completely eliminate a recovery for people who have suffered.[47]

Rothman finds that, after starting his own practice, he has more autonomy in selecting cases and generally avoids cases portending moral injury. Many other attorneys lack that degree of autonomy, he observes, and they "feel the impact of taking on certain types of cases. Many lawyers can feel the downsides of moral injury, which might explain some of the burnout that seems to be so ubiquitous in the legal profession."

The risk of moral injury may be heightened for ethnic minority attorneys like Black associate attorneys whose alignment with client and firm values (only 11 percent report "close alignment" with client and firm values) is considerably more attenuated than the alignment reported by White associate attorneys (22 percent report close alignment with client values, and 41 percent report close alignment with firm values). Male and female associate attorneys also react differently to client values. Only 19 percent of female associates believe that their personal values are closely aligned with client values, but 27 percent of male associates see their personal values as being closely aligned with client values. When the disparities between an attorney's personal values and professional services are prolonged or intensified, attorneys may experience the depression, stress, shame, familial breakdowns, and suicidality reported by other professionals experiencing moral injuries.[48]

Boring work, a limited number of role models, and a lack of shared values may explain why the percentage of Millennial generation attorneys describing themselves as loyal to their current firms is decreasing, and only one-third see themselves, in ten years, as a partner in their current firm.[49] If only one

47 Rothman, Jordan. (2023, July 19). Do some lawyers suffer from moral injury? *Above the Law*.

48 See Williamson, Victoria, et al. (2021, June). Moral injury: The effect on mental health and implications for treatment. *Lancet Psychiatry*, *8*(6), 453.

49 Major, Lindsey & Africa. *Searching for balance: Millennial lawyers' perspectives on the legal industry*, *supra* note 5 at 34, 36.

in three Millennial attorneys intend to continue their work and expand their influence within their current firms, compensated at magnetic partner income levels, their law firms are not only failing to inspire them but, more fundamentally, failing to engage them.

Gender bias

If the world was seeking a model of gender bias, it might select law firms. That's because a typical class of first year associates will be evenly distributed among similarly compensated males and females, and the equality of that class eventually will be subsumed and lost within a law firm controlled and led primarily by old, male attorneys. Only 24 percent of law firm equity partners are female attorneys, and only 12 percent of firms' managing partners are female.[50] Women occupy only one in four positions on firms' governance committees.

Female equity partners' compensation ranges from 75 percent to 78 percent of the amount paid to male equity partners; and a female equity partner is the most highly paid partner in only 2 percent of law firms. Female attorneys' average hourly billing rates are less than male attorneys' rates. The hourly rate disparity between female and male attorneys increases with seniority. And seniority abounds. The average age of partners is 52, and 3 percent of partners—often the partners exercising de facto control over major clients, assignments, marketing opportunities, and law firm strategies—are 71 to 88 years old.[51] A demographer could conclude that law firms are not only patriarchies but gerontocracies as well.

The income disparity between female lawyers and male lawyers cannot be explained by practice areas, academic achievement, billable hours, and demographic characteristics. In a study of 9,000 Texas attorneys, for example, researchers found that "differences in demographic backgrounds and human capital assets explain only 13 percent of the gender earnings gap. After adding

50 The data in the first three paragraphs of this section appears in NALP. (2024, March). Women and people of color in U.S. law firms. *NALP Bulletin*. O'Brien, Amanda. (2024, January 10). Women make up the majority of associates for first time. *The American Lawyer*. Peery, Destiny. (2021). *2021 report: National Association of Women Lawyers (NAWL) survey on the promotion and retention of women in law firms*. Chicago: National Association of Women Lawyers. The data showing that female partners' compensation is 75 percent of male partners' compensation is reported in Lowe, Jeffrey, A. (2022). *2022 partner compensation survey* (p. 13). Washington, DC: Major, Lindsey & Africa. See also Bell, Jacqueline. (2021, September 13). Law 360's glass ceiling report: What you need to know. *Law 360*. Trivedi, Upmanyu. (2022, October 25). UK's female trial lawyers earn half as much as male colleagues. *Bloomberg Law*.

51 Weiss, Debra Cassens. (2016, March 2). Average age of BigLaw partner is about 52; which firms are outliers? *ABA Journal*.

controls for occupational sector, 83 percent of the earning difference remains unexplained."[52] Female lawyers with high academic records earn less than similarly situated male lawyers; their income is similar to male lawyers with the weakest academic records, and this bias against high-achieving female lawyers is stronger in private practice than in government. The income disparity in the legal profession also is greater than the disparity in other professional fields. Male lawyers, in short, "earn far more than similarly situated female lawyers across legal practice settings and roles."

The persistent gender bias in law firms leads the National Association of Women Lawyers to conclude, "A review of the last 15 years of data from the NAWL Survey on the Promotion and Retention of Women in Law Firms (NAWL Survey) shows that year after year, the promotion and retention of women in the legal profession have not changed. While women are entering the legal field as law school graduates at a rate equal to, and often exceeding that of men, women are leaving the profession sooner and more frequently."[53]

Gender bias in law firms is particularly acute for women of color.[54] They comprise only 2 percent of all equity partners and leave law firms at disproportionately high rates relative to White male attorneys. Although only 3 percent of White male attorneys experience demeaning comments or harassment at their law firms, nearly half of women of color are subjected to that misconduct. Women of color also are more likely than White males to be excluded from firm networking opportunities, desirable client assignments, and client development events. Their experiences are encapsulated in these comments:

- "Having to deal with assumptions of inferiority, intellectual or otherwise, and constantly having to prove myself no matter how senior or qualified or experienced I am is something my white male peers do not have to do. It is psychologically exhausting."
- "While sexism was a common thread, my white female counterparts didn't have to deal with the elements of race. Moreover, they also benefitted from the racial hierarchy. They didn't have a presumption of being angry if they were focused on work and not chit-chatty. When white women leave the

52 Data and quotations in this paragraph appear in Markovic, Milan, & Plickert, Gabriele. (2023). The gender pay gap and high-achieving women in the legal profession. *Law & Social Inquiry*, *8*(2), 561. See also Lowe, *supra* note 50.

53 National Association of Women Lawyers (2021), *supra* note 50 at 2.

54 Data in this paragraph is reported in American Bar Association Commission on Women in the Profession. (2006). *Visible invisibility*. Chicago: American Bar Association. The quotations appear in Peery, Destiny, et al. (2020). *Left out and behind*. Chicago: American Bar Association.

profession I hear it is because of balance and cultural issues. When people of color, especially black and Hispanic, attorneys leave our firms I heard people have discussions about whether they were qualified to begin with."

- "Despite working on a team headed by a woman, there existed (in my opinion) a bias towards the white women on the team who often received better assignments, better mentorship, and greater visibility."
- "The bias that I face as a woman of color has become the elephant in the room. It means that I have to keep proving myself to clients, peers, superiors, subordinates, even after each success. Sometimes others assume that I am not a threat because they don't see me as real contender for business or leadership roles. I am not seen as a viable team member until I prove that I am. Then, even once I get buy-in from others, there are those who doubt my abilities or wait for me to fail."
- "As one small example, African Americans are often told, and I have been told this literally thousands of times, 'You're so articulate!' or 'You speak so well!' Why, thank you, that's super nice, but is anyone surprised when white people know how to string together a sentence? It only ever seems to be a subject of pleasant surprise when it comes to people of color being able to do so. Why? Because the surprised person started with the assumption that we don't have a solid grasp of the English language. Think what a handicap that is for a practicing lawyer. It's huge! And that's just one of many burdens we are obliged to carry. Every. Single. Day."

When asked why she stayed in the legal profession, a 42-year old Latinx female attorney responded, "I refuse to leave because my continued presence is beneficial for younger generations. I also try to be the mentor that I wanted when I started out. My daughter should NOT have to deal with the same crap that I have."

Sexual harassment

Sexual harassment in the legal profession occurs frequently. The International Bar Association reports that one in three female legal professionals and one in 14 male legal professionals have been sexually harassed at work.[55] Sexual harassment disproportionately affects younger, female legal professionals, and most perpetrators are senior colleagues.

Only 21 percent of sexual harassment incidents are reported, and "there is remarkably little variation in reporting rates by age, region or workplace,

55 The data in the first two paragraphs and the quotation in the second paragraph of this section appear in International Bar Association. (2019). *Us too? Bullying and sexual harassment in the legal profession*. London: International Bar Association.

suggesting that underreporting of sexual harassment is a profession-wide—and possibly societal-wide—problem." The most commonly cited reason for not reporting is the perpetrator's status. As a female attorney in South Korea recalls, "After I was sexually assaulted, I feared that his rank and reputation made me vulnerable. My disgust at remembering this horrible event prevented me from reporting it to the bar association or police. He frequently harassed junior female colleagues. I should have stopped him."

Surveys conducted by the American Bar Association confirm high rates of sexual harassment in U.S. law firms:

"• 50% of women versus 6% of men had received unwanted sexual conduct at work. In essence, one of every two women said they had experienced sexual harassment.
• 16% of women versus 1% of men have lost work opportunities as a result of rebuffing sexual advances.
• At the same time, more than a quarter of all women (28%) avoided reporting sexual harassment due to fear of retaliation while 1% of men reported the same avoidance behavior."[56]

The ABA survey results confirm that "the problem of sexual harassment in law firms is far from solved. Sexual harassment is not confined to 'certain' firms, but instead is widespread throughout the profession."[57]

A detailed survey of the Women's Bar Association of Massachusetts reveals the pervasiveness and gravity of sexual harassment[58]:

- 29 percent of female attorneys said they have been made to feel that they "needed to engage in sexual behavior or develop a personal relationship with someone at work to advance."
- 22 percent have been "the recipient of or witnessed unwelcome physical contact at work."
- 38 percent have been "the recipient of or copied on unwelcome emails, texts, or instant messages of a personal or sexual nature at work."
- 40 percent have been present "when comments or jokes were made that were sexual in nature or disparaging of other people or groups."

In most of these incidents, the attorney experiencing sexual harassment was in a subordinate or junior position relative to the perpetrator. Many of the

56 Liebenberg, Roberta D., & Scharf, Stephanie A. (2019). *Walking out the door* (p. 8). Chicago: American Bar Association.

57 Ibid at 9.

58 Rikleen, Lauren Stiller. (2018). Survey of workplace conduct and behaviors in law firms. Boston: The Women's Bar Association.

incidents "were perpetrated by partners and, frequently, important rainmakers or senior leaders in the firm. Because of their status, respondents did not report the behaviors, often because they feared retribution or because the people they would report to were involved in the incidents described."[59] As one survey respondent remarked, "Partner who did this was very popular/made lots of money for the firm and if one of us had to go it would have been me."[60]

Bullying

Nearly 7,000 legal professionals responded to the International Bar Association's survey regarding bullying and sexual harassment in the legal profession. One in two female respondents and one in three male respondents said they had been bullied in connection with their employment.[61] Thirty-seven percent of these incidents had occurred within the previous 12 months.

Attorneys in North America reported a higher incidence of bullying than the global average; and attorneys at large law firms (> 100 partners) were considerably more likely to experience bullying than attorneys at small firms (≤ 100 partners). Most of the survey respondents who experienced bullying did not report it, citing the "profile/status of the perpetrator (e.g., senior member of the workplace)." As a law firm employee remarked, "Senior management talk a good story about bullying but when it is a big billing lawyer or senior partner involved then the real values show themselves. Until firms start living their values, what they are really saying is 'all staff are equal, but some are more equal than others!'"

The attorneys who did report bullying were generally dismayed by the results. Seventy percent of those who reported bullying rated their employer's response as "insufficient" or "negligible." In two-thirds of the cases, the complaining attorneys thought that "the situation was unchanged or exacerbated." Even in the more extreme cases involving violence, the employers' responses were muted: "Interestingly, although targets of threatened or actual violence were almost 20% more likely than average to report this conduct, perpetrators were only slightly more likely to be sanctioned."

The effects of bullying were most severe in law firms. "Targets working at law firms," the International Bar Association reports, "were more likely than other respondents to leave their workplace as a result of bullying; indicating a higher

59 Ibid at 8.
60 Ibid at 12.
61 The data reported and the comments quoted in this section appear in International Bar Association (2019), *supra* note 55 at 11, 34, 35, 37, 44–46, and 48. The incidence of bullying reported by female legal professionals in the International Bar Association Survey (55%) is higher than the incidence of bullying reported in Rikleen's survey of female attorneys in Massachusetts (39%), *supra* note 58 at 23.

level of career disruption caused by bullying in these workplaces." A female attorney subjected to bullying describes her career disruption: "I left the workplace, considered changing careers and contemplated suicide." Another female attorney working at a law firm discloses, "I was systematically bullied to the extent I considered, for the first time, taking my life. My confidence was shattered. I began to doubt myself in every aspect of my life, work and personal."

Toxic lawyers

In recruiting associate attorneys and lateral partners, law firms try to project an aura of collegiality. The reality, though, is that many law firms are inhabited by unpleasant lawyers lacking conventional social skills and controlling a large volume of business. They have power and autonomy and do not need another attorney's approbation.

Not surprisingly, given the unlikable behavior of many attorneys, only one in four partners select "the partner or partners with whom I work" when asked, "What do you like most about your job?"[62] When asked to share "what aspects of their job prevented them from doing well or thriving at their job," the top five negative aspects included "actions of other attorneys at my firm."[63] A senior partner in a 200-attorney law firm laments the competitive and antagonistic interactions at his firm: "A key to happiness in being embedded in a community and the key to forming a good community is to establish one based on trust and acceptance. Unfortunately, it is increasingly difficult to trust others who pose a threat and seem more willing to judge than accept."[64]

Associate attorneys frequently encounter problems in working with other attorneys, especially supervising attorneys. One in seven associates identifies "they had problematic relationships with other lawyers at the firm" and "they did not like the firm" as the reasons other lawyers have left the firm.[65] In extreme circumstances, partners "have referred to colleagues using misogynistic, homophobic and antisemitic language."[66] Even well-intentioned attorneys may inadvertently frustrate and antagonize subordinate attorneys. As Katie Herzog, a consultant to law firms and a former psychology professor, notes, "Most people who supervise associates have never had any training in it. There's not a thoughtfulness about the impact of their behavior on others."[67]

62 Cartusciello, *supra* note 5 at 87.

63 Thiese, Matthew S. (2020, March/April). The Utah lawyer well-being study: Preliminary results show Utah lawyers at risk. *Utah Bar Journal*, p. 30.

64 Henderson & Henderson, *supra* note 5.

65 Ibid at 122–123.

66 Henry, Justin. (2023, June 5). Leaked emails show years of sexist, racist language by Barber Ranen leaders. *The American Lawyer*.

67 McLellan, Lizzy. (2019, May 18). Battling an 'epidemic' of loneliness among lawyers. *The American Lawyer*.

David Maister, a law firm consultant who spent decades analyzing and advising lawyers, finds that their legal training and practice prevent them from functioning effectively in groups. He describes them as "professional skeptics" who accentuate possibilities and disregard probabilities: "In a room full of lawyers, any idea, no matter how brilliant, will be instantly attacked. Lawyers are expert loophole finders, trained to find counterexamples of or exceptions to any proposition. Accordingly, within a short time, most ideas, no matter who initiates them, will be destroyed, dismissed, or postponed for future examination."[68] As a result of lawyers' skepticism, distrust, and lack of collegiality, Maister concludes, law firms "will remain what they are today: bands of warlords, each with his or her followers, ruling over a group of cowed citizens and acting in temporary alliance—until a better opportunity comes along."[69]

Although firms prefer to characterize attorneys' stress as being client-driven, it often originates and metastasizes within the firm itself. Perhaps that is the reason attorneys select in-house remedies like "improve workplace culture," "create a culture of mutual respect," and "address poor behaviour" as the most important steps to promote attorney well-being.[70] Remedial action, attorneys indicate, must start within their law firms.

Inadequate firm leadership

The quality of leadership skills in law firms ranges from exemplary to abysmal. Law firms underestimate the demoralizing effect that poor leadership has on their attorneys, imagining that they are so absorbed in their client work that leadership deficiencies go unnoticed. The reality is that the sense of despair, frustration, and helplessness that younger attorneys often experience is intensified by leaders who lack vision and fixate on short-term profitability.

The magnitude of the leadership crisis in law firms is demonstrated by these results, compiled in the surveys of Millennial generation attorneys cited in Chapter 1[71]:

- Fifty-six percent of associates and 48 percent of partners believe that "the current generation of law firm leadership has outstayed their effectiveness."

68 Maister, David. (2006). Are law firms manageable? *The American Lawyer*.
69 Ibid.
70 International Bar Association (2021), *supra* note 5 at 44.
71 These survey results appear in Major, Lindsey & Africa. (2023). *Searching for balance: Millennial lawyers' perspectives on the legal industry*, *supra* note 5 at 41, 44, 48, 49. Major, Lindsey & Africa. (2019). *New expectations, evolving beliefs, and shifting career goals* (p. 28). Hanover, MD: Major, Lindsey & Africa.

- Seventy-one percent of associate attorneys believe that "law firm partnership is much less desirable than it was a generation ago."
- Only 32 percent of associate attorneys believe that their firm "has made strides in the past year to address workplace gender issues."
- Seventy-two percent of associate attorneys agree that "the pandemic has revealed how law firm leverage models favor partners at the expense of associates."
- Fifty-one percent of associates and partners agree that "the law firm business model is fundamentally broken."

These survey results reflect a lack of confidence in law firm leaders and business models, a perception that partners exploit associate attorneys, and a diminishment of traditional career incentives like partnership. The results indicate that many law firm leaders may be aggravating the problems they were expected to solve. Unfortunately, as Scott Westfahl, the Director of Harvard Law School's Executive Education Program, informs us, leadership "is a foreign concept to lawyers," and "the lawyer leadership gap is real and critical."[72]

72 Westfahl, Scott. (2015). Learning to lead: Perspective on bridging the lawyer leadership gap. In Normand-Hochman, Rebecca (Ed.). *Leadership for lawyers* (pp. 84, 88). Surrey, UK: Globe Law and Business Ltd.

4

STRESSED JUDGES

Judges exhibit higher levels of mental health than attorneys, but the unique stresses of their jobs ultimately threaten their effectiveness. Many judges respond to the pressures and traumas of their work by becoming impatient, indignant, intolerant, and insensitive. As one judge stated at a pre-trial hearing, "I'm tired of this case. I'm tired of this defendant. I'm tired of getting the run around."[1] The judge remarked later, "This guy looks like a criminal to me. This is what criminals do." When the defendant's attorney moved for recusal of the judge, he denied the motion, asserting that "just because I got mad does not mean I'm biased against [the defendant]. I'm not, trust me. I give [him] the same rights and opportunities here to demonstrate his innocence or lack of guilt as any other litigant."

Some judges also cope by unilaterally defining their responsibilities so narrowly that they avoid accountability for the legal system they lead, manage, and endorse. Their reliance on precedent not only promotes uniformity and predictability but also serves to minimize their responsibility for the harmful and unjust consequences of some decisions. In distancing themselves from the citizens disoriented, displaced, and impoverished by their decisions, many judges ignore or perpetuate the problems that cause their mental distress and compromise their service. They may have succumbed to the conditions about which the U.S. Department of Justice warned Congress in 1977: "We

1 Weiss, Debra Cassens. (2023, August 7). Federal judge who said defendant 'looks like a criminal' can't preside in new trial, 6th Circuit says. *ABA Daily News*. Raymond, Nate. (2023, August 4). US court tosses conviction after judge says Black man 'looks like a criminal'. *Reuters*. *United States v. Liggins*, No. 22–1236 (6th Cir. 2023).

DOI: 10.4324/9781003514848-4

are creating a workload that is even now changing the very nature of courts, threatening to convert them from deliberative institutions to processing institutions, from a judiciary to a bureaucracy."[2]

This chapter first analyzes judicial demographics to determine whether judges approximate the general population based on gender, race, and age—a measure of the legal system's perceived legitimacy and the degree of connection between judges and the citizens they evaluate, regulate, stigmatize, and imprison. It then examines judges' mental health—giving special attention to secondary trauma, self-imposed isolation, and the role of positive emotions—and considers how the demands, stresses, and traumas of judging affect their performance. The chapter concludes by considering the possibility that many judges have drafted their job descriptions too narrowly, participating daily in a system that they know is deficient while taking little or no action to improve it. Are those judges complicit in maintaining a legal system that fails its citizens and serves as an international model of delay, inequality, and privilege? Or do the stresses and traumas of their work excuse them from objectively evaluating the legal system and being innovative and expeditious in improving it?

Judicial demographics

Judges are demographic anomalies in American society, superimposed over citizens that bear little resemblance to them. Although females comprise 51 percent of the U.S. population, only 28 percent of federal judges are females.[3] Eighty percent of federal judges are White, but only 62 percent of the general population is White. In 27 percent of the federal district courts, including the Southern District of Georgia, whose Black residents constitute one-third of the district's population, all of the judges have always been White.

The average age of federal court judges is 68, and very few will leave the bench voluntarily through resignation or retirement.[4] In 2020, for example, only one federal court judge resigned and six retired; 35 died during their

2 Mayer, Martin. (2006). *The judges* (p. 149). New York: St. Martin's Press. Writing about 2,500 years ago, the philosopher Lao-tzu observed, "ritual appears when justice is lost; ritual marks the waning of belief; and the onset of confusion." Pine, Red. (2009). *Lao-tzu's Taoteching* (p. 76). Port Townsend, WA: Copper Canyon Press.

3 Unless otherwise noted, data in this paragraph and the next paragraph regarding judges' gender and race appears in American Bar Association. (2021). *ABA profile of the legal profession 2021*. Chicago: American Bar Association. American Bar Association. (2022). *ABA profile of the legal profession 2022*. Chicago: American Bar Association. Headley, Tiana. (2023, September 5). A quarter of US federal courts have never had a non-white judge. *Bloomberg Law*. For additional information regarding diversity on the federal bench, see Hofer, Scott, & Achury, Susan. (2020). Examining diversity, inclusion, and equity in the legal profession. In Solberg, Rorie Spill, & Waltenburg, Eric (Eds.). *Open Judicial Politics*. Corvalis, OR: Oregon State University. https://open.oregonstate.education/open-judicial-politics/chapter/examining-diversity/.

4 Federal Judicial Center. *Demography of Article III judges, 1789–2020*. www.fjc.gov/history/exhibits/graphs-and-maps/age-and-experience-judges.

term. Former federal judge Richard Posner aptly describes the federal judiciary as "the nation's premier geriatric occupation."[5]

In state supreme courts, 59 percent of justices are males, and only 18 percent of justices are Black, Hispanic, Asian American, Native American, or multiracial. Twenty states do not have a single supreme court justice that identifies as a person of color, and in 15 states, a Black lawyer has never served on the supreme court. The Supreme Court of the State of Nevada is emblematic of these anomalies: although 49 percent of the population is non-White, all seven justices were White until Justice Patricia Lee was appointed to replace Chief Justice Abbi Silver in November 2022.

Judges' demographic peculiarities extend beyond gender, race, and age and encompass law schools and practice settings[6]:

- "The legal educations and formative experiences of federal appellate judges are largely homogeneous as well, with approximately 30 percent of circuit court judges being educated at just four law schools: Columbia, Harvard, Stanford, and Yale."
- "Only about 1 percent of sitting circuit court judges have spent the majority of their careers as public defenders or within a legal aid setting. In contrast, the federal appellate bench is swamped with those who spent the majority of their careers in private practice or as federal prosecutors—making up more than 70 percent of all sitting appellate judges. No sitting judge spent the majority of their career with a nonprofit civil rights organization."
- "Nearly 70 percent of the 181 white men on the federal appellate bench spent their careers in private practice, but less than half of the only 12 women of color on the bench came from the same sector."

At least two major trends are evident in federal court appointments. First, "the educational diversity of federal judges is at an all-time low. Over the past century, a smaller and smaller number of law schools have claimed a larger and larger share of judgeships and clerkships."[7] Second,

5 Berman, Russell. (2020, September 25). No other western democracy allows this. *The Atlantic*.

6 Buchanan, Maggie Jo. (2020, August 13). Pipelines to power: Encouraging professional diversity on the federal appellate bench. *Center for American Progress*.

7 Iuliano, Jason, & Stewart, Avery. (2016). The new diversity crisis in the federal judiciary. *Tennessee Law Review*, *84*, 247. See George, Tracey E., et al. (2023). *Some are more equal than others: U.S. Supreme Court clerkships*. https://papers.ssrn.com/sol3/papers.cfm?abstract_id=4338222. ("We find that educational pedigree, as opposed to academic performance or any other qualification, has an overwhelming impact on attainment. The Court clerkship selection process proves to be a blend of status and merits where status often prevails.")

"the composition of the federal judiciary is massively imbalanced in favor of former government advocates [prosecutors, government lawyers, and other lawyers representing the government] compared with former government opponents [public defenders, criminal defense lawyers, and civil liberties litigators]. Former courtroom advocates for government (389, 44.20 percent) now outnumber former advocates for individuals against government (57, 6.47 percent) by nearly seven to one."[8] As a result of this imbalance, civil liberties advocates and criminal defense lawyers now submit their cases to "a judiciary half-filled with former government advocates." Although one-third of President Joe Biden's nominees had experience as public defenders, they remain a small fraction of the federal judiciary.[9]

Perhaps the most fundamental disparity between judges and the general population is economic status. The annual salary of federal trial and appeals judges, for instance, is nearly four times greater than the median annual household income in the United States.[10] The disparity in wealth between judges and ordinary citizens fosters what former federal judge Alex Kozinski calls "unselfconscious cultural elitism" and causes judges to overlook the impact of their decisions on poor people:

> There's been much talk about diversity on the bench, but there's one kind of diversity that doesn't exist: No truly poor people are appointed as federal judges, or as state judges for that matter. Judges, regardless of race, ethnicity or sex, are selected from the class of people who don't live in trailers or urban ghettos. The everyday problems of people who live in poverty are not close to our hearts and minds because that's not how we and our friends live.[11]

Amplifying Judge Kozinski's concerns, law professor Michele Neitz states, "Socioeconomic bias may be more obscure than other forms of bias, but its impact on judicial decision-making processes can create very real harm for disadvantaged populations."[12]

8 Neily, Clark. (2021, May 27). Are a disproportionate number of federal judges former government advocates? *Cato Institute.*

9 See Litvan, Laura. (2022, December 27). Biden builds judicial legacy with diversified federal courts. *Bloomberg Law.* Wheeler, Russell. (2022, January 27). Biden's first-year judicial appointments: Impact. *Brookings.*

10 Weiss, Debra Cassens. (2012, October 4). Law prof sees socioeconomic bias on the bench, suggests changes to ABA Model Code. *ABA Journal Daily News.*

11 Cohen, Joel. (2014). *Blindfolds off* (p. 193). Chicago: American Bar Association.

12 Neitz, Michelle. (2013). Socioeconomic bias in the judiciary. *Cleveland State Law Review, 61*(1), 137, 141.

Judges' mental health

In Krieger and Sheldon's study of 7,805 attorneys and judges, discussed in previous chapters, judges reported the highest level of well-being.[13] They specifically reported the highest levels of autonomy, relatedness, competence, and intrinsic motivation and the lowest levels of depression and alcohol consumption. Although judges appear to be happier and more satisfied than lawyers, judges experience a series of problems that highlight the unique challenges of overseeing courtrooms and rendering judgments. Nearly one-half of surveyed judges, for instance, state that they have "suffered secondary traumatic stress from being a judge."[14] The most stressful situations and sources, as ranked by judges, are crimes against children, sexual crimes, violent crimes, attorneys' behavior during trial, and trial interruptions and delays.[15]

Judges also encounter personally threatening behavior and conditions. More than one-quarter of judges have received inappropriate/threatening letters; 13 percent have been subjected to inappropriate/threatening calls; and 9 percent have received death threats. Five percent of judges report being physically attacked in their courtrooms.[16] During the last two years, the number of serious threats against federal judges—exemplified by a letter warning, "You ruined my life [so] your life must be taken"—has doubled.[17] These threats extend to judges' families as well. "We know where they live, work, or go to school," another letter to a judge menaced. "If you try to alert the authorities, we will know and your loved ones will disappear."

When asked to identify the effects of stress, about one-third of judges cite fatigue and low energy; sleep disturbance; decreased attention and concentration; rumination and worry about cases after they are decided; and increased health concerns.[18] About one in five surveyed judges report that stress has caused feelings of apprehension or anxiety; lack of initiative and interest;

13 Krieger, Lawrence S., & Sheldon, Kennon M. (2015). What makes lawyers happy?: A data-driven prescription to redefine professional success. *The George Washington Law Review*, *83*, 554, 591.

14 The National Judicial College. (2017, October 20). Nearly half of all judges have suffered from this condition. *Judicial Edge*.

15 Data in this sentence and the following sentences appears in Flores, David M., et al. (2009). Judges' perspectives on stress and safety in the courtroom: An exploratory study. *Court Review*, *45*, 83, 85.

16 Ibid at 84–86.

17 Data regarding the number of threats is reported by the U.S. Marshals Service. Lybrand, Holmes. (2024, February 14). US Marshals director calls increase in threats to judges and prosecutors 'a substantial risk to our democracy.' *CNN*. Monyak, Suzanne. (2024, May 14). Chief judges ramp up efforts to bolster security as threats rise. *Bloomberg Law*. The quotations in this paragraph appear in Wheeler, Lydia. (2023, December 7). US Marshals' blind spots leave judges vulnerable to threats (1). *Bloomberg Law*.

18 Data in this sentence and the next two sentences appears in Swenson, David, et al. (2020). Stress and resiliency in the U.S. judiciary. *2020 Journal of the Professional Lawyer*.

physical discomfort; irritability; being short-tempered; acting sarcastically; and being preoccupied with negative thoughts. Female judges are more likely than male judges to report symptoms of stress and to acknowledge the severity of those symptoms. They also score higher on depressive impairment scales than male judges.[19] This difference may be attributable to heightened self-awareness among female judges.

Summarizing the results of a survey of 1,034 judges, researchers found that 23 percent of judges "met criteria for stress at a level that could be debilitating."[20] The surveyed judges also exhibited serious depressive symptoms:

> Survey items reflecting depression in respondents included: not having initiative (22.9%), preoccupation with negative thoughts (20%), work is no longer meaningful (17.8%), can't wait for the day's work to end (16.7%), depressed mood (15.3%), nothing to look forward to (12.6%), feel increasingly numb to pleas of urgency (11.2%), and care little about trial outcomes (6.9%). Each of these criteria is concerning. The finding that over one in five judges meet at least one criteria for depressive disorder deserves our full attention.

Ten percent of the judges reported problematic alcohol use. While this level is less than the level of attorneys' problematic use (21 percent), it is higher than the level for the general population (7 percent).

In a different study of state court judges, researchers found that judges were "only moderately able to perform their jobs to the best of their abilities."[21] A minority of judges, moreover, expressed "quite measurable" fears about "feelings of failure or inability to achieve their goals." Although judges reported moderate stress levels overall, one in four judges acknowledged that they had missed ten or more days of work, during the last year, due to stress. Both job satisfaction and job efficacy decreased as judges' stress increased. Stress, in short, "relates to negative, undesirable outcomes for judges."

19 Flores, *supra* note 15 at 82, 87.

20 Quotations and data in this paragraph appear in Swenson, *supra* note 18 at 12, 13, and 15. For a study of Australian judges see Schrever, Carly, et al. (2019). The psychological impact of judicial work: Australia's first empirical research measuring judicial stress and wellbeing. *Journal of Judicial Administration*, *28*, 141. ("Three-quarters of judicial officers' burnout scores indicated some level of burnout risk. The great majority endorsed at least one symptom of STS [secondary traumatic stress], with approximately a third scoring in moderate to severe ranges. Almost one in three judicial officers reported problematic alcohol use. Alongside this, however, judicial officers' rates of depressive and anxious symptoms were similar to and, in the moderate to extremely severe ranges, considerably lower than population norms, which is dramatically lower than rates reported for the legal profession.")

21 Edwards, Charles P., et al. (2018). Judges and stress: An examination of outcomes predicted by the Model of Judicial Stress. *Judicature*, *102*(3), 50.

The riskiest aspect of judicial stress may be judges' denial of its effects. Despite the frequency and intensity of stressful events in their courtrooms, judges claim that their ability to fulfill their responsibilities is "only slightly compromised by stress."[22] Their self-assessment, however, is contradicted by their self-reports of "decreased productivity, inappropriate courtroom demeanor, decreased concentration, and compromised courtroom decisions." Researchers attribute this disparity between judges' self-assessment and the actual effects of stress to two causes: "(1) judges may not fully recognize the negative impact of stress; and (2) reporting such vulnerability is not socially desirable because such an admission would have negative implications for their personal legal decisions as well as for the integrity of the legal system." Stress harms the quality of judges' performance, and being unaware of its effects prevents judges from identifying and mitigating them.

Although studies of judges' mental health emphasize stress, depression, and alcohol use, they also suggest that boredom contributes to judges' feelings of emotional distress. Forty-one percent of judges cite "boring trials" as a source of their stress, and 32 percent report problems with attention, concentration, and distraction.[23] About one in five judges have "felt my work is no longer meaningful," and about one in ten judges say that they "feel out of touch with current legal issues and innovations" and "care little about the outcome of most trials."[24]

Judges' sense of boredom poses a discernible risk for society because boredom is not just associated with a lack of empathy and sadism; in experimental studies with 4,000 participants, boredom has been shown to *cause* sadistic behavior.[25] Researchers conducting those studies contend that deficits in meaning and attention—two factors cited by a significant minority of judges—"can motivate sadism, in that sadistic behavior can serve to directly counter inattention and can be used indirectly (as a distraction) in coping with deficits in meaning." Stated differently, judges who feel bored, inattentive, and purposeless might counter those feelings with sadism or relatively less disturbing behavior like antagonism, hostility, dominance, or impulsivity.

The advanced age of many judges poses an additional risk of mental impairment. Twenty-four percent of U.S. circuit court judges are 65–69 years

22 The quotations in this paragraph appear in Flores, *supra* note 15 at 82, 87.

23 Flores, *supra* note 15 at 83. Swenson, *supra* note 18 at 13.

24 Swenson, *supra* note 18 at 13–14.

25 Pfattheicher, Stefan, et al. (2021, September). On the relation of boredom and sadistic aggression. *Journal of Personality and Social Psychology*, *121*(3), 573. See Lobbestael, Jill, et al. (2023, October 19). Sadism and personality disorders. *Current Psychiatry Reports*, *25*, 573. ("Finally, there is emerging evidence that boredom can augment sadism.")

old, and 26 percent are 70 years of age or older.[26] A ProPublica study found that 12 percent of federal district and circuit judges were 80 years or older, and "the share of octogenarians and nonagenarians on the federal bench has doubled in the past 20 years."[27] Older judges have a relatively higher risk of mild cognitive impairment or dementia. The prevalence of mild cognitive impairment in the elderly population is "6.7% for ages 60–64, 8.4% for 65–69, 10.1% for 70–74, 14.8% for 75–79, and 25.2% for 80–84."[28] Fifteen percent of individuals initially exhibiting mild cognitive impairment proceed to dementia within two years. About 11 percent of people age 65 and older currently have Alzheimer's Dementia.

Even among relatively healthy individuals, the aging process inexorably degrades cognition. Neurologist Robert Friedland finds that changes with aging include decreased reasoning abilities, memory, numerical abilities, speed of perception, spatial awareness, learning and processing speed, spatial and working memory, brain size, density of synapses, and neurotransmitters involved in memory and learning.[29] This catalog of cognitive decline and the incidence of mild cognitive impairment and dementia among elderly adults call into question many senior judges' belief that their judgment continues to improve with experience. Their self-assessments are further challenged by empirical research showing that judges' performance "falls with age," and older judges "reduce the performance of younger colleagues."[30]

Secondary trauma

About one-half of surveyed judges experience secondary trauma—a threat to their psychological well-being caused by intense or chronic exposure to

26 McMillion, Barry J. (2017, August 1). *U.S. circuit and district court judges: Profile of select characteristics* (p. 11). Washington, DC: Congressional Research Service.

27 Goldstein, Joseph. (2011, January 18). The oldest bench ever. *Slate*.

28 For data regarding mild cognitive impairment and Alzheimer's Dementia see Alzheimer's Association. (2022). *2022 Alzheimer's disease facts and figures*. Chicago: Alzheimer's Association. Petersen, Ronald C., et al. (2018). Practice guideline update summary: Mild cognitive impairment. *Neurology*, *90*, 126.

29 Friedland, Robert P. (2022). *Unaging* (pp. 5–6). New York: Cambridge University Press. See Deary, Ian J., et al. (2009). Age-associated cognitive decline. *British Medical Bulletin*, *92*, 135. Meeks, Thomas W., & Jeste, Dilip V. (2009). Neurobiology of wisdom: A literature overview. *Archives of General Psychiatry*, *66*(4), 362. ("Older age has been traditionally associated with wisdom but the limited available empirical research does not consistently support this notion.")

30 Ash, Elliott, & MacLeod, W. Bentley. (2022, November 24). Mandatory retirement for judges improved the performance of U.S. state supreme courts, pp. 3, 31. https://elliottash.com/wp-content/uploads/2023/01/Ash-MacLeod-Mandatory-Judges-Improved-Performance-US-State-Supreme-Courts.pdf.

traumatic events and traumatized individuals.[31] Secondary trauma is sometimes called vicarious trauma, secondary traumatic stress, and compassion fatigue. Judges in criminal, juvenile, and family law cases are particularly susceptible to secondary trauma, and the sources of that trauma typically are witness testimony, physical evidence, and details of crimes. More experienced judges are more likely to report secondary trauma than less experienced judges.[32] Judges, ironically, become more susceptible to vicarious trauma and less susceptible to general stress over time.

These judges' comments illustrate some of the circumstances causing vicarious trauma[33]:

- "I heard a 15-year-old male child testify about acts he had seen committed by members of the gang MS13. After his testimony I went to Chambers and cried and cried."
- "I handle [juvenile] dependencies and delinquencies. Almost on a daily basis, I hear stories of pain, anquish (sic) and heartache. I have kids who have run away. I have kids who get injured. . . . I had a young foster child drown. I constantly see children who have been sexually abused, usually by a trusted family member or family friend. Do I have any trauma over this? Would I be human if I didn't?"
- "I will be out running, and suddenly I see the burned-off face of a 5-year-old child in my head, and it won't go away."
- "Mostly, though, I think about those four beautiful young girls and what they could have become, and I am haunted to this day by the gruesome photographs of their skeletal remains."

One judge reflects, "Unfortunately, we are not able to unhear or unsee the things we see and hear in the courtroom. There is no button to turn off the effects of this when you go to bed at night."[34]

The effects of secondary trauma include disengagement, depersonalization, helplessness, fatigue, isolation, anger, decreased concentration, avoidance,

31 Jaffe, P.G., et al. (2003). Vicarious trauma in judges: The personal challenge of dispensing justice. *Juvenile and Family Court Journal*, *54*(4), 1. The National Judicial College. (2017, October). Nearly half of all judges have suffered from this condition. *Judicial Edge*.

32 Jaffe, *supra* note 31 at 1. Eells, Tracy D., & Showalter, Robert C. (1994). Work-related stress in American trial judges. *Bulletin of the American Academy of Psychiatry and the Law*, *22*(1), 71.

33 Edwards, Charles P., & Miller, Monica K. (2019). An assessment of judges' self-reported experiences of secondary traumatic stress. *Juvenile and Family Court Journal*, *70*(2), 7. Weisberg, Frederick H. (2018). Crazy or cruel: The trial of an unexplained filicide. In Canan, Russell F., et al. (Eds.). *Tough cases* (p. 235). New York: The New Press.

34 The National Judicial College. (2017, October 20). Nearly half of all judges have suffered from this condition. *Judicial Edge*.

and impaired performance.[35] Physical symptoms include sleep disturbances, muscle pain, breathing difficulties, rapid heartbeat, and an impaired immune system. One of the most pervasive responses is emotional numbness, as former trial court judge Karen Adam explains:

> [A] judge is required to hear about terrible things that happen to people but cannot respond physically or emotionally in a naturally human way.
>
> However horrific the testimony and exhibits, a judge must remain dignified, calm, respectful. Emotions must be buried. . . .
>
> Remaining stoic in the midst of this much trauma was incredibly difficult, but I did it. At a steep cost.
>
> Suppressing emotions for days, months and years carries a heavy toll. A kind of numbness can develop. Sleeping and eating suffer. Some people develop substance abuse or addictive exercise regimens. By the time I left the bench, I rarely cried or was visibly upset by anything that happened in my personal life.[36]

Reflecting on her service for 34 years, Judge Adam observes, "I was a good judge; dignified, respectful and focused. I didn't realize how this was affecting my emotional health."

Isolation

When asked to identify stress symptoms they experience daily, judges most frequently select "feeling distant or cut off from people around you."[37] They also identify "a sense of isolation" as one of the most frequently experienced symptoms of trauma.[38] Isaiah Zimmerman, a clinical psychologist who treats and consults with judges, estimates that 70 percent of judges suffer appreciably from isolation. He recalls these judges' remarks from his practice[39]:

- "After all of these years on the bench, the isolation is my major disappointment."

35 See Skilnick, Kenneth D. (2017). Judicial wellness: Vicarious trauma and secondary traumatic stress in judges. *PCJ News*, *19*(2), 35. Bock, Christian, et al. (2020, April). Secondary traumatic stress, mental state, and work ability in nurses—Results of a psychological risk assessment at a university hospital. *Frontiers in Psychiatry*, *11*, Article 298.

36 Adam, Karen. (2017, April 20). The price I paid for being a 'good judge'. *Reflections from the Bench*.

37 Flores, *supra* note 15 at 76.

38 Jaffe, *supra* note 31 at 1.

39 Quotations in this paragraph appear in Zimmerman, Isaiah M. (2000, Winter). Isolation in the judicial career. *Court Review*, *36*, 4.

- "You gradually lose your original group of friends, and you have no time or energy to make new ones. Discretionary time goes down to zero. With all the ethical restrictions that are obviously necessary, who has time to go out and break new ground?"
- "Often, I am bored and exhausted; but I can't talk to anyone about it. I have to keep up the act of being on top of my game."
- "Before becoming a judge, I had no idea or warning, of how isolating it would be."
- "I live and work in a space capsule—alone with stacks of paper."

Zimmerman remembers the regimen described by two state trial court judges who were married to each other: "We work late in the courthouse every week day. But on the weekends, we see no one. We sleep or stay in bed most of the weekend, and absolutely bring no legal work home. As a result, we hardly see any friends and have almost given up on social life, but we've tried to preserve our intimate life."

Although isolation can be seen as a personal psychological problem for judges, the larger issue is how it affects the citizens dependent on judges' perceptual, analytical, and decision-making skills. In that respect, isolation has been shown to "wreak havoc" on an individual's cognitive health.[40] Isolation is specifically correlated with depression, anxiety, stress, impaired executive function, poor sleep quality, and accelerated cognitive decline.[41] Isolation also is associated with a 40 percent increased risk of dementia, independent of gender, race, ethnicity, and education.[42] Judges' isolation, in short, renders them highly susceptible to cognitive impairment. This risk increases substantially when judges have lifetime appointments and are allowed to self-diagnose their own cognitive fitness.

Positive emotions

Despite the difficulties judges encounter in maintaining their emotional health, positive emotions are critical to their performance. Vanderbilt Law School professor Terry Maroney, who conducts programs for judges on the role of emotions in decision making, contends that positive emotions are predictive

40 Novotney, Amy. (2019, May). The risks of social isolation. *Monitor on Psychology, 50*(5), 32.
41 Hawkley, Louise C., & Capitanio, John P. (2015, May 26). Perceived social isolation, evolutionary fitness and health outcomes: A lifespan approach. *Philosophical Transactions of the Royal Society B, 370*, 20140114.
42 Sutin, Angelina R., et al. (2020). Loneliness and risk of dementia. *The Journals of Gerontology: Series B, 75*(7), 1414.

of a sound judicial temperament and desirable judicial behaviors.[43] She finds that temperamentally positive judges, as opposed to their angry or fearful colleagues, more consistently display the traits that promote respect for the courts and instill in litigants the sense they have been heard and understood: compassion, patience, kindness, altruism, understanding, humility, caring, respect, and open-mindedness.

Positive emotions also protect judges and the public against outcomes tainted by a judge's depression, cynicism, and despair, as Maroney explains: "The work of judging often shows humanity at its worst. To perform that work well over time requires a fundamental disposition to believe in humanity's essential decency, and a propensity to care about the public being served. Indeed, tributes to great judges typically praise their benevolence." The positive emotions of benevolence, kindness, and caring tend to be accompanied by a heightened level of self-awareness, an ability to "have a broadened perspective on their own thoughts and actions" and to "feel and project calm and patience."

Judges who lack positive emotions tend to be hostile and argumentative, displaying frustration, impatience, disdain, closed-mindedness, and anger toward attorneys and litigants. They undermine public confidence in courts, Maroney asserts, and may allow their hostility to affect their decision making:

> Judges who regularly indulge in over-the-top anger displays are the frequent-flyers of disciplinary complaints, as are those who use insults, sarcasm, and humiliation to cement their power over lawyers and parties. These behaviors erode faith in the courts, and the damage does not stop there. Negativity can close minds as surely as positivity can open them. Left unchecked, anger can curtail deliberation and increase punitive behavior, regardless of whether it is relevant or justified—a particular danger for judges who feel it with greater frequency and less justification.

Maroney's belief that positive emotions are essential to sound judging is corroborated by research linking those emotions to understanding, perspective-taking, open-mindedness, flexible thinking, efficiency in processing information, and careful problem solving.[44] Among these qualities, perspective-taking is particularly important for judges, as United States District Judge George B. Daniels, relates: "Objectivity is one of the most

43 Quotations in this paragraph and the next two paragraph appear in Maroney, Terry A. (2021, Summer). Judicial temperament explained. *Judicature*, *105*(2), 49, 52–54.

44 See Isen, Alice M. (2001). An influence of positive affect on decision making in complex situations: Theoretical issues with practical implications. *Journal of Consumer Psychology*, *11*(2), 75. Lyubomirsky, Sonja, et al. (2005). The benefits of frequent positive affect: Does happiness lead to success? *Psychological Bulletin*, *131*(6), 803.

important aspects of being a good judge; this comes from understanding each party's perspective. The greatest challenge is being able to represent a variety of opposing perspectives and to understand and empathize with the rich and the poor, the accused and the prosecutor, the individual and the corporation, the perpetrator and the victim."[45]

Positive emotions also are correlated with a sense of meaning and purpose. Those qualities, in turn, facilitate emotion regulation, impulse control, and engagement and reduce anxiety, depression, suicidal ideation, substance abuse, and risk of burnout.[46] They also increase motivation, promote healthy sleep, and delay cognitive decline. For judges, the benefits of positive emotions are not merely desirable but imperative.

Protective job descriptions

Law professor William Henderson, the leading scholar of the American legal system, finds that judges in general and state Supreme Court justices in particular have defined their responsibilities too narrowly. They typically limit their work to the intellectually stimulating exercise of deciding cases while avoiding the more difficult problem of designing and operating a better legal system. Henderson notes that judges tend to defer to lawyers and bar associations on the critical issues of legal ethics, dispute resolution systems, and bar admissions. In deferring to the lawyers and bar associations that they should be leading, regulating, and upgrading, judges foster a lawyer-centric legal system and subordinate ordinary citizens' requirements, as Henderson explains:

> For reasons rooted in separations of power, the authority to oversee lawyers has historically resided in the courts with state Supreme Court justices pretty much getting the final say. However, most supreme court justices think of themselves as jurists who decide the state's hardest legal questions. They seldom think of themselves as regulators of a complex economic sector undergoing significant structural change.
>
> Because the judges are not expert regulators, they naturally turn to bar associations for advice and expertise, often creating governance mechanisms that rely heavily upon practicing lawyers. This is the basis for lawyers being part of a self-regulated profession.
>
> The courts' regular activity can be placed into three different categories. First, the structure of the legal services market is substantially shaped by

45 Pereira, Rachel. (2019, February 12). Four federal judges talk about their journey to the bench. https://www.americanbar.org/groups/litigation/resources/newsletters/diversity-inclusion/four-federal-judges-talk-about-their-journey-bench/.

46 Brafford, Anne, & Rebele, Robert W. (2018). Judges' well-being and the importance of meaningful work. *Court Review*, *54*, 60, 61.

> the legal ethics rules. Specifically, the ABA Model Rules of Professional Conduct set forth limitations on who can own a law firm, who can practice law, the permissibility of noncompete agreements among lawyers, and also how lawyers can market and sell their services.
>
> The second category of regulation is the courts deciding the system for resolving disputes. Naturally, justices are going to default to the traditional court system as this is what they're familiar with. Yet Richard Susskind [legal futurist] and others have raised a provocative question: Is court a service or a place? And if it is a service, can it be redesigned for the benefit of ordinary citizens?
>
> The third category of regulation is courts deciding the educational requirements for entering the profession. The risk here is that the rules will be very lawyer-centric when, in fact, what is needed is entry to allied professionals who have the expertise to help us reduce costs and improve quality and access.[47]

This close relationship between judges and lawyers is different from conventional "regulatory capture," whereby regulators are eventually dominated by the interests they were charged with regulating. For judges and lawyers, there is no discernible interregnum, no period of tension and uncertainty where their objectives diverge and the public interest is preeminent. Both judges and lawyers attend the same law schools, are acculturated in the same law firms and departments, and have benefitted from the same legal system and the hierarchies within that system. They share values, allegiances, and affinities, and even after retirement, judges may join lawyers' firms or seek their business as mediators and arbitrators.

Judges' relationships with lawyers are more akin to "original antigenic sin" than regulatory capture. In medicine, original antigenic sin describes how the body's original response to a virus determines its response to subsequent exposures to antigenically related strains of that virus. The term "refers to the preference of the immune system to recall existing memory cells, rather than stimulating de novo responses when encountering a novel but closely related antigen."[48] This response is a "sin" because it becomes less effective

47 Henderson, William. (2022, April 7). Module 1: Legal services market, Chapter 2: Historical arc of the legal profession. (Edited version of video prepared by Indiana University). Henderson identifies four major deficiencies: Judges "1. Don't perceive themselves as regulators; 2. Lack expertise in designing and running systems; 3. Have little time to focus on the issues; 4. Look to the organized bar for guidance ('self-regulation')." IAALS. (2024, March 7). Tackling root causes & overcoming the middle-class access to justice problems. (webinar).

48 Aydillo, Teresa, et al. (2021, June). Immunological imprinting of the antibody response in COVID-19 patients. *Nature Communications*, *12*, Article 3781. See Zhang, Ali, et al. (2019). Original antigenic sin: How first exposure shapes lifelong anti-influence virus immune responses. *The Journal of Immunology*, *202*, 335.

over time; viruses mutate, and the induction of the same antibodies hinders the induction of antibodies ("negative interference") that would be effective against the divergent virus. It is, in short, a repetitive failure to develop a de novo response to a new threat.

Many judges display the immunological imprinting known as original antigenic sin. They have been responding to threats to the current legal system in the same way they responded in the early phases of their legal careers. As attorneys, they were protective of the legal profession's prerogatives, granting a largely self-regulated industry an exclusive right to provide and profit from legal services. In that regulatory scheme, lawyers control legal services within a state but are not responsible for providing them to the citizens of that state. When those lawyers become judges, they continue to protect those prerogatives. As Henderson points out, they defer to lawyers' legal ethics rules, dispute resolution systems, and bar admission requirements. Although attorneys' prerogatives should be less important to judges than citizens' needs, very few reforms occur when attorneys become judges. Their roles change, but their responses are determined by the primary exposure, the original sin.

5

ELEMENTS OF WELL-BEING

What does an emotionally healthy lawyer, deriving satisfaction from serving clients and society, look like? What perceptions, values, and attributes do they have that enhance their well-being, promote client service, and activate a sense of social responsibility? Those questions and the extensive research supporting a model of constructive, fulfilling attorney behavior are the subjects of this chapter.

Attorneys who are happier and experience fewer mental health problems are quite different from other attorneys in eight respects: (1) they make less money; (2) they are more likely to work in public interest and government positions; (3) their professional roles are closely aligned with their personal values and goals; (4) their work is meaningful to them; (5) they enjoy higher levels of autonomy in their work; (6) their social relationships are more extensive and satisfying; (7) they see themselves as being successful in influencing outcomes that are important to them; and (8) they are intrinsically motivated.

One other factor merits our attention: attorneys who left the legal profession are happier than those who stayed in it. A Gallup study of attorney purpose well-being (a measure of "liking what you do each day and being motivated to achieve your goals") found that "more non-practicing than practicing J.D. holders have thriving purpose well-being (59% vs. 51%, respectively)."[1] This indicates, Gallup reports, that "more law graduates like

1 Gallup & AccessLex Institute. (2018). *Examining value, measuring engagement* (pp. 17, 18). Washington, DC: Gallup. The survey data regarding suicidal ideation appears in Krill, Patrick, et al. (2023). Stressed, lonely, and overcommitted: Predictors of lawyer suicide risk. *Healthcare*, *11*, 536.

DOI: 10.4324/9781003514848-5

what they do every day when they are outside of the legal profession." In another study, none of the attorneys who left law practice reported suicidal ideation ("thoughts that you would be better off dead or of hurting yourself") while 9 percent of the practicing lawyers reported suicidal ideation. The relatively happier cohort of non-practicing lawyers constitutes a large portion of law school graduates; 24 percent of lawyers who passed the bar in 2000, for example, were not practicing law in 2012.[2]

The nine factors predictive of attorney well-being, identified above, are generally consistent with two major theories of psychological health, Self-Determination Theory (SDT) and the PERMA theory of well-being. SDT identifies three needs that must be satisfied for people to attain optimal levels of fulfillment and performance: autonomy, relatedness, and competence.[3] The PERMA theory identifies five elements of well-being: positive emotion, engagement, relationships, meaning, and accomplishment. As we discuss in this chapter the qualities and actions that contribute to attorney well-being, it might be helpful to keep in mind the SDT and PERMA theories and see how well they delineate attorney well-being.

Income

The first irony of attorney well-being, as we saw in Chapter 2, is that money does not buy happiness—at least not for attorneys. In fact, increased income seems to diminish happiness, as law professor Lawrence Krieger and psychology professor Kennon Sheldon observe:

> The competition and stress related to high earnings and high grades—both zero-sum, limited resources—appear overdone. These data consistently indicate that a happy life as a lawyer is much less about grades, affluence, and prestige than about finding work that is interesting, engaging, personally meaningful, and focused on providing needed help to others. The data therefore also indicate that the tendency of law students and young lawyers to place prestige or financial concerns before their desires to "make a difference" or serve the good of others will undermine their ongoing happiness in life. This is a clear direction for increased education of law students and young lawyers. If a lawyer isn't happy, "what is the point?"[4]

2 Weiss, Debra Cassens. (2014, February 9). 24 percent of JDs who passed the bar in 2000 aren't practicing law, survey finds. *ABA Journal*.

3 Ryan, Richard M., & Deci, Edward L. (2008). Self-determination theory and the role of basic psychological needs in personality and the organization of behavior. In John, Oliver P., et al. (Eds.). *Handbook of personality: Theory and research* (pp. 654–678). New York: The Guilford Press.

4 Krieger, Lawrence S., & Sheldon, Kennon M. (2015). What makes lawyers happy?: A data-driven prescription to redefine professional success. *The George Washington Law Review*, *83*, 554, 592.

Even within the lucrative world of private law firms, paying the highest average compensation to lawyers, more money does not buy happiness: "Junior partners reported well-being that was identical to that of senior associates, who were paid 62 percent less."[5]

The income disparities between attorneys in public service positions, who report higher well-being levels, and attorneys in private practice, who report lower well-being levels, are dramatic. As the American Bar Association reports, "The median salary of $165,000 for first-year associates at private law firms was roughly triple the median salary for a first-year lawyer in a public service job ($48,000 to $58,300 for lawyers at legal aid offices, public interest groups, local prosecutor's offices and public defender's offices in 2018)."[6] These income disparities also are chronic, as the National Association for Law Placement explains: "among attorneys working in civil legal services organizations, as public defenders or local prosecuting attorneys, or as attorneys in public interest organizations, those providing civil legal services have the lowest median entry-level salary, earn the smallest increases in salary based on experience, and have seen the slowest growth in salary levels over the past 14 years."[7]

The fact that higher income does not result in higher levels of well-being may be news to attorneys, but it does not surprise psychologists who have studied income effects for decades. Their research results are mixed but generally indicate that incomes above a certain level have no effect or a relatively minor effect on well-being. Cognitive scientist Laurie Santos, who teaches a popular class on happiness at Yale University, summarizes these results in response to a journalist's question, "Is there anything surprising to you that people are just not getting about happiness?":

> For my students, it's often money. . . . There's a lot of evidence it doesn't affect your positive emotion too much. There was a recent paper by [psychologist] Matt Killingsworth where he was trying to make the claim that happiness continues as you get to higher incomes. And yeah, he's right, but if you plot it, it's like if you change your income from $100,000 to $600,000 your happiness goes up from, like, a 64 out of 100 to a 65. For the amount of work you have to put in to sextuple your income, you could instead just write in a gratitude journal, you could sleep an extra hour. Yeah, the money thing is one that students fight me on. It hits at a lot of the worldview they've grown up with.[8]

5 Quenqua, Douglas. (2015, May 12). Lawyers with lowest pay report more happiness. *The New York Times*.
6 American Bar Association. (2021). *Profile of the legal profession 2021*. Chicago: American Bar Association.
7 NALP. (2018, July 9). New public service attorney salary figures from NALP show slow growth since 2004. (Press release). https://www.nalp.org/uploads/PSASR_7-9-18_FINAL.pdf.
8 Marchese, David. (2022, February 18). Yale's happiness professor says anxiety Is destroying her students. *The New York Times*.

Even researchers who observe a linear relationship between income and happiness acknowledge that "the relationship is weak, even if statistically robust."[9]

Before closing this section on income effects, it might be enlightening to question some other icons of status in law schools and law firms and their effects on well-being: law school ranking, grades, law review membership, partnership, and law firm size. The correlation between law school ranking and lawyer well-being, based on a survey of 8,000 attorneys, is "almost meaningless."[10] A different study found that "only 27 percent of graduates of the top-ten law schools reported that they were extremely satisfied with their career choice, compared to 43 percent of graduates from fourth-tier law schools."[11] Another large survey actually showed an inverse relation between law school ranking and well-being. The attorneys who had graduated from non-elite law schools "were on the whole more satisfied with their large-firm jobs than those working in the same sorts of firms who had graduated from 'elite law.'"[12] The theory is that "graduates of the less elite schools were more grateful for their opportunities and less likely to have illusions about how hard the work was going to be."[13]

Law school grades also may have less of an effect than previously presumed: "Public service lawyers had the lowest grades and earnings of the lawyer groups, but nonetheless reported greater well-being than even the 'prestige' group, with the highest grades and earnings."[14] And despite the pressure placed on law review membership and becoming a law firm partner, neither "bore any relationship to the well-being of subjects."[15] Law firm size, moreover, does not result in increased well-being; "in the larger firms lawyers earn much more money but nonetheless experience no greater well-being and slightly more negative mood than those in smaller private firms."[16]

Self-perception and role-distancing

Law students who intend to practice law in the government and public interest sectors see themselves differently than attorneys who plan to join

9 Killingsworth, Matthew A., et al. (2023). Income and emotional well-being: A conflict resolved. *PNAS*, *120*(10), 4.

10 Krieger & Sheldon, *supra* note 4 at 605.

11 Levit, Nancy, & Linder, Douglas O. (2010). *The happy lawyer* (p. 15). New York: Oxford University Press.

12 Chambers, David L. (2013). *Satisfaction in the practice of law: Findings from a long-term study of attorneys' careers*. U. of Mich. Public Law Research Paper No. 330. *Bibliography of Research Using UMLS Alumni Survey Data*. 26, 39. (Citing Dinovitzer, Ronit & Garth, Bryant G. (2007). Lawyer satisfaction in the process of structuring legal careers. *Law and Society Review*, *41*, 25).

13 Ibid.

14 Krieger & Sheldon, *supra* note 4 at 614–615.

15 Ibid at 627.

16 Ibid at 596–597.

private law firms. Students planning government/public interest careers see their roles, values, and work as being closely aligned, while students planning private sector careers tend to separate their roles and values from their work. The attenuation of self and work in private practice is illustrated by a law firm partner who said that "when he hung up his jacket on the back of his door in the morning, with it went his personality, both of which he put on at the end of the day as he left the office."[17] These self-perceptions can affect their respective levels of commitment and engagement, the morality of their careers, and as we have seen in chapters 2 and 3, their well-being.

Law professor John Bliss has conducted extensive research regarding law students' self-perceptions and their effects on legal careers.[18] He categorizes students into three groups: students committed to careers in government or public interest (GPI); students who express a preference from the beginning of law school to work in large corporate law firms ("large firm"); and students who initially plan on a GPI career and, often for financial reasons, change their initial plan and prefer to join a large corporate law firm ("drifting"). The number of students in each category is roughly the same, and Bliss' sample "is approximately reflective of the law school's demographics and those of new lawyers across the profession."

As part of his research, Bliss asks the students to list the different roles in their lives—e.g., "Latina," "good Catholic," "family member," and "law student"—and then he presents them with a piece of paper with a large circle drawn on it to represent their identity. The students depict their most important roles by drawing them in the center of the large circle. They draw their less important roles near the edge of the circle and show the degree of connection between their core roles and their less important roles by the distance between them. An illustrative circle, with drawings by "Sam," a student planning to work in a large law firm, is shown in Figure 5.1. Sam's handwriting depicts his role as "Lawyer" at the edge of the circle, distant from his roles in the center as "vet [war veteran]," "family (old)," "family (new)," "politics," "religion," DOMA [Defense of Marriage Act]," and "military."

Bliss combines the students' lists and drawings with his interviews of them and quantitative analyses to form a composite view of GPI, large law firm, and drifting students. In follow-up interviews with the students, after they graduate and join law firms, he observes "a surprising consistency" between

17 Maister, David. (2006). Are law firms manageable? *The American Lawyer*.

18 The description of John Bliss' research and the quotations in this section, except for the quotations in fn. 17, 20 and 21, are derived from Bliss, John. (2018). Divided selves: Professional role distancing among law students and new lawyers in a period of market crisis. *Law & Social Inquiry*, 42(3), 855. Bliss, John. (2016, March/April). The professional identity formation of lawyers: How does becoming a lawyer change you? *The Practice*, 2(3).

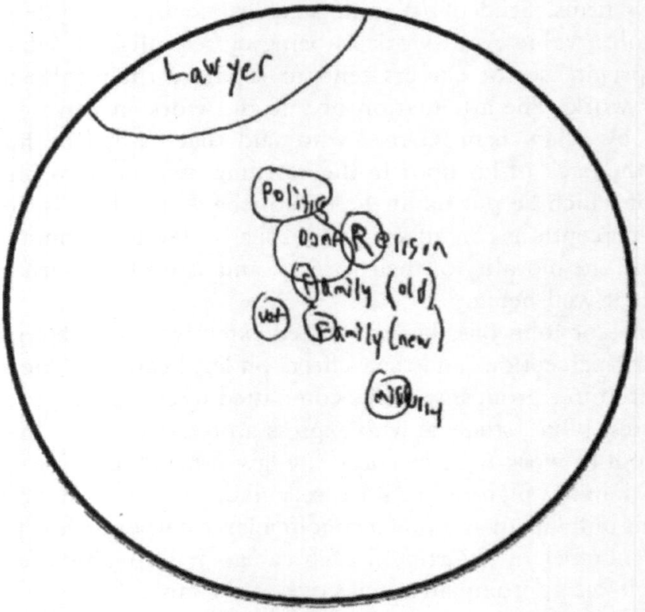

FIGURE 5.1 Large Law Firm Identity Map (Sam)

Source: John Bliss, University of Denver Sturm College of Law. Bliss, John. (2018). Divided selves: Professional role distancing among law students and new lawyers in a period of market crisis. *Law & Social Inquiry*, 42(3), 855.

their law school interviews and their post-graduation interviews. He summarizes his findings:

> Students who pursued public-interest careers generally maintained a central conception of lawyer identity, which often overlapped with political, racial, religious, and gender roles. In contrast, students who pursued positions in large firms tended to describe substantial distancing from professional identity in their 2L [second year] interviews. For students who had initially stated a preference for positions in the public-interest sector but later decided to pursue large firms, this distancing was often accompanied by a distressing sense of temporariness and fraudulence in their professional identities.[19]

The GPI students, Bliss explains, have "highly integrated professional identities that changed little over the course of their legal education." Their

19 Bliss (2016), *supra* note 18.

professional role is "in the center of their identity maps." The large law firm students, in contrast, exhibit "greater compartmentalization" and "a more bifurcated conception of the lawyer role." As a consequence, they "view their upcoming legal positions as instrumental and distant from what they conceived as their core identities."

Government/public interest (GPI) students

In their hour-long interviews with Bliss, the law students reveal the different aspirations, values, and professional identities underpinning their careers. These comments by GPI students illustrate the close connection between their self-perceptions and intended careers:

> "It never occurred to me [to apply to large firms]. The whole reason I am [in law school] is I feel like working people get treated badly or . . . disrespectfully."
>
> "The [recession] is exposing all kinds of ugly power and inequality . . . I feel like I need to be a part of a . . . movement right now to help steer things in a better direction."
>
> "Everything is definitely tied up with my role as a family member since my family is really defined by being activists and community members. . . . My friends, the community that I've grown up with, these people are all so proud of me back at home for getting into this law school and for pursuing my dream of being that social justice advocate."

Bliss describes GPI students as presenting "deeply held views regarding professional purpose" and notes that "race and gender may contribute to experiences of professional role integration in alignment with a cause lawyering conception of one's career."

Large law firm students

The integrated professional identity that characterizes GPI students contrasts sharply with the role distancing exhibited by large law firm students. This role distancing, Bliss observes, enables them to view their lawyer role "as distinct and distant from other constitutive identities." These interview comments by large law firm students depict their bifurcated, sometimes fragmented identities:

> "Even things that I'm passionate about in the law are secondary to me. I'm ok with that . . . .[Being a lawyer] is not central to my being at all. I want to be a lawyer just so that I can provide for the things that I want out of life."

> "You should never sell your soul, but you certainly [can] rent it. I'll rent them my soul for you know, a couple hours, or you know, a couple years of my life, if it means that I get to have a good quality of life for the rest of it."
>
> "I plan to be a lawyer for however long it takes to do something else. It's more of a launching pad for me. Step 1: Go to law school. Step 2: Pay off massive debt. Step 3: Get out of massive law firm and pursue other opportunities like smaller firms or business."

One large law firm student candidly acknowledges, "Despite all my rhetoric about being involved in society and about how that's why I want to [be] a lawyer, I kind of also just want to have a job that's not involved in the big issues."

Drifting students

Drifting students assume an uneasy professional identity. Their unease, Bliss states, reflects their concerns about "actually becoming a 'corporate lawyer' rather than temporarily portraying one" and is "accompanied by accounts of fraudulence, moral compromise, and concerns about the habitability of the lawyer role." Their sense of fraudulence and disappointment is encapsulated in these interview comments:

> "That makes me really sad, to think that I'm [planning to work in a large firm] because I was scared . . . or I wasn't able to take a leap of faith on something else, or I'm doing this because my practical side won over my romantic side, but the truth is, there is some level of accuracy to that."
>
> "When I was talking to [law firm interviewers] I told them I was interested in class actions, which is true . . . but I told them I was interested in them because I saw it as a legal mechanism that is often stretched beyond its proper scope. . . . If I told them what I believe, I definitely don't think I would have gotten a job. I think [that] before I had just been figuring out ways not to tell [interviewers] what I really thought. And then I shifted to affirmatively telling them lies. So I guess that helps. I guess that's what it takes."
>
> "[The firm where I will be working] defends the biggest companies . . . and they're being sued by the public interest organizations that I might have worked at. . . . I know it's all part of the legal system and everyone deserves a defense, but I also kind of feel like I switched sides . . . like I have to actively fight for the wrong side now."

Nearly all drifting students regarded their intended employment in a large law firm as a "temporary stint." As one second year law student explained, "It's really just a means to an end . . . it's a necessary evil for a couple years."

Reflecting the "moral and psychological role distancing" that Bliss observes in drifting students, "Rose" joined a large law firm and chose to work in the firm's intellectual property group. She lacked experience and expertise in intellectual property but selected that group because it was the "least dirty practice area" within the firm. Since she lacked legal or technical expertise in intellectual property, she has been consigned to the tedious task of "making binders" that Elizabeth Wurtzel described in Chapter 3. "I've been doing really menial stuff, like I make binders," Rose says. "I would say about 50 percent of what I do is making binders."

Rose avoided the firm's white-collar criminal defense practice because "I'm thinking, 'No. You'd feel so bad about yourself if you did that.' I can see myself doing criminal defense if I were a public defender, but not defending corporate criminals, even though someone has to do it because everyone is entitled to a defense." After two years of employment at the firm, she reflects, "The worst thought is that I'm going to work here every day until I'm too old to work."

The role-distancing displayed by drifting and large law firm students—in tandem with an instrumental approach that views a legal career as a way of obtaining financial benefits rather than animating personal values—may result in unethical or immoral behavior. In one study of attorneys' negotiation behavior, for example, the attorneys who saw negotiations as a "game" ("How I behave when negotiating is not a reflection of who I am, it is just how the 'game' is played") were more likely to act dishonestly and unethically.[20] "Lawyers with higher levels of moral character," the study authors concluded, "applied a game frame to negotiation to a lesser degree than did lawyers with lower levels of moral character and reported more willingness to disclose honest information to correct misimpressions held by counterparties."

The study authors also note that conventional legal education, teaching law students "how to think like a lawyer," may increase their risk of adopting a game frame and disregarding their personal values and ethics. The absence of an internalized moral identity or violations of one's moral identity, the study authors explain, "could temper their effectiveness at problem solving and may adversely impact their mental health as well."[21]

Meaningful work

Meaningful work, as discussed in Chapter 3, may be the central element in lawyer happiness. The University of Michigan Law School has surveyed

20 Cohen, Taya R., et al. (2022). Honesty among lawyers: Moral character, game framing, and honest disclosures in negotiations. *Negotiation Journal*, *38*(2), 206.

21 Ibid at 220. See Kammeyer-Mueller, John D., et al. (2010). The psychic cost of doing wrong: Ethical conflict, divestiture socialization, and emotional exhaustion. *Journal of Management*, *38*(3), 784.

more than 50 successive graduating classes to assess their level of job satisfaction and the predictors of happiness in legal careers. Their findings upset the conventional belief that working for large, prestigious law firms and earning a relatively large income lead to career success and personal satisfaction:

> Some findings may be surprising. We have found, for example, that, among Michigan's graduates five, fifteen and twenty-five years out of law school, for both men and women, overall work satisfaction is much more closely related to perceptions of the social value of their work and the quality of their relations with co-workers than it is to their satisfaction with income or with their prestige in the community. This finding helps make more explicable another of our findings—that, on the whole, women practitioners are somewhat more satisfied than men—since it appears that, in general, women place a higher priority than men [on] finding employment in settings where the work (as they view it) has comparatively high social value and where they are likely to have especially good relations with coworkers.[22]

Since meaning is critical to attorney well-being, attorneys who see their work as a "calling" report higher levels of job satisfaction.[23] As law professor Nancy Levit, co-author of *The Happy Lawyer* and *The Good Lawyer*, explains, "If you work at something you care about, you are much more likely to be happy."[24] The happiest lawyers, she states, "tend to be those who do work that they think make the world at least marginally a better place." Their values are aligned with their work, and they derive a sense of meaning and fulfillment from the close connection between the clients they represent and the values they espouse. Ninety-two percent of legal aid attorneys, for instance report that their work is meaningful.[25]

The centrality of meaning is corroborated by another survey showing that 82 percent of partners and 83 percent of associate attorneys agree that "it is important to me to find meaning in my work."[26] Their actual experience in finding meaning, however, is often disappointing. Only 66 percent of

22 Chambers (2013), *supra* note 12 at 2. The University of Michigan surveys are consistent with the Harvard Study of Adult Development's finding that the strongest predictors of longevity, health, and happiness "turned out to be the quality of their relationships." Tergesen, Anne. (2022, December 29). Your 401(k) isn't enough: To invest for retirement, build friendships and hobbies. *The Wall Street Journal*.

23 Ibid. at 15. See Levit & Linder, *supra* note 11 at 49–111.

24 Both quotations in this paragraph appear in Levit & Linder, *supra* note 11 at 106–107.

25 Coe, Aebra. (2022, July 22). Pay is a pain point in retention for Ill. [Illinois] Legal Aid orgs. *Law 360*.

26 Cartusciello, Yolanda, et al. (2020, March). *Multiple generations in law firms* (pp. 82, 113). Washington, DC: NALP and PP&C Consulting.

male attorneys and 58 percent of female attorneys, for example, are satisfied with "the value of their work to society."[27] Only 60 percent of all attorneys cite "meaningful, impactful work" and only 42 percent cite "personal values aligned with job" as a reason for being happy with their job.[28] When asked whether they are satisfied with the recognition they receive for their work, 71 percent of male attorneys, but only 50 percent of female attorneys, respond affirmatively.[29]

Surveys regarding attorney satisfaction and meaning can leave us with a hollow feeling because we're not sure whether the survey respondents' opinions match our understanding of those opinions, and it's difficult to know the context in which survey respondents are assessing themselves and their careers. Reading what attorneys have said about the intersections of meaning, purpose, career choices, money, and ambition helps to convey the personal impact sometimes lost in statistics[30]:

- "The fun part of practicing revolves around feeling like you've accomplished something that's significant. Whether that's helping someone save a building and turn it into a hotel or helping the guys at a struggling shopping mall that's a liability to the city turn it into a useful asset."
- "I think a lawyer's satisfaction with the legal profession is more closely correlated with how honest the individual is with him- or herself and less to do with how long the individual has aspired to practice law. It's not surprising that lawyers who enter the profession with a general "desire to help people" but wooed by lucrative offers from large firms are unhappy. I left private practice for legal aid, and have never been happier."
- "Every day I go to work at the ACLU, I strive to advance values that make this country great: freedom, democracy, and equality. . . . Those who work at the ACLU and other public interest organizations are not motivated by the desire to get rich, but rather by the desire to achieve the greater good. I believe that this difference helps to create a wonderful, collaborative, and supporting atmosphere in the office. Though we often work long hours, we do so because we want to and without resentment. Our work to preserve civil liberties and civil rights is a labor of love."

27 Liebenberg, Roberta D., & Scharf, Stephanie A. (2019). *Walking out the door* (p. 5). Chicago: American Bar Association.

28 Debney, Claire, & Sharpe, Emma. (2020). *The Mosaic mood index*, p. 4. London: The Mosaic Collective.

29 Liebenberg & Scharf, *supra* note 27 at 5.

30 The second quotation in this paragraph appears in Neil, Martha. (2008, January 22). Which lawyers love their jobs? *ABA Journal Law News Now*. All other quotations appear in Levit & Linder, *supra* note 11 at 224–225.

- "I went to law school intent on becoming a civil rights lawyer. . . . I ended up a victim of my own success. High grades and law review, followed by a federal judicial clerkship, opened doors to the highest-paying, most prestigious job opportunities. People I respected, my judge and my brother (a successful lawyer) told me no one in their right minds would turn down an offer from the [Biggest & Best] law firm. But it was never for me. I knew that at the interview. The partners were stuffy, arrogant, and conservative. It was not a good fit. But instead of following my own heart, I did what other people thought I should do. Big mistake."
- "I know so many people who feel stuck in jobs they don't want. In the beginning, they knew it was not for them, but said, 'I'll work here, advocating positions I don't like and working 2000+ hours a year for just a while. Once I make lots of money, I will move on.' They get in it and find themselves vested and unable or unwilling to take the risk. Years of their lives will get by them with little reward except perhaps money, and that does not compensate them for having no life. I say, take a job that satisfies you and allows you to embrace your interests now, not later."

The attorney survey results, combined with attorneys' personal insights, show that attorneys are like most people in identifying "important and meaningful work as the single most valued feature of their employment."[31] The need for meaning, observes Anne Brafford, a former partner at Morgan Lewis, "too often has been overlooked in a profession that narrowly favors rationality and logic."[32] Fulfillment of this need, for many attorneys, is dependent on beneficence, "the sense of having a positive pro-social impact on others." Beneficence is closely aligned with altruism and is a strong predictor of meaningfulness and well-being.[33]

Autonomy

In their survey of 7,805 attorneys, law professor Lawrence Krieger and psychology professor Kennon Sheldon discovered that the factors most strongly correlated with well-being were (in this order) autonomy, relatedness,

31 The statements in this paragraph appear in Brafford, Anne M. (2018, July). A full life: Five ways to foster meaningful work and boost lawyer well-being. *Texas Bar Journal*, *81*(7), 520.

32 Martela, Frank, & Ryan, Richard M. (2016, December). The benefits of benevolence: Basic psychological needs, beneficence, and the enhancement of well-being. *Journal of Personality*, *84*(6), 750.

33 Martela, Frank, & Riekki, Tapani J.J. (2018, July). Autonomy, competence, relatedness, and beneficence: A multicultural comparison of the four pathways to meaningful work. *Frontiers in Psychology*, *9*, Article 1157.

competence, and intrinsic motivation. These factors, Krieger and Sheldon point out, are not only the most powerful predictors of well-being:

> In addition to clear implications for the universal search for life satisfaction and happiness, these findings have "important implications for attorney ethics and professionalism and for the "bottom line" productivity and profits of legal employers. The most powerful predictors of well-being in these data—autonomy (r =.66), relatedness to others (r =.65), competence (r =.63), and internal motivation for work (r =.55) are also sources of professional behavior and positive performance in lawyers; lawyers experiencing high well-being are also likely to produce more, remain longer, and raise the morale of others.[34]

The four critical factors identified by Krieger and Sheldon—autonomy, relatedness, competence, and intrinsic motivation—are critical for well-being and provide concurrent benefits in ethics, professionalism, productivity, profitability, and collegiality.

This section discusses autonomy, and later sections address relatedness, competence, and intrinsic motivation. Autonomy, for purposes of understanding attorney well-being, has two facets: personal satisfaction of the need for autonomy; and autonomy support provided by someone in a supervisorial role like a practice group leader or other law firm partner. Personal satisfaction of the need for autonomy occurs when people "experience their behavior as emanating from themselves, so that they feel they are acting out of their own choice."[35] It requires both the freedom to choose how to develop professional expertise and the freedom to choose how to deploy it. Autonomy support, which contributes to personal satisfaction of the need for autonomy, occurs when a person in authority "(1) acknowledges the perspectives or preferences of the other; (2) provides meaningful choices to the other; and (3) when asserting control rather than providing choices, explains to the other the reasons why that is necessary."[36] Perhaps the easiest way to understand personal autonomy and autonomy support is to recall situations in which you thrive and then consider the degree of freedom you exercise in performing the work and the respect and discretion accorded to you by others.

Analyzing attorney survey data, Krieger and Sheldon found that personal autonomy and overall well-being increased with an attorney's legal

34 Krieger & Sheldon, *supra* note 4 at 585.

35 Pomerantz, Eva M., et al. (2007). The role of parents in how children approach achievement. In Elliot, Andew J., & Dweck, Carol S. (Eds.). *Handbook of competence and motivation* (p. 260). New York: The Guilford Press.

36 Krieger & Sheldon, *supra* note 4 at 582.

experience and decreased with firm size and alcohol consumption. They also confirmed an inverse relation between autonomy support and attorney depression. In other words, attorneys whose work is directed by overbearing, micromanaging partners tend to report high levels of depression. Krieger and Sheldon's conclusions regarding the importance of autonomy are buttressed by other surveys showing that lack of control over workload and assignments is frequently cited by attorneys as the worst aspect of their work. In one survey, for instance, associate attorneys were asked "What do you dislike the most about your job?" The top five responses, in order of detestation, are: lack of control over my work schedule; number of hours; firm politics; lack of control over my assignments; and lack of diversity of my colleagues.[37]

Krieger and Sheldon's emphasis on autonomy is directly corroborated by the Canadian Bar Association's survey of 6,365 lawyers. A statistical analysis of the survey results demonstrates that "autonomy is the resource that has the most decisive impact on health as it is associated with significantly lower levels of stress, psychological distress, depressive symptoms, and burnout."[38] The survey further shows that "autonomy and consistency of one's values with those of their work environment seem to have a very significant effect on reducing burnout symptoms, even surpassing the effect of certain risk factors such as hours worked and qualitative overload." The protective effect of autonomy was particularly strong in private practice settings, indicating that increased autonomy can mitigate the negative effects of long hours associated with private practices. The beneficial effects of autonomy are also corroborated by studies of lawyers in England, France, and Wales.[39]

Our sense of autonomy has objective and subjective facets. It can depend on the sheer volume of responsibilities unilaterally imposed on an associate attorney by partners; and it can depend on perceptions of how other attorneys' preferences are treated when partners make assignments and whether other attorneys are given discretion in prioritizing, scheduling, defining, and modifying their assignments. Our sense of autonomy invariably reflects the degree of freedom and discretion we think we have earned, as well as our personal tolerance for control, conformity, reporting, and compliance.

37 Cartusciello, *supra* note 26 at 120.

38 Cadieux, Nathalie, et al. (2022). *Research report (preliminary version): Towards a healthy and sustainable practice of law in Canada* (pp. 73, 75). National Study on the Psychological Health Determinants of Legal Professionals in Canada, Phase I (2020–2022). Sherbrooke, QC: Université de Sherbrooke, Business School.

39 Soon, Lucinda, et al. (2021). The effects of basic psychological needs satisfaction and mindfulness on solicitors' well-being. *International Journal of the Legal Profession*, 29(2), 143. Nickum, Marion, & Desrumaux, Pascale. (2023). Burnout among lawyers: Effects of workload, latitude and mediation via engagement and over-engagement. *Psychiatry, Psychology and Law*, *30*(3), 1.

Associate attorneys encounter formidable obstacles in their quest for autonomy. They rarely have the opportunity to choose among assignments, and partners' assignments frequently are arbitrary or unfair. Barely one-half (51 percent) of partners and associates agree with the statement, "My firm's assignment system is fair." A scant majority (51 percent) of associates agree that "my firm treats attorneys of color and non-minority attorneys equally when it comes to staffing matters."[40] When only one-half of attorneys perceive their firm's assignment system as fair and non-discriminatory, law firms are failing to provide autonomy support and intensifying attorney depression.

Relatedness

Attorney well-being is strongly correlated with relatedness, "an interpersonal dimension reflecting the extent to which a person feels that one is connected to others, has caring relationships, and belongs to a community."[41] The sense of belonging is closely linked to a belief that life is meaningful.[42] Conversely, social isolation or exclusion causes "cognitive deconstruction" and results in "finding less meaning in life."[43]

Relatedness takes on a special significance among lawyers because law practice is ranked as the loneliest profession. As Shawn Achor, author of *The Happiness Advantage*, writes, "In a breakdown of loneliness and social support rates by profession, legal practice was the loneliest kind of work, followed by engineering and science. This is perhaps not surprising, given the known high prevalence of depression among lawyers."[44] In Achor's study, 61 percent of the lawyers ranked "above average" on the UCLA Loneliness Scale.[45] Their sense of loneliness can be deadly; lawyers who "screened as lonely on the UCLA loneliness scale were 2.8 times more likely to endorse suicidality than lawyers who did not screen as lonely."[46] Loneliness, moreover,

40 Major, Lindsey & Africa. (2023). *Searching for balance: Millennial lawyers' perspectives on the legal industry* (pp. 24, 26). Hanover, MD: Major, Lindsey & Africa.

41 Martela, Frank, et al. (2018). Autonomy, competence, relatedness, and beneficience: A multicultural comparison of the four pathways to meaningful work. *Frontiers in Psychology*, *9*, Article 1157.

42 Lambert, Nathaniel M., et al. (2013). To belong is to matter: Sense of belonging enhances meaning in life. *Personality and Social Psychology Bulletin*, *39*(11), 1418.

43 Ibid at 1419.

44 Achor, Shawn, et al. (2018, March 19). America's loneliest workers, according to research. *Harvard Business Review*.

45 Paquette, Danielle. (2018, March 30). American workers are already lonely. Here come the robots. *The Washington Post*. Weiss, Debra Cassens. (2018, April 3). Lawyers rank highest on 'Loneliness Scale,' study finds. *ABA Journal*.

46 Krill, et al., *supra* note 1 at 8.

is correlated with anxiety, heart disease, dementia, Parkinson's disease, high blood pressure, stroke, and depression.[47]

Lawyers, law professors, psychologists, and therapists acknowledge the loneliness epidemic in the profession and identify many reasons why it persists:

- "The loneliness, lack of meaning. . . . That's why people are turning to all these coping mechanisms and ending their lives and having anxiety and depression."[48]—Rebecca Simon, law professor
- "What that translates to is: You're working all the time. You get to the point where you're too exhausted to socialize."[49]—Daniel Lukasik, lawyer and creator of the online community Lawyers With Depression
- "It's harder to get that camaraderie and that exchange of ideas and the brainstorming when you are a slave to the billable hour because you don't have enough time in your day to brainstorm and then make your hours. I constantly feel like I'm cutting people off, or they're cutting me off or they just don't want to be bothered, and it's very frustrating. [Y]ou can't just shoot the breeze with people."[50]—Senior law firm female lawyer (anonymous) participating in the American Bar Association Initiative on Achieving Long-Term Careers for Women in Law
- "I do hear from a lot of early career associates that their work, by the nature of their work, document review and so on, often precludes them from having sustained interaction with colleagues. You can imagine the scenario of the overworked associate working by themselves, they're quite literally in their head. And depending on what's in their head it can be problematic."[51]—Tyger Latham, clinical psychologist
- "It can be very lonely. You just feel besieged."[52]—William Meyerhofer, psychotherapist and former practicing lawyer

Many attorneys' responses to loneliness—excessive use of prescription medicines, alcohol, and illegal drugs—are maladaptive. Their coping mechanisms intensify their isolation and compulsive need to work. "Eventually their personal relationships begin to suffer as a result," explains psychotherapist Lucy

47 Abbott, Brianna. (2023, November 9). Loneliness isn't just bad for your health—it's deadly. *The Wall Street Journal.*
48 McLellan, Lizzy. (2019, May 18). Battling an 'epidemic' of loneliness among lawyers. *The American Lawyer.*
49 Paquette, *supra* note 45.
50 Sterling, Joyce, & Chanow, Linda. (2001). *In their own words* (p. 15). Chicago: American Bar Association.
51 McLellan, *supra* note 48.
52 Ibid.

Myers, "which can exacerbate the feeling that the job has to be the priority. And so the cycle continues."[53]

The sense of loneliness and isolation is particularly acute for women of color. "I'm in an office now where we, I think, we have more of a camaraderie and I'm included more," a Black female lawyer remarks. "But even still, even the white women will get together after work and go have a drink and I will see people making plans and talking after hours and I'm almost never included." This isolation, she says, "is the worst part for me."[54]

The prevalence of loneliness among lawyers is confirmed by a Gallup study assessing attorneys' social well-being (defined as "having strong and supportive relationships" and "access to necessary resources").[55] Only 55 percent of attorneys were "thriving" in social well-being (strong and consistent well-being); 38 percent were "struggling" (moderate or inconsistent well-being); and 7 percent were "suffering" (low and inconsistent well-being). Their level of social well-being was worse than other advanced degree holders.

Although strong relationships with other people are essential to well-being, attorneys may lack sufficient sociability, sensitivity, empathy, and care to build relationships with other people. Law firm consultant David Maister describes this phenomenon:

> As many researchers have shown, lawyers score very low in the areas of intimacy skills and sociability. They tend to prefer role-to-role interactions with people, inside and outside the firm, rather than eagerly seeking out person-to-person connections. This doesn't mean they don't like people. It just means that, statistically speaking, lawyers prefer focusing on the job at hand rather than investing in relationships with those they are working with (other partners or associates) or for (clients).[56]

Maister recalls a lawyer who attended one of his seminars and laughed at the idea of developing closer relationships with colleagues and clients. That lawyer later sent him this email: "My laughing was cynical. . . . The first thing you learn when you become a lawyer is not to care. The legally sound judgment, the intellectual sparkle, that is what counts. The personal, the emotional, what is right: Throw it away, because it will taint your professionalism. 'Do not get involved' is the credo."[57]

53 Mawardi, Adam, & Burton, Lucy. (2023, March 10). The City lawyers working themselves to death. *The Telegraph*.
54 Sterling, *supra* note 50 at 18.
55 Gallup & AccessLex Institute, *supra* note 1.
56 Maister, David. (2006). Are law firms manageable? *The American Lawyer*.
57 Ibid.

A study of 1,800 attorneys in four large law firms suggests that they may encounter significant difficulties in realizing relatedness and social well-being. Their lowest average score on the Hogan Personality Inventory was on "Interpersonal Sensitivity," measuring the "degree to which a person is socially sensitive, tactful, and perceptive."[58] On the Hogan Motives, Values, Preferences Inventory, the attorneys scored below average on "Altruistic," indicating that lawyers "place more value on their own work than in helping others" and have a relatively low interest in building a better workplace or improving society.

The lawyers' scores on five other traits were above average. Those traits and their definitions in the Hogan Development Survey signal some challenges in enhancing social well-being among large law firm lawyers:

- *Reserved*. "Tends to be tough, remote, detached, and hard to reach. Result: seems to be a poor communicator."
- *Leisurely*. "Tends to be independent, ignore others' requests, and becomes irritable if they persist. Result: seems stubborn, procrastinating, and uncooperative."
- *Cautious*. "Tends to be overly worried about making mistakes and criticism. Result: seems resistant to change and risk adverse."
- *Excitable*. "Tends to be initially enthusiastic about people or projects but then becomes disappointed with them. Result: seems to lack persistence."
- *Skeptical*. "Tends to be socially insightful but cynical, mistrustful, and overly sensitive to criticisms. Result: seems to lack trust."[59]

Interpreting some of these study results, the researchers determined that many attorneys "come across as cold, critical and argumentative" and "physically or emotionally distance themselves from others and become uncommunicative." In a deeply lonely profession where attorneys score below other advanced degree holders in social well-being, this behavior will petrify their isolation.

Attorneys' aversion to the human and altruistic dimensions of law practice is shown again in a survey of major law firm partners identified by senior in-house counsel as "stand-out lawyers."[60] When asked which non-billable activities they want to "drop" or "don't have or want," the most unpopular activities included diversity, equity, and inclusion

58 Foster, Jeff, et al. (2010). Understanding lawyers: Why we do the things we do. *Hildebrandt Baker Robbins*. All quotations in this paragraph appear in that article.

59 All bulleted quotations appear in Foster, *supra* note 58 at 4.

60 Thomson Reuters Institute. (2021, November). Stellar performance: Skills and progression mid-year survey. https://www.thomsonreuters.com/en-us/posts/wp-content/uploads/sites/20/2021/11/Standout-Lawyers-2021_LawFirms_FINAL-web.pdf.

initiatives; pro bono work; graduate recruitment; and well-being initiatives. The survey also detected serious gaps between the law firms' needs for mentoring and team development and the partners' willingness to meet those needs. These eminent lawyers were self-absorbed, intending to decrease human connections and prosocial activities that engender relatedness and meaning.

Competence

The third critical element of attorney well-being, as Krieger and Sheldon determined in their survey of 8,000 attorneys, is competence. Although this term seems self-explanatory, it has a slightly more nuanced meaning in the self-determination theory applied by Krieger and Sheldon. In that theory, competence refers to the need that individuals have "to experience themselves as competent—that is, to feel that they are capable of successfully influencing their environment."[61] The perception that we can influence outcomes underpins our sense of competence and, ultimately, enhances our self-esteem and well-being.[62] Competence is closely related to autonomy because the individual initiative, discretion, and freedom that attend autonomy also lead to the successful problem solving and goal achievement that foster feelings of competence.[63]

We might expect that attorneys with high incomes and exceptional academic records, including law review experience, would have the most positive perceptions of their competence. But that expectation is not supported by Krieger and Sheldon's data:

> Another point of interest emerged in the data: although the "prestige" lawyers had substantially higher law school grades than any other group, they reported significantly lower satisfaction of the competence need ($p < .01$) than the group with the lowest grades and pay, the "service" lawyers. This suggests a core dissonance between "competence" as measured in law school (largely by grade performance) and a lawyer's ability to feel competent in actual law practice.[64]

The lawyers with law review experience, moreover, "experienced no greater competence in law practice than non-journal members."[65]

61 Pomerantz, *supra* note 35 at 260.

62 Eccles, Jacquelynne S. (2005). Subjective task value and the Eccles et al. model of achievement—related choices. In Elliott & Dweck, *supra* note 35 at 109.

63 Pomerantz, *supra* note 35 at 263.

64 Krieger & Sheldon, *supra* note 4 at 591.

65 Ibid at 578.

Linking competence and autonomy, Krieger and Sheldon contend that service lawyers' higher sense of competence is due, in part, to increased latitude and responsibilities: "This difference in reported competence likely results from the fact that attorney competencies accrue from the development of practice skills, rather than from the more typical theoretical learning provided by most law schools, coupled with the fact that lawyers in public service positions are often provided case responsibilities sooner than those in 'prestige' positions."[66]

Intrinsic motivation

Internal motivation—frequently termed "intrinsic motivation"—is the fourth-strongest predictor of well-being in Krieger and Sheldon's study. Intrinsic motivation is "the motivation to approach a task out of sheer interest in the activity itself and excitement about the challenges that lie ahead. When fueled by intrinsic motivation, people perceive that their involvement is free of strong external control; they get the sense that they are playing rather than working."[67] Extrinsic motivation, in contrast, "is the motivation to do something for some external goal, some incentive outside of the task itself, such as an impending evaluation or the promise of a reward."[68] In law practices, extrinsic rewards can include income, staffing, office space, status, leadership positions, titles, praise, attention, media coverage, and power. Most large law firm partners in one study, for example, designated "high salaries as having had the most positive impact on their lives."[69] One-third of those partners selected "ability to pay for children's education/nicer living arrangements or luxury goods" as the "main positive" of their careers.

Krieger and Sheldon find that intrinsic motivation and competence are strongly correlated: "Beyond its powerful contribution to well-being, internal motivation also promotes competence because it generates focus and persistence in work."[70] They also find that intrinsic motivation decreases with firm size, income, and billable hour requirements and increases with the number of unpaid public service/pro bono hours an attorney provides in a typical month. Although White attorneys earned more money than other

66 Ibid at 591.

67 Hennessey, Beth A. (2019). Motivation and creativity. In Kaufman, James C., & Sternberg, Robert J. (Eds.). *The Cambridge handbook of creativity* (p. 376). New York: Cambridge University Press.

68 Ibid.

69 Walker, Rose. (2022, October 18). Regrets? Maybe a few, say older partners looking back at their work-life balance. *Law.com*.

70 Krieger, Lawrence. (2018, January). The surprising master key to happiness and satisfaction according to the lawyer research. *Florida Bar Journal*, 92(1), 16.

racial groups in the Krieger and Sheldon study, they "also had less internal motivation for their work and consumed alcohol more intensely than others."[71]

Does it matter whether an attorney is primarily driven by intrinsic motivation or extrinsic motivation? The answer is that these two different types of motivation have fundamentally different effects on well-being and society. The attorneys showing the highest levels of intrinsic motivation in Krieger and Sheldon's study exhibited the highest levels of well-being. This is consistent with extensive research demonstrating a strong association between intrinsic motivation and "richer experience, better conceptual understanding, greater creativity, and improved problem solving, relative to external controls."[72] Extrinsic motivation, in contrast, generally has a deleterious effect on performance. It promotes short-term thinking; limits the breadth and depth of analysis; hinders creativity; encourages unethical behavior; undermines intrinsic motivation; and eventually becomes addictive, requiring ever-increasing rewards to deliver the same satisfaction previously obtained from smaller rewards.[73]

Self-determination Theory and PERMA Well-being Theory

Self-determination Theory (SDT) has been tested, accepted, and refined for about 40 years, and the PERMA Well-Being Theory has been applied for nearly 15 years. SDT, as previously discussed, posits that well-being is largely determined by the satisfaction of three needs: "*autonomy* (the need to perceive one's self as the originator of one's actions), *competence* (the need to feel capable to perform well in an activity), and *relatedness* (the need to feel close to and understood by important others)."[74] SDT also posits that intrinsic motivation—an inherent interest in a subject or task—is essential to well-being. Krieger and Sheldon's research demonstrates that all four elements of SDT comprise the factors most closely correlated with attorney well-being. As they state, "The data contradict beliefs that prestige, income, and other external benefits can adequately compensate a lawyer who does not regularly experience autonomy, integrity, close relationships, and interest and meaning in her work."[75] SDT, moreover, has proven to be valid and

71 Krieger & Sheldon, *supra* note 4 at 602.

72 Deci, Edward L. (1995). *Why we do what we do* (p. 51). New York: Penguin Books.

73 See Park, Tae-Youn, et al. (2022). Incentive effects on ethics. *Academy of Management Annals*, *16*(1), 297. Pink, Daniel H. (2009). *Drive*. New York: Riverhead Books.

74 Pietrabissa, Giada, et al. (2020, June 30). Development and validation of a self-determination theory-based measure of motivation to exercise and diet in children. *Frontiers in Psychology*, *11*, 1299.

75 Krieger & Sheldon, *supra* note 4 at 623–624.

reliable in studies of lawyers and judges in multiple jurisdictions, including Australia, Canada, England, France, the United States, and Wales.[76]

A short outline of the PERMA Well-being Theory shows that it, too, provides a sound framework for understanding and achieving satisfaction and fulfillment in practicing law[77]:

P—Positive Emotions (feeling happiness, pleasure, pride, gratitude, satisfaction, interest, and hope about the past, present, and future).
E—Engagement (participation, concentration, and absorption in an activity that is gratifying for its own sake).
R—Relationships (joy and a sense of purpose, security, and belonging in supporting, serving, and interacting with other people).
M—Meaning (being able to effectuate personal values that give significance to one's life).
A—Achievement (the feeling of having achieved personal goals that were established for their own sake).

Some PERMA elements overlap with SDT while other elements remind us that well-being may be more complex and personal than a single theory can comprehend. We can quickly detect similar themes in Engagement and intrinsic motivation; Relationships and relatedness; Meaning, autonomy, and intrinsic motivation; and Achievement, competence, and intrinsic motivation. Positive Emotions, however, may be seen as independent factors or, perhaps more accurately, outcomes of the other elements. As psychologist Martin Seligman, the creator of the PERMA theory, explains, "No one element defines well-being, but each contributes to it."[78]

76 See Cadieux, *supra* note 38. Krieger & Sheldon, *supra* note 4. Nickum & Desrumaux, *supra* note 39. Schrever, Carly, et al. (2019). The psychological impact of judicial work: Australia's first empirical research measuring judicial stress and wellbeing. *Journal of Judicial Administration, 28*, 141. Soon, *supra* note 39.

77 The definitions in this paragraph are derived from Benoit, Valerie, & Gabola, Piera. (2021). Effects of positive psychology interventions on the well-being of young children: A systematic literature view. *International Journal of Environmental Research and Public Health, 18*, 12065. Csikszentmihalyi, Mihaly. (1990). *Flow*. New York: Harper Perennial. Seligman, Martin E.P. (2011). *Flourish*. New York: Free Press. University of Pennsylvania Positive Psychology Center. (2022). *PERMA theory of well-being and PERMA workshops*. https://ppc.sas.upenn.edu/learn-more/perma-theory-well-being-and-perma-workshops.

78 Seligman, *supra* note 77 at 24.

6
ALTRUISM

The Presidential Medal of Freedom is the highest civilian honor in the United States. President John F. Kennedy established the honor in 1963, declaring that it commends "any person who has made an especially meritorious contribution" to national security, world peace, or "cultural or other significant public or private endeavors."[1] Recipients of the medal typically have "overcome significant obstacles to achieve impressive accomplishments in the arts and sciences, dedicated their lives to advocating for the most vulnerable among us, and acted with bravery to drive change in their communities—and across the world—while blazing trails for generations to come."[2]

Although the award is known as the Medal of Freedom, it functions as an award honoring exceptional altruism. As President Ronald Reagan commented before awarding the medal to seven Americans in 1986, "You've all made America better—a better place—and you've made it seem a better place in the eyes of the people of the world."[3] The elements of altruism—protection of vulnerable individuals; dedication to improving the quality of life in communities; belief in the dignity and efficacy of individual action; commitment to change and innovation; personal integrity despite criticism, derision, or ostracism; bravery in the face of resistance and danger; and the acceptance of

1 Baker, Peter. (2022, July 1). Biden will award Medal of Freedom to Simone Biles, John McCain and others. *The New York Times*. See Boorstein, Michelle. (2022, July 1). Medal of Freedom awarded to Catholic nun and Muslim human rights advocate. *The Washington Post*.
2 The White House. (2022, July 1). President Biden announces recipients of the Presidential Medal of Freedom [Press release].
3 Reagan, Ronald. (1986, May 12). Remarks at the presentation ceremony for the Presidential Medal of Freedom. *Archives of the Ronald Reagan Presidential Library and Museum*.

DOI: 10.4324/9781003514848-6

personal risks without the expectation of commensurate rewards—permeate the lives of most award recipients.

Twelve presidents have awarded the Medal of Freedom to 692 citizens during the last 61 years. Only 19 of the recipients were judges, and only 44 were attorneys. At this rate, it would take another 260 years to have identified 100 judges qualified for the award. And it would take 78 more years to have found 100 attorneys deserving of this award, despite a current pool of 1.3 million attorneys. Only a tiny cohort of judges and lawyers is sufficiently altruistic to be honored nationally for their courage, compassion, and contribution.

Although the Medal of Freedom awards are not a scientific test of altruism and largely serve as an inspiration for altruistic behavior, they do raise questions and epitomize concerns about why society expects so little of its judges and attorneys. How has a profession characterized by fiduciary duties to place others' needs above their own been so successful in dampening society's expectations and evading accountability for the legal system? The paucity of Medal of Freedom recipients in the legal community reminds us that, although judges and attorneys are among the most powerful people in controlling individuals, businesses, religious organizations, governments, and societies, they have relatively little current value in promoting major progress and improvement. An ordinary citizen, for instance, might be hard pressed to identify a single sitting U.S. Supreme Court justice or prominent attorney who is universally respected or admired for their foresight and contribution to society.

This chapter explores altruism and its effects on attorney well-being and society. It first examines the issue of whether attorneys are altruistic and whether their sense of altruism fades during law school and law practice. It then discusses the types of altruism, describes the heritability of altruistic traits, and identifies other traits correlated with altruism. The chapter concludes by explaining the effects of altruism on mental and physical health and the impact of altruistic behavior on other people and society.

Altruism and attorneys

Altruism is the pivotal factor in restoring attorney well-being and repairing the legal system, but attorneys and law firms diminish its importance. In a survey of 24,137 lawyers, for example, 61 percent stated that having a "passion for public service" was either "not relevant" or "not necessary" to a lawyer's success.[4] Seventy-three percent said that engaging in pro bono work was either not relevant or not necessary to success. Nearly one in four lawyers,

4 Gerkman, Alli, & Cornett, Logan. (2016). *Foundations for practice: The whole lawyer and the character quotient*. Denver, CO: Institute for the Advancement of the American Legal System.

moreover, believed that having a "commitment to justice and the rule of law" was neither relevant nor necessary to success. In another survey, 14,846 lawyers were asked to rank the importance of various attributes of newly licensed lawyers.[5] "Social consciousness/community involvement" (defined as demonstrating a "desire to improve society by contributing skills to the community") was ranked as one of the least important qualities. "Instructing/mentoring" (defined as an ability to "manage, train, and instruct to assist others in realizing their full potential") also received one of the lowest ratings.

The study of 1,800 lawyers in large law firms, described in Chapter 5, found that the attorneys' lowest score on the Hogan Motives, Values, Preferences Inventory was on the "Altruism" scale. This score indicates that "lawyers place more value on their own work than in helping others."[6] Since they scored considerably below average on altruism, they are "less interested in others' well-being" and unlikely to spend their time "actively helping others and improving society."

The large law firm lawyers also scored high on the "Reserved" scale of the Hogan Development Survey, suggesting that they

> prefer to work alone and they value their private time. They prefer work environments where people attend to their own business and solve their own problems. They are unconcerned with social approval and they don't care to work in a team environment. In addition, they value productivity over staff morale and they tend to be disinterested in the problems and needs of others.[7]

People scoring high on the Reserved scale are "imperceptive or uninsightful about social, interpersonal, or political cues. Their imperceptiveness may be a function of deliberately ignoring other people; whatever the reason, they seem unconcerned about the welfare of others, indifferent to their moods and feelings, and unaware of or indifferent to how others react to them." On the positive side, they can be implacable in adverse circumstances because they are not easily affected by others' needs and criticisms.

5 National Conference of Bar Examiners Testing Task Force. (2020). *Testing Task Force phase 2 report: 2019 practice analysis*. https://nextgenbarexam.ncbex.org/wp-content/uploads/TestingTaskForce_Phase_2_Report_031020.pdf.

6 This quotation and the following quotation appear in Foster, Jeff, et al. (2010). Understanding lawyers: Why we do the things we do. *Hildebrandt Baker Robbins*. Hogan Assessment Systems. (2013). *MVPI subscale interpretation handbook*. Tulsa, OK: Hogan Assessment Systems.

7 The quotations in this paragraph appear in Hogan, Robert, & Hogan, Joyce. (2009). *Hogan development survey manual*. Tulsa, OK: Hogan Press.

Lawyers' aversion to altruism is also evident in their non-billable time preferences. Nearly one in three partners concedes, "I have not worked on any pro bono matters" within the last 24 months, despite the American Bar Association's admonition to render "at least (50) hours of pro bono publico legal services per year."[8] Seventy-two percent of law firm lawyers identified by senior corporate counsel as "stand-out lawyers" do not want pro bono work in the future or want to drop the pro bono work that they're currently handling.[9] About 80 percent of those attorneys do not want to be involved in "client innovation development" or "alternative delivery model development," both of which could result in more responsive and less expensive ways of delivering legal services to clients. And two out of three would like to divest themselves of responsibilities for "internal relationship development." The second most disliked non-billable activity is "wellbeing initiatives" (disdained only slightly less than "alternative delivery model development").

Altruism is neither a value nor a practice for many lawyers. They do not want to be associated with altruism and related traits, perceiving those qualities to be unimportant or possibly harmful to their reputations. When asked to identify how they want to be described, attorneys frequently select adjectives like intelligent, honest, reliable, and trustworthy.[10] The least popular adjectives include compassionate, thoughtful, helpful, decent, kind, and caring. When asked to identify "what adjectives they do *not* want to be called," the most frequently mentioned words are dishonest, lazy, unethical, incompetent and sloppy. The adjectives that bother attorneys the least include selfish, uncaring, self-centered, unhelpful, unfair, and insensitive. Attorneys also rank "making a positive impact" as less important for a positive reputation than being "smart and savvy" and "effective at achieving clients' goals." The importance of having a positive impact varies with practice settings. Attorneys in large law firms place relatively less emphasis on having a positive impact than attorneys in corporate law departments, solo practices, and small and midsize firms.

8 Cartusciello, Yolanda, et al. (2020, March). *Multiple generations in law firms* (p. 94). Washington, DC: NALP and PP&C Consulting. A.B.A. Model Rules of Prof'l Conduct R. 6.1.

9 Thomson Reuters Institute. (2021, November). Stellar performance: Skills and progression mid-year survey. https://www.thomsonreuters.com/en-us/posts/wp-content/uploads/sites/20/2021/11/Standout-Lawyers-2021_LawFirms_FINAL-web.pdf.

In another survey, female attorneys working at the 200 largest law firms rated "more pro bono hours" as the least important factor for them in their law firms. Leopard Solutions. (2023). *The challenges of women in Big Law* (p. 16). https://www.leopardsolutions.com/thought-leadership/women-in-big-law-2023/.

10 Data in this paragraph is derived from Above the Law, & Embroker. (2022). *Give a damn about your reputation.* https://470182.fs1.hubspotusercontent-na1.net/hubfs/470182/Embroker%202022/ATL_Embroker_ReputationReport2022.pdf.

Since altruism is not central to many attorneys' identities and their financial success, it generally is a low priority for their law firms. When asked to rank their business priorities, for instance, law firms place "growing revenue or identifying new revenue streams" at the top and "community engagement and social responsibility" at the bottom.[11] When asked to identify ten traits that "best embody your firm's culture," 65 percent of attorneys select "firm is well-managed from a financial standpoint," while only 36 percent select "civic-minded." The low priority that attorneys assign to being civic-minded is unlikely to change; only 27 percent of attorneys believe that civic-mindedness should be more prominently reflected or valued in their firm's culture.

Instilling altruism in attorneys is an extraordinarily difficult challenge because the legal profession does not seem to prize altruism. As law professor William Henderson observes, "the U.S. legal profession has virtually no experience engaging in significant collective action that strengthens and improves our ability to better serve either the public or our members."[12] His observation is corroborated by a Bloomberg Law survey where attorneys were asked, "Which rule categories of the ABA Model Rules of Professional Conduct do you believe should be revised?"[13] Only 16 percent of lawyers stated that the rules in the public service category should be revised; and it's unclear whether their contemplated revision was an upward or downward change in the ABA's aspirational designation of 50 annual pro bono hours. The survey indicates that only a small percentage of lawyers favor changes in the ABA's currently low level of aspirational public service, and some lawyers may prefer an even lower level.

The peculiar arc of attorneys' careers indicates that the character strengths supporting altruism reach their peak in first year law students and then wane in law school and law practice. As shown in Figure 6.1, incoming law students score higher than practicing attorneys on these critical strengths: valor and bravery; fairness and equity; social and emotional intelligence; kindness and generosity; perseverance and diligence; passion and enthusiasm; and hope and future-mindedness.[14] Although the differences between law students and lawyers may not seem to be large for every character strength, the

11 Data in this paragraph appears in Actionstep. (2023). *2023 Midsize law firm priorities report*. https://www.actionstep.com/blog/new-2023-midsize-law-firm-priorities-report/. Major, Lindsey & Africa. (2022). *2022 Law firm culture survey*. Hanover, MD: Major, Lindsey & Africa.

12 Henderson, Bill. (2023, January 15). Mindshare matrix for legal professionals (349). *Legal Evolution*. www.legalevolution.org/2023/01/mindshare-matrix-for-legal-professionals-349.

13 Heelan, Melissa. (2023, September 20). Lawyers worry most about the profession's reputation. *Bloomberg Law*.

14 Kern, Margaret L., & Bowling, Daniel S. (2014). Character strengths and academic performance in law students. *Journal of Research in Personality*, 55, 29.

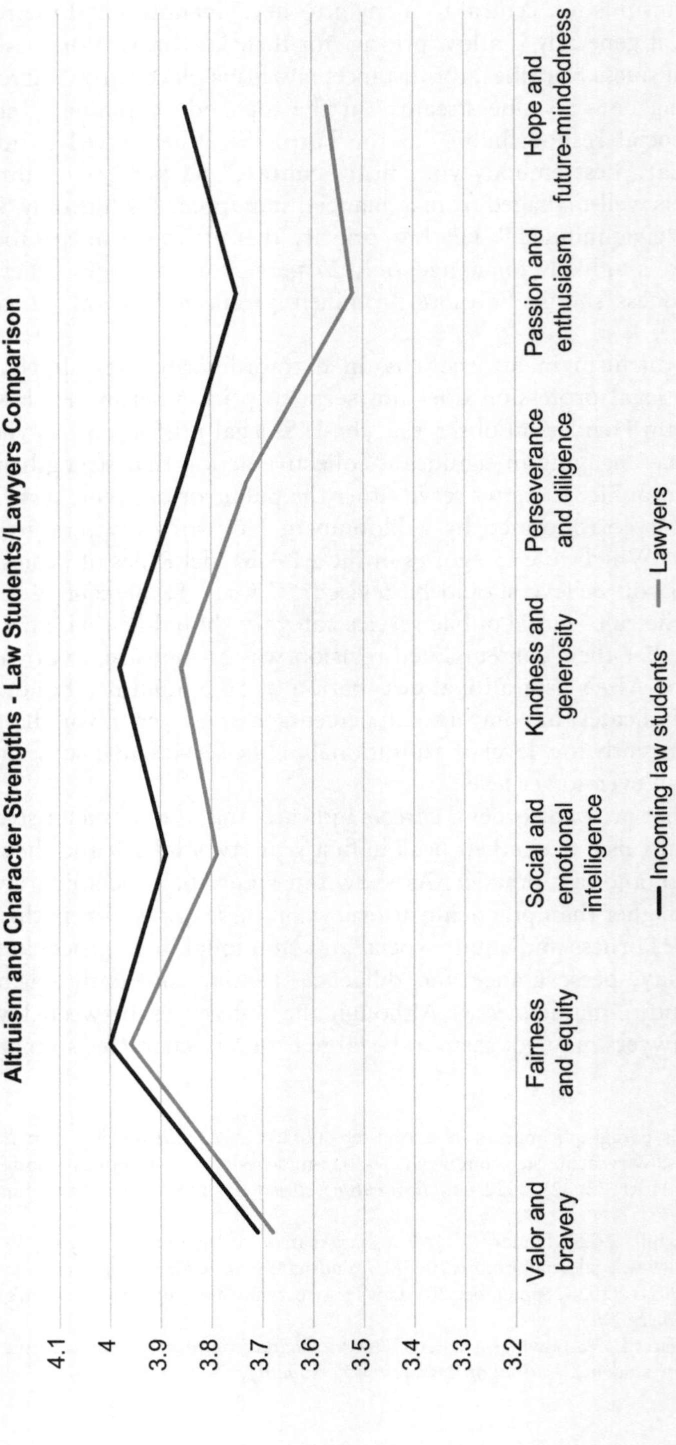

FIGURE 6.1 Comparison of Law Students and Lawyers' Traits
Source: Kern, Margaret, & Bowling, Daniel. "Character Strengths and Academic Performance in Law Students."

evident regression of those character strengths in law school and law practice is both revelatory and disconcerting. These strengths should be expanding over time rather than atrophying.

The arc of altruism depicted in Figure 6.1, culminating in weaker character strengths to support altruism, is consistent with prior research indicating that law students became less caring and social and "lost interest in other people" during the first year of law school.[15] Law students, like medical students, also become less altruistic.[16] Earlier reports from the American Bar Association corroborate this devolution; in one survey, attorneys identified their *least* important goals as "advance to a position of power" and "improve the public good."[17]

Even when lawyers are acting altruistically, their desire to be helpful may be eclipsed by their need for public recognition and extrinsic rewards. In one notable study, economics professor William Harbaugh analyzed how attorneys' donations to their alma mater, a prestigious law school, changed after the law school stopped reporting each donation by donor and amount and started reporting donors and their donations within categories (e.g., donors who made gifts of $500 to $999 were listed in the "Sponsor" category, and gifts of $1,000 to $1,999 qualified for the "Patron" category).[18] Theoretically, this change in the reporting format would have no effect on the attorney donors because their altruistic intentions function independently of anticipated public recognition. But after the change, most contributions were "exactly the minimum amount required for inclusion in each category."[19]

The change in reporting donations demonstrated that the attorney donors were motivated, in large part, to signal their wealth status. As a result, the "change to category reporting increased the proportion of donations made at the minimum amount necessary to get into a category and decreased the proportion of donations made at other amounts."[20] Economists at the Federal Reserve Bank of St. Louis concluded that the "warm glow" usually derived

15 Guthrie, Chris. (2001). The lawyer's philosophical map and the disputant's perceptual map: Impediments to facilitative mediation and lawyering. *Harvard Negotiation Law Review*, 6, 45.

16 See Daicoff, Susan. (1997). Lawyer, know thyself: A review of empirical research on attorney attributes bearing on professionalism. *The American University Law Review*, *46*, 1337. Daicoff, Susan. (2004). *Lawyer, know thyself*. Washington, DC: American Psychological Association. Hojat, Mohammadreza, et al. (2009). The devil is in the third year: A longitudinal study of erosion of empathy in medical school. *Academic Medicine*, *84*(9), 1182.

17 Daicoff (1997), *supra* note 16 at 1392.

18 Harbaugh, William T. (1998, May). The prestige motive for making charitable transfers. *AEA Papers and Proceedings*, *88*(2), 277.

19 Murillo, Ruben Hernandez, & Roisman, Deborah. (2005, October 1). The economics of charitable giving: What gives? *Regional Economist*.

20 Vesterlund, Lise. (2006). Why do people give? In Powell, Walter W., & Steinberg, Richard (Eds.). *The non-profit sector* (p. 573). New Haven, CT: Yale University Press.

from voluntary contributions did not generate sufficient incandescence and internal gratification for this donor group.[21]

Types of altruism

We have been using the term "altruism" in its ordinary sense: "the promotion of another's self-interest at risk or cost to oneself."[22] For psychologists, altruism has multiple meanings, and it may be instructive to understand various meanings as we refine our concepts of altruism. Nine different types of altruism alert us to the nuances in altruistic behavior:

- *Conventional altruism*—intentional action undertaken at tangible cost or risk to assist others without a reasonable expectation of a reciprocal benefit.
- *Empathic altruism*—"helping others out of a truly compassionate concern for the other," an expression of empathic concern for the welfare of someone we value.[23]
- *Reciprocal altruism*—an exchange "between unrelated individuals when there will be repayment (or at least the promise of repayment) of the altruistic act in the future," as occurs in grooming among non-human primates and referral networks among attorneys.[24]
- *Moral altruism*—"the capacity to take the moral point of view and be disposed to act accordingly," an "internalized pull of morality" that extends beyond a desire to help others.[25]
- *Altruistic urge*—a compulsion to help a "vulnerable victim in urgent need of aid that the observer can provide," frequently occurring "without the time to bask in feelings of empathy or sympathy or to imagine how the other must feel."[26]
- *Kin selection altruism*—behavior that, at a cost to the altruist, increases the likelihood of relatives' survival and reproduction, intensifying "with greater genetic overlap (degree of kinship) between giver and receiver."[27]

21 Murillo & Roisman, *supra* note 19.
22 Feldman, Mitchell D. (2017). Altruism and medical practice. *Journal of General Internal Medicine*, *32*(7), 719.
23 Preston, Stephanie D. (2022). *The altruistic urge* (p. 210). New York: Columbia University Press.
24 Segerstrale, U. (2016). History of sociobiology. In Kliman, Richard (Ed.). *Encyclopedia of evolutionary biology* (p. 140). Cambridge, MA: Academic Press.
25 Schramme, Thomas. (2017). Empathy and altruism. In Maibom, Heidi (Ed.). *The Routledge handbook of philosophy of empathy* (p. 203). New York: Routledge.
26 Preston, *supra* note 23 at 14, 33.
27 Rachlin, Howard, & Jones, Bryan A. (2008). Altruism among relatives and non-relatives. *Behavioural Processes*, *79*(2), 120.

- *Altruistic professionalism*—the concept that professions are moral communities "emphasizing altruism or the 'service' orientation of professionalism" and displaying a force "capable of subjecting rampant individualism to the needs of the community."[28]
- *Altruistic punishment*—the voluntary sacrifice of resources to punish violations of social norms, especially human cooperation and fairness norms, even when the punishment imposes greater costs on the altruist than on the transgressor.[29]
- *Pathological altruism*—"extreme, emotionally exhausting empathy" or altruism that results in unanticipated harm.[30]

The type of altruism directly applicable to lawyers and law firms is altruistic professionalism, but that concept may antagonize attorneys by prioritizing community needs over individual attorneys' needs. We have seen that attorneys' well-being is too precarious to adopt such an ambitious, community-focused concept of altruism. Instead, we need a broader concept of altruism that we will call "regenerative altruism" because it incorporates the benefits of conventional, empathic, moral, and professional altruism to restore attorney well-being and repair the legal system.

Regenerative altruism, a concept presented here to specifically address lawyers' responsibilities and needs, is a moral commitment accompanied by individual action to continually upgrade the legal system and ensure that everyone can identify and enforce their legal rights. Regenerative altruism captures in a single concept the benefits of professionalism, courage, empathy, compassion, perseverance, engagement, meaning, self-fulfillment, creativity, and ethics. In making the moral commitment and undertaking the actions that define regenerative altruism, attorneys experience a sense of purpose, integrity, consequence, and well-being that currently eludes many of them. The process of understanding and serving the legal needs of otherwise legally powerless citizens—an exercise in empathy, compassion, and altruism—produces a state of well-being that "mitigates the altruist's own distress and reflexively activates the reward system."[31]

28 Evetts, Julia, et al. (2006). Professionalization, scientific expertise, and elitism: A sociological perspective. In Ericsson, K. Anders, et al. (Eds.). *The Cambridge handbook of expertise and expert performance* (p. 107). New York: Cambridge University Press.

29 De Quervain, Dominique J.F., et al. (2004). The neural basis of altruistic punishment. *Science*, *305*, 1254. Fehr, Ernst, & Gachter, Simon. (2002). Altruistic punishment in humans. *Nature*, *415*, 137.

30 Oakley, Barbara H., et al. (Eds.). (2012). *Pathological altruism*. New York: Oxford University Press. Oakley, Barbara A. (2013). Concepts and implications of altruism bias and pathological altruism. *Proceedings of the National Academy of Sciences*, *110*(Supplement 2), 10408.

31 Sonne, James W.H., & Gash, Don M. (2018). Psychopathy to altruism: Neurobiology of the selfish-selfless spectrum. *Frontiers in Psychology*, *9*, Article 575.

Altruistic genes and heritability

A threshold question for some attorneys contemplating altruism is whether it is a genetically determined, "you either have it or you don't" personality trait. Economics professor Scott Shane answers that question:

> Our genes influence how interested we are in work that involves helping others, perhaps because our genes affect how altruistic we are. Studies show that about 30 percent of the difference between people on this dimension is genetic. Stated differently, a little under one-third of the variation in whether individuals put themselves or others first appears to be innate.[32]

Other academics contend that differences in altruistic behavior "can be attributed to genetic factors, with a heritability of 31%—61%."[33]

Shane notes that social responsibility is a trait similar to altruism: "both involve acting in ways that might be counter to one's own self-interest, but social responsibility focuses on a person's sense of duty to others." Social responsibility, Shane elaborates, has two forms: normative altruistic obligation (the duty to participate in charitable activities and social causes) and normative civic obligation (the duty to perform civic responsibilities). The genetically influenced variance in altruistic obligation is more than 30 percent, while 37 percent of the variation in civic obligation is genetic.

Thirty percent or 37 percent may seem like a high degree of genetic influence, but it is relatively low in comparison to many other traits like leadership styles, creativity, and numeracy. The takeaway is that individual attorneys, if motivated, can enhance and direct their sense of altruism and social responsibility. Attorneys have sufficient volition to be held accountable for their lifetime decisions to meet or disregard other citizens' legitimate needs and improve or disenfranchise themselves from society. They also are accountable for the impact of those decisions on their mental health and relationships with people close to them.

Traits correlated with altruism

Have scientists discovered an altruistic personality, a set of values, traits, beliefs, and behaviors, that define and distinguish altruists? The short answer is that, although many personal qualities are correlated with altruistic

32 The quotations in this paragraph and the following paragraph appear in Shane, Scott. (2010). *Born entrepreneurs, born leaders* (pp. 50–51). New York: Oxford University Press.

33 Liu, Jinting, et al. (2017). A field study of the association between CD38 gene and altruistic behavior: Empathic response as a mediator. *Psychoneuroendocrinology*, *85*, 1. See Cesarini, D., et al. (2009). Genetic variation in preferences for giving and risk-taking. *Quarterly Journal of Economics*, *124*, 809.

actions, scientists have not developed a checklist of attributes that reliably determine whether someone is altruistic or will act altruistically under exigent conditions. But they have identified a host of attributes that tend to be associated with altruistic action. Absent a reliable list of attributes conclusively determining whether we are altruistic or egoistic, we would benefit from recognizing that people who are convinced that they are altruists may not act like altruists in a crisis; and people who see themselves as egoists may discover altruistic impulses under compelling circumstances. Since altruism ultimately requires action, self-evaluations of altruism have little value until tested empirically.

The correlations between altruism and other traits are critical to our understanding of altruism and its effects on other people and society. Altruism does not exist in isolation but rather is a bundle of qualities and behaviors that manifest regularly but not invariably. When we discuss altruism and evaluate its efficacy, we must consider the correlated attributes as well because most of them will be operating concurrently with altruism. Neuroscientist Raymond Dolan finds that empathy, for example, is "the attribute that underpins a human disposition to altruism and compassion."[34]

The personal traits, qualities, and states correlated with altruism include empathy; concern; kindness; selflessness; creativity; tolerance for ambiguity; sympathy; compassion; self-efficacy; longevity; novelty seeking; moral elevation; and gratitude. Altruism also is correlated with decreased narcissism; diminished binary thinking; greater awareness of nonverbal distress signals like fearful facial expressions; higher oxytocin (the "tend and befriend" hormone) levels; highly developed social-brain regions; more gray matter in the right temporoparietal cortical junction (implicated in enhanced perspective-taking); heightened sense of awe; increased sensitivity to fairness; and an internal locus of control (a belief that outcomes in life depend on individual characteristics, decisions, and actions rather than external factors).[35]

34 Linder, Douglas O., & Levit, Nancy. (2014). *The good lawyer* (p. 2). New York: Oxford University Press.

35 For traits, states, emotions, and behaviors correlated with altruism, as discussed in this paragraph and the following paragraph see Decety, Jean, et al. (2015). Empathy as a driver of prosocial behaviour: Highly conserved neurobehavioural mechanisms across species. *Philosophical Transactions of the Royal Society B: Biological Sciences*, *371*, 20150077. Keltner, Dachner. (2009). *Born to be good*. New York: W.W. Norton & Co. Kitayama, Shinobu, et al. (2020). The gray matter volume of the temporoparietal junction varies across cultures: A moderating role of the dopamine D4 receptor gene (DRD4). *Social Cognitive and Affective Neuroscience*, *15*(2), 193. Knafo, Ariel, & Israel, Salomon. (2012). Empathy, prosocial behavior, and other aspects of kindness. In Zentner, Marcel, & Shiner, Rebecca L. (Eds.). *Handbook of temperament* (pp. 168–179). New York: The Guilford Press. Knafo-Noam, Ariel, et al. (2015, February). The prosocial personality and its facets: Genetic and environmental architecture of mother-reported behavior of 7-year-old twins. *Frontiers in Psychology*, 6, Article 112. Liu, *supra* note 33. Marsh, Abigail A., et al. (2014, October 21). Neural

These traits, qualities, and states generally are correlated with and predictive of positive emotions and well-being.

Altruists behave and relate to people differently than egoists. Actions and attitudes empirically associated with altruism include generosity; cooperation; helpfulness; self-transcendence; ethical decision making; decreased entitlement; increased demands for equitable wealth distribution; greater resource sharing; tendencies to be less aggressive; an inclination to trust strangers; and increased involvement in charitable activities and civic duties. These correlated actions are collectively called "pro-social behavior," as opposed to the combative, zero-sum conflicts and transactions that epitomize adversarial legal systems. Although these pro-social behaviors could be seen as devaluing individual superiority and hence jeopardizing self-worth, they actually enhance self-esteem, happiness, and well-being. "A large self is not necessarily the best self," explains psychology professor Paul Piff. "That is, a reduced sense of self may allow people to transcend self-interest and behave in accordance with their higher moral values, which may actually increase self-esteem."[36]

If pro-social behavior enhances self-esteem and happiness, could those positive emotions induce a sense of complacency and ultimately decrease benevolent actions? Cognitive scientist Laurie Santos, whom we met in Chapter 5, answers that question:

> There's been some lovely work on this by Kostadin Kushlev, who's a positive psychologist who has been interested in, Do these practices make you complacent when it comes to the big issues? What he finds is that the people who self-report the highest positive emotions, they're the ones who are taking action. This comes up in other domains too: There's evidence

---

and cognitive characteristics of extraordinary altruists. *Proceedings of the National Academy of Sciences*, *111*(42), 15036. Piff, Paul K., et al. (2015). Awe, the small self, and prosocial behavior. *Journal of Personality and Social Psychology*, *108*(6), 883. Poulin, Michael J., et al. (2013, September). Giving to others and the association between stress and mortality. *American Journal of Public Health*, *103*(9), 1649. Sonne & Gash, *supra* note 31. Steel, G. Daniel, et al. (2012). Personality, nations, and innovation: Relationships between personality traits and national innovation scores. *Cross-Cultural Research*, *46*(1), 3. Thompson, Graham L., et al. (2013). Genes underlying altruism. *Biology Letters*, *9*, 20130395. Valk, Sofie L., et al. (2017). Structural plasticity of the brain: Differential change after socio-affective and cognitive mental training. *Science Advances*, *3*(10), e1700489. Yamasue, Hidenori. (2008). Sex-linked neuroanatomical basis of human altruistic cooperativeness. *Cerebral Cortex*, *18*(1), 2331. Yusimi, Rodriguez-Ricardo, et al. (2019, September). Altruism and internal locus of control as determinants of the intention to participate in crowdfunding: The mediating role of trust. *Journal of Theoretical and Applied Electronic Commerce Research*, *14*(3), 1. Zhong, Songfa, et al. (2010). Dopamine D4 receptor gene associated with fairness preference in ultimatum game. *Proceedings of the National Academy of Sciences*, *5*(11), 13765.

36 Piff, *supra* note 35 at 896.

> that people who experience more gratitude have a high level of what's called self-regulation—kind of like sucking it up and doing the hard things now. There's also evidence that people who are more grateful are more likely to do things for other people. So I worry about complacency, but the evidence suggests it doesn't work in the way we might expect. When you do have some positive emotion, you have the bandwidth to deal with other things.[37]

Positive emotions and altruism exhibit "reciprocal causation," meaning that the cause-effect relationships can be bi-directional. Law professor Nancy Levit applies this concept to the practice of law: "Along with the positive feeling that comes with helping acts, you're likely to come home feeling better about where life has taken you. Yes, there is some status that comes with churning out the billable hours for zillionaires who want a few more zillions than the next zillionaire—but odds are you'll be a little happier helping Farmer McDonald save the family back forty from the I.R.S., helping that well-intentioned Latin family obtain citizenship, or making sure that the little boy crushed by the falling anvil will get his medical expenses paid for by ABC Anvil Company (or whatever negligent bastard let loose the anvil)."[38] The "warm glow" engendered by altruism has a scientific basis, as law professor Douglas Linder explains: "brain scans have allowed us to see how behavior consistent with our own sense of justice activates our reward (dopamine-driven) systems. In short, seeing justice done makes us feel good."[39]

Applied altruism in the Holocaust

When we discuss altruism and altruistic personalities, many people immediately think of the individuals who risked torture, disability, and death to protect Jewish refugees during World War II. A poignant question inevitably arises, "What compelled the rescuers to act altruistically when their fellow citizens chose to ignore or participate in the moral depravity of the Holocaust?" That question, sparked by intensive acts of altruism despite the threat of deadly force, should serve to illuminate an archetypal altruistic personality.

Unfortunately, the studies of Holocaust rescuers have utilized a variety of methodologies that make meta-analyses difficult if not impossible. We can,

37 Marchese, David. (2022, February 18). Yale's happiness professor says anxiety is destroying her students. *The New York Times*.

38 Levit, Nancy, & Linder, Douglas O. (2010). *The happy lawyer* (p. 89). New York: Oxford University Press.

39 Linder & Levit, *supra* note 34 at 230.

however, identify some of their personality features in studies completed by psychologist Eva Fogelman and sociologists Nechama Tec and Andre Stein. Fogelman and her staff volunteers interviewed 300 rescuers and confirmed the rescuers' accounts by interviewing the people they saved or verifying their stories with archival material. She disputes the theory that the rescuers' altruistic actions were primarily reactive, caused by uniquely heinous conditions:

> Rather, as I view it, the act of rescue was an expression of the values and beliefs of the innermost core of a person. It is a core nurtured in childhood, which came to expression during the Holocaust in the act of rescue, and then continued in the postwar years. Saving Jews came from that inner core and became part of it. This rescuer self was and, over the years has continued to be, an integral part of their identity.[40]

For many of the rescuers, the decision to put their lives at risk came down to a solitary inquiry, "Can I live with myself if I say no?"

Although Fogelman identified an inner core of values and beliefs among rescuers—"the basic compassion and moral integrity that triggered rescuing activity was repeated over and over during the rescuers' lifetimes"—she observed five different types of rescuers:

- *Moral rescuers*—"people who were prompted to rescue Jews by thoughts or feelings of conscience." Moral rescuers were the largest group, constituting 32 percent of interviewees. "Their concept of right and wrong," Fogelman writes, "was so much a part of who they were and are, that it was as if I had asked them why they breathed."
- *Judeophilic rescuers*—"people whose rescue activity arose out of a special feeling or love for individual Jews or the Jewish people as a group." Judeophiles were the second largest group, representing 28 percent of the interviewees.
- *Network rescuers*—"people fueled by anti-Nazi ideology, joining others who were politically opposed to the Third Reich." These rescuers, comprising 22 percent of the interviewees, joined and operated secret societies of Jews and non-Jews. Most of the network rescuers were highly educated individuals from business or professional families; they became the most cohesive and homogenous group of rescuers.
- *Children rescuers*—"children who helped rescue Jews at the behest of their families." These children, Fogelman learned, "became couriers, espionage

40 The quotations in the three paragraphs referencing Fogelman's studies appear in Fogelman, Eva. (1994). *Conscience & courage* (pp. xviii, 60, 82, 159, 161, 182, 194, 223, and 315). New York: Anchor Books.

agents, and guides. They learned to lie convincingly to authorities or feign innocence if caught." Children rescuers constituted 12 percent of the interviewees. About one-quarter of all interviewees said that they had put the lives of their children at risk to save other people.

- *Concerned professionals*—"people such as doctors or social workers who held jobs in which helping was a natural and logical extension." This was the smallest group, representing only 5 percent of interviewees. Fogelman distinguishes the concerned professionals from other rescuers: "the rescuer selves that emerged from this group's helping activities were little different from their usual professional demeanors. They were competent, independent, and dedicated to doing their jobs well. They were also a bit aloof, keeping an emotional distance between themselves and their charges."

Fogelman's five categories are illuminating, but they may obscure one overarching influence she observed: 89 percent of her subjects "had a parent or other adult who acted as an altruistic role model."[41]

Fogelman's studies led her to conclude, "The motivational drive behind acts of conscience and courage are the same for today's heroes as they were for Holocaust rescuers. I have found that all altruistic individuals share the same reasons: morality, a special affinity with the victims, professional concern, a network or community with a shared anti-Nazi ideology, or children who help parents or other adults." These reasons characterize many of the types of altruism identified earlier in this chapter, although Fogelman's labels are different.

Research conducted by sociology professor Nechama Tec complements Fogelman's studies. Tec finds that the Holocaust rescuers came from "all walks of life, all religious, political affiliations, and all family configurations."[42] She identifies six interdependent characteristics shared by Holocaust rescuers:

1 *Individuality*. They are not controlled by their environment and "are more inclined to act on their own principles."
2 *Independence*. They are self-reliant and "do what they feel they must do, what is right, and the right thing is to help others."

41 Hurowitz, Richard. (2023). *In the garden of the righteous* (p. 354). New York: HarperCollins.
42 The references to Nechama Tec in this section appear in Block, Gay, & Drucker, Malka. (1992). *Rescuers* (pp. 5–6). New York: Holmes & Meier Publishers. Tec, Nechama. A glimmer of light. Shoah Resource Center, International School for Holocaust Studies. Nechama, Tec. Nechama Tec discussing rescuers. Facing History and Ourselves. www.facinghistory.org/resource-library/video/nechama-tec-discussing-rescuers. For additional perspectives on Holocaust rescuers, see Oliner, Samuel, & Oliner, Pearl M. (1988). *The altruistic personality*. New York: Free Press. Samuel Oliner identifies these rescuer traits: deeply empathetic and altruistic; internalized ethic of caring and social responsibility; learned in childhood to consider the consequences of their misbehavior; capacity for love and compassion; and sense of self-esteem and efficacy. See also Hurowitz, *supra* note 41.

3 *Commitment*. Their actions are consistent; they have a long record of helping the needy and performing good deeds.
4 *Modesty*. They have a modest appraisal of their courage and actions; "because they have done the right thing for a long time, it doesn't seem extraordinary to them."
5 *Selflessness*. Their decision to assist others is "irrational" because it is driven by non-economic considerations.
6 *Justice*. They have universalistic perceptions that transcend race and ethnicity, and they protect vulnerable people because they identify with victims of injustice.

Tec finds that the rescuers were "independent in terms of their own values." They had previously "participated in what I think you would describe as prosocial behavior," she writes, and "when the time came to help Jews, it fit into their behavior."

A third perspective on altruism among Holocaust rescuers is provided by Andre Stein in his book, *Quiet Heroes*. Nearly everyone in Stein's family was murdered by Nazis in World War II, and Stein himself was tortured and presumed dead when he was captured as an eight-year-old child. Many years after he had moved to Canada, he interviewed Christians who had protected Jews during World War II. The interviews revealed distinctions between the rescuers and their neighbors that seem applicable to contemporary tragedies as well:

> But what seemed even more notable about these quiet heroes, and what truly set them apart, was their unwillingness, or perhaps even their inability, to engage in the same sorts of rationalizations as virtually all their neighbors. . . .
>
> Their neighbors claimed to be powerless to do anything or to have felt obligated to put the safety of their own families above the safety of strangers. The quiet heroes said they had just done what they saw could be done and that the risks they undertook, at least initially, were small in light of the fates facing those they sheltered if no one came to their aid. Their neighbors focused on day-to-day concerns and didn't allow themselves to see the issue in broader moral terms. The quiet heroes could not maintain that narrow perspective. They asked themselves, "What would it say about me if I remained indifferent to the fate of these children? What kind of person would I be?"[43]

Stein's descriptions of the rescuers are similar to Tec's descriptions. When Tec asked them why they took risks that endangered themselves and their

43 Gilovich, Thomas, & Ross, Lee. (2015). *The wisest one in the room* (pp. 128–129). New York: Free Press.

families, they responded, "It was my duty. It is a simple thing. Everybody should have done it." Tec confides, "And they would embarrass me. They would say, you would have done the same thing. Wouldn't you?"[44]

Effects of altruism

Psychologist Martin Seligman, the proponent of the PERMA model of well-being discussed in Chapter 5, relates a story about his friend, bioethicist Stephen Post: "When he was a young boy, and his mother saw that he was in a bad mood, she would say, 'Stephen, you are looking piqued. Why don't you go out and help someone?'"[45] Seligman likes this story because it illustrates the therapeutic effects of altruism. "Empirically, Ma Post's maxim has been put to rigorous test," Seligman declares, "and we scientists have found that doing a kindness produces the single most reliable momentary increase in well-being of any exercise we have tested." Helping other people, in short, "is the best antidote to the downs of life and the single most reliable up."

If a single trait could materially upgrade personal well-being and the public interest at the same time, the most promising candidate would be altruism. That's because altruism exerts remarkably strong effects on individual well-being and social welfare. At a personal level, altruism promotes positive affect, self-esteem, meaningfulness, life satisfaction, work performance, physical health, and longevity.[46] It also heightens a sense of connectedness with other people and decreases a sense of loneliness.[47] Volunteering, a form of altruism, "is one of the best, most certain ways we can find a purpose and meaning in our life," states Val Walker, author of *The Art of Comforting* and *400 Friends and No One to Call*.[48]

44 Nechama Tec discussing rescuers, *supra* note 42.

45 The quotations in this paragraph appear in Seligman, Martin E.P. (2011). *Flourish* (p. 20). New York: Free Press.

46 Liu, *supra* note 33. Post, Stephen G. (2005). Altruism, happiness, and health: It's good to be good. *International Journal of Behavioral Medicine*, *12*(2), 66. Reich, Jarrod F. (2019). Capitalizing on healthy lawyers: The business case for law firms to promote and prioritize lawyer well-being. *Villanova Law Review*, *65*(2), 361. Schwartz, Carol, et al. (2003). Altruistic social interest behaviors are associated with better mental health. *Psychosomatic Medicine*, *65*, 778.

47 Cacioppo, John T., & Patrick, William. (2009). *Loneliness*. New York: W.W. Norton & Company. Shin, Lilian J., et al. (2019). Good for self or good for others? The well-being benefits of kindness in two cultures depend on how the kindness is framed. *The Journal of Positive Psychology*, *15*(4), 1.

48 Caron, Christina. (2021, December 21). An overlooked cure for loneliness. *The New York Times*. See Yeung, Jerf W.K., et al. (2018). Volunteering and health benefits in general adults: Cumulative effects and forms. *BMC Public Health*, *18*, Article 8. ("Consistent with prior research, the present study supports the beneficial effects of volunteering on mental and physical health, life satisfaction, social well-being and depression.")

Attorneys seem to recognize that pro bono services contribute to their well-being; the five most highly ranked "motivating factors" for performing pro bono services are helping other people in need; ethical obligation; professional duty; participating in reducing social inequalities; and "it would make me feel like a good person."[49] Pro bono work has been directly linked to increased levels of happiness for attorneys, and for trial lawyers like the legendary Clarence Darrow in the early 20th century it was cathartic.[50] Darrow tried about 2,000 cases, and he worked for free in more than one-third of those cases. His clients faced and ultimately avoided the death penalty in 102 cases. Darrow said his work was gut-wrenching but gratifying:

> I had a strongly emotional nature which has caused me boundless joy and infinite pain. I had a vivid imagination. Not only could I put myself in the other person's place but I could not avoid doing so. My sympathies always went out to the weak, the suffering, and the poor. Realizing their sorrows I tried to relieve them in order that I myself might be relieved.[51]

In Darrow's five sentences, we can see many critical elements of altruism: empathy, compassion, perspicacity, morality, sympathy, commitment, reliability, and energy. We also see in Darrow's words ("in order that I myself might be relieved") a phenomenon confirmed by contemporary researchers: giving help is a stronger predictor of mental health than receiving help. And the happiness that people experience after providing a benefit to someone lasts longer than the happiness they sense after receiving a comparable benefit.[52]

Darrow eventually reduced his case load and "went on to do his best work, speaking and writing against fundamentalism, eugenics, the death penalty, and Jim Crow." Those issues—in substance—continue to rally many altruists nearly one hundred years after Darrow's death. Like the Holocaust rescuers whose compassion "was repeated over and over," Darrow's entire career was an iteration of compassion. "He just didn't want to see bigotry thrive or watch a man die," says historian Jill Lepore.

49 American Bar Association Standing Committee on Pro Bono & Public Service. (2018). *Supporting justice: A report on the pro bono work of American's lawyers* (p. 19). Chicago: American Bar Association.

50 Levit & Linder, *supra* note 38 at 90.

51 The quotations in this paragraph and the next paragraph are from Lepore, Jill. (2011, May 16). Objection. *The New Yorker*. See Kersten, Andrew E. (2011). *Clarence Darrow: American iconoclast*. New York: Hill and Wang.

52 O'Brien, Ed, & Kassirer, Samantha. (2019, February). People are slow to adapt to the warm glow of giving. *Psychological Science*, *30*(2), 193. Schwartz, *supra* note 46.

The benefits of altruism and its correlated traits go far beyond personal well-being and directly benefit society. As neuroscientists James Sonne and Don Gash explain, "prosocial altruistic capability provides for complex interactions that have come to form the foundation of our civil, societal interactions."[53] Advanced societies, Sonne and Gash elaborate, are distinguished by high levels of empathy and compassion, two traits strongly correlated with altruism: "Empathy and compassion are feelings with basic genetic and neural underpinnings crucial for the development of large interacting social communities characterizing our species. Successful cultures have strong and effective implicit and explicit mechanisms for promoting and enhancing empathetic and compassionate behavior."

To facilitate the development of these complex, highly interactive communities and our survival and reproduction in those communities, our brains began to change about 350 million years ago. They started to upgrade the capacity for altruism, empathy, compassion, and abstraction, all of which are necessary to form an ethos, an embryonic moral code, that curtails selfish behavior when necessary to protect and advance society. These changes in our brains initially favored close relatives but eventually refined a larger set of interactions, as neurophilosopher Patricia Churchland explains:

> A compelling line of evidence from neuroendocrinology, which studies hormone-brain interactions, suggests that in mammals (and quite possibly social birds), the neuronal organization whereby individuals see to their own well-being was modified to motivate new values—the well-being of certain others. In early stages of the evolution of mammals, those others included only helpless offspring. Depending on ecological conditions and fitness considerations, strong caring for the well-being of offspring has in some mammalian species extended further to encompass kin or mates or friends or even strangers, as the circle widens. This widening of other-caring in social behavior marks the emergence of what eventually flowers into morality.[54]

Demonstrating the evolutionary advantages of altruism and the partial innateness of generosity, children start displaying altruistic behavior within 18 months after birth, and our brains show activity in reward-processing areas when we make charitable contributions.[55] In one study, those reward-processing areas were activated even when the study participants

53 The quotations in this paragraph appear in Sonne & Gash, *supra* note 31.

54 Churchland, Patricia S. (2011). *Braintrust* (p. 14). Princeton, NJ: Princeton University Press.

55 See Allen, Summer. (2018, May). *The science of generosity* [White paper]. Greater Good Science Center at U.C. Berkeley. https://ggsc.berkeley.edu/images/uploads/GGSC-JTF_White_Paper-Generosity-FINAL.pdf. Pfaff, Donald W. (2015). *The altruistic*

were forced to give items to others.[56] The imperative to help and cooperate in a competitive world is so strong that law professor Yochai Benkler suggests "we might add 'natural cooperation' as a third fundamental principle for evolution beside mutation and natural selection."[57]

Eliciting altruism

If altruism has evolutionary roots and is essential to the operation of complex societies, we need to know how altruistic tendencies can be increased. The answer to that inquiry may be found in the brain reward regions and research regarding moral exemplars. Brain-imaging studies indicate that altruism is habit forming: "being generous and being described as generous can engage the so-called reward circuitry in the brain, prompting the release of dopamine-like neurotransmitters that are associated with positive feelings."[58] This suggests that altruistic behavior is self-reinforcing and triggers the same neural responses that engender other repetitive actions central to human survival:

> Acting generously also appears to stimulate the neural circuits involved in reward, the same circuits that are activated when we eat food or have sex, which helps to explain why giving feels good. This neural response is also a sign that generosity is important for survival—when an act feels good, we're more likely to do it again—and thus, thanks to evolution, the behaviors that are most fundamental to our survival also tend to make us feel good. For example, one study found that parts of the brain called the mesolimbic reward system, which are activated by stimuli like sex, drugs, food, and receiving money, are also engaged when people make charitable donations.[59]

Altruistic behavior not only enhances our sense of pleasure and well-being; it also makes other people feel better because we "perceive them more positively and charitably."[60] In that sense, altruism can be considered contagious as it enhances another person's well-being and fosters more pro-social behavior.

---

brain. New York: Oxford University Press. Warneken, Felix, & Tomasello, Michael. (2006, March 31). Altruistic helping in human infants and young chimpanzees. *Science*, *311*, 1301.

56 Harbaugh, William T., et al. (2007). Neural responses to taxation and voluntary giving reveal motives for charitable donations. *Science*, *316*(5831), 1622.

57 Benkler, Yochai. (2011, July–August). The unselfish gene. *Harvard Business Review*.

58 Helliker, Kevin. (2011, October 11). 'It's mine!' The selfish gene. *The Wall Street Journal*. See Filkowski, Megan M. (2016). Altruistic behavior: Mapping responses in the brain. *Neuroscience and Neuroeconomics*, *5*, 65.

59 Allen, *supra* note 55.

60 Lyubomirsky, Sonja. (2008). *The how of happiness*. New York: Penguin Books.

Being a moral exemplar of altruistic behavior also stimulates pro-social behavior by other people. When study participants recall other people who have acted selflessly, generously, charitably, empathetically, or responsively, they are motivated to "do good things for other people, become a better person oneself, and emulate the virtuous role model more generally."[61] They also report a heightened sense of calmness and an increased openness and warmth toward other people. As psychology professor Jonathan Haidt observes, "we are easily and strongly moved by the altruism of others."[62]

If we had to distill the research regarding altruism into a single sentence, we would have to rely on a four-year-old child participating in a study with 135 other children.[63] The children were given six sets of stickers and then invited to share their stickers with another child. The largest group of children gave away one set, and the second largest group kept all of their stickers. Only two children gave away all of their stickers. When asked in a videotaped interview why he shared all of his stickers, one of those two children responded, "That's how you become happy."[64]

61 Algoe, Sara B., & Haidt, Jonathan. (2009). Witnessing excellence in action: The 'other-praising' emotions of elevation, gratitude, and admiration. *The Journal of Positive Psychology*, *4*(2), 105. See Hoffman, Edward, et al. (2017). The psychological benefits of receiving real-life altruism. *Journal of Humanistic Psychology*, *60*(2), 187. Vianello, Michelangelo, et al. (2010). Elevation at work: The effects of leaders' moral excellence. *The Journal of Positive Psychology*, *5*(5), 390.

62 Haidt, Jonathan. (2003). Elevation and the positive psychology of morality. In Keyes, Corey L.M., & Haidt, Jonathan (Eds.). *Flourishing: Positive psychology and the life well-lived* (p. 275). Washington, DC: American Psychological Association.

63 Avinun, Reut, et al. (2011). AVPR1A variant associated with preschoolers' lower altruistic behavior. *PLoS ONE*, *6*(9), e25274.

64 Helliker, *supra* note 58.

7

ALTRUISM IN PRACTICE

"Justice is a bone-deep urge towards fairness in things large and small," states renowned litigator Elizabeth Cabraser. "It's the human journey toward a better world."[1] Few attorneys embark on that journey, and even fewer stay the course for their entire career. In this chapter, we'll meet attorneys who have that bone-deep commitment to justice and personify altruism in their law practices. Although altruistic attorneys practice in all areas of law, our focus here is on attorneys in practice areas that are correlated with high levels of attorney well-being and career satisfaction: public interest, nonprofit, and public defender practices. We will also look at attorneys who seek to achieve justice by providing pro bono legal services and judges who promote altruism in their courtrooms.

MacArthur Fellows

Every year, the MacArthur Foundation awards a $800,000 stipend to about 25 individuals who have shown extraordinary creativity, insight, self-direction, and achievement. The purpose of the award is "to enable recipients to exercise their own creative instincts for the benefit of human society."[2] Frequently called "the Genius Grants," they have been awarded to 1,131 people since 1981.

The awards identify individual achievement in about 90 different fields in the humanities, arts, social sciences, natural sciences, and technological

1 Jefferson, Jon. (2012, Spring). Trouble on oiled waters. *Transcript*, *44*(1), 27.
2 MacArthur Foundation. *About MacArthur fellows program.* www.macfound.org/programs/fellows/strategy. The stipend was raised from $625,000 to $800,000 in 2022.

DOI: 10.4324/9781003514848-7

sciences. Seven areas of achievement are distinctly legal: civil rights and civil liberties; criminal justice; human rights and human security; peace and international security; immigration; privacy and intellectual property; and legal studies. Seventy-five awards have been made in these legal fields, but only 10 law professors and 31 lawyers received those awards. Nearly one-half of the MacArthur geniuses in these legal fields were neither law professors nor lawyers. Although law professors and lawyers dominate those fields, their significance often declines when the criteria changes from legal expertise to creativity, insight, self-direction, and durable achievements.

Four attorneys who exercise "creative instincts for the benefit of society" are highlighted below to show the range of imagination, talents, and altruism in MacArthur Fellows:

- *Marie-Therese Connolly (2011 award).* Connolly is the founder of the Elder Justice Lab and was a driving force behind the Elder Justice Act, federal legislation enacted in 2010 to detect and prevent elder abuse. Before passage of that legislation, she worked in the U.S. Department of Justice as a prosecutor and head of the Elder Justice and Nursing Home Initiative. She describes elder abuse as "a national blind spot," noting that "people are still far more aware of child abuse and domestic violence than they are of what happens to an older neighbor or relative."[3] Her career has been dedicated to eliminating that blind spot by increasing awareness of all forms of elder abuse—physical, psychological, and financial. "I was shocked that the problem is so invisible," Connolly states. "There is so much opportunity for change, and I can't think of another issue that affects so many people and where less is being done."[4]
- *Margaret Stock (2013 award).* Stock is an immigration attorney and a retired Lieutenant Colonel in the United States Army Reserve. She has taught law at the United States Military Academy in West Point, New York. She is credited with creating the Military Accessions Vital to the National Interest Program (MAVNI), which authorizes the military services to recruit legal aliens who have skills deemed critical to the national interest. It also expedites the naturalization process for those service members. In another collaboration with the military, Stock initiated the American Immigration Lawyers Association's Military Assistance Program ("MAP"). That program enables military attorneys in the Judge Advocate General Corps, who "have been inundated with complex immigration legal questions," to obtain advice from The American Immigration Lawyers Association

3 Olson, Elizabeth. (2012, March 7). A prosecutor becomes a champion for the elderly. *The New York Times*.

4 Davenport, Christian. (2011, September 20). MacArthur 'genius' grant goes to D.C. activist who fights elder abuse. *The Washington Post*.

(AILA).[5] She also started an AILA program that provides pro bono legal advice to service members; within six years of the program's inception, 375 AILA attorneys had helped clients in 700 cases.[6] "She's a great leader and a changemaker," says retired Lieutenant General Benjamin Freakley.[7]

- *Jonathan Rapping (2014 award)*. Rapping is the founder of Gideon's Promise, a nonprofit organization that provides coaching, training, mentors, and networking for public defenders. It started as a training program for 16 public defenders in two states and now has 1,000 participants in 27 states. As he explains in his book, *Gideon's Promise*, Rapping formed the organization with the goal of "grooming a generation of public defenders who had a revolutionary understanding of what justice looks like for poor people. Sadly, ensuring that marginalized communities receive the protections enshrined in our Constitution, and are afforded the dignity and respect in the process that we expect for the more privileged members of society, is revolutionary."[8]
- *Ahilan Arulanantham (2016 award)*. Arulanantham was a human rights lawyer at the American Civil Liberties Union of Southern California for 20 years. He currently serves as Professor from Practice and Co-Director of the Center for Immigration Law and Policy at UCLA School of Law. While representing clients at the ACLU, he "litigated several landmark cases, including *Nadarajah v. Gonzales*, the first Ninth Circuit case establishing limits on the government's power to detain immigrants as national security threats; *Rodriguez v. Robbins*, which required the government to provide bond hearings to thousands of immigration detainees; and *Franco v. Holder*, the first case to establish a right to appointed legal representation for any group of immigrants facing deportation, which required the federal government to provide legal representation to mentally ill immigrants."[9]

The four recipients highlighted in this section, along with the 37 other lawyers and law professors who have received a MacArthur Fellowship award, are anomalies. They have emerged from an arduous search that the MacArthur Foundation "once called a 'truffle hunt' in recognition of their rarity and the talent required to recognize them."[10] They have the distinction of meeting

5 Tabo, Tamara. (2013, September 26). Who says lawyers can't be geniuses? An attorney wins a MacArthur genius grant. *Above the Law*.
6 Bacon, Katie. (2014, May 15). Stock in trade: Ingenuity. *Harvard Law Today*.
7 Ibid.
8 Rapping, Jonathan. (2020). *Gideon's promise* (p. 86). Boston: Beacon Press.
9 ACLU News and Commentary, Ahilan Arulanantham Bio. www.aclu.org/bio/ahilan-arulanantham.
10 Conrad, Cecilia A. (2018, September 25). Are truffles getting harder to find? *Perspectives*. MacArthur Foundation. www.macfound.org/press/perspectives/are-truffles-getting-harder-find.

the MacArthur Foundation's criteria for making "an investment in a person's originality, insight, and potential," but their ideas and actions should be representative, not anomalous, in a profession defined by fiduciary duties and charged with a public service orientation.

The purpose of the MacArthur Fellowship award—to enable recipients to "exercise their own creative instincts for the benefit of human society"—is already embodied in the American Bar Association's duty to "seek improvement of the law, access to the legal system, the administration of justice and the quality of service rendered by the legal profession."[11] This duty is imposed on every attorney and is grounded in a professional ethos of public service, equal justice, and adherence to the rule of law. Although the duty is continuous and profession-wide, its execution has been sporadic and idiosyncratic.

Public interest law fellowships

Numerous law schools and law firms sponsor public interest law fellowships for graduating law students. These fellowships may be self-directed (the fellow designs and directs their own project) or project-based (the fellow participates in a pre-existing project or implements a personally selected project while working within a non-profit organization). These fellowships pay a stipend or modest salary and last one or two years. The more well-known fellowships are underwritten by The Skadden Fellowship Foundation, Equal Justice Works, The Justice Catalyst, and The Open Society Foundations. Collectively, those four organizations select and sponsor about 200 graduating or recently graduated law students every year.

The Skadden Fellowship Foundation exemplifies the benefits of public interest fellowships. Founded by the Skadden law firm in 1988, the Skadden Fellowship Foundation has funded 990 fellows and "has become the largest public interest law firm in the United States."[12] About 90 percent of the Skadden fellows are still involved in public interest law, and 20 fellows are now serving as judges. The Skadden fellowship program—the *Los Angeles Times* calls it the legal "Peace Corps"—has expanded to include training programs for recent Skadden fellows, conducted by Skadden fellows who have practiced public interest law for more than ten years.[13] The Skadden Fellowship Foundation also initiated the first legal fund-within-a-fund, awarding grants to former Skadden fellows for new public interest projects.

11 A.B.A. Model Rules of Prof'l Conduct, Preamble & Scope.

12 The information in this paragraph appears in the Skadden Foundation's website at www.skaddenfellowships.org.

13 Haederle, Michael. (1993, April 12). Taking on the legal battles of those in need. *Los Angeles Times*.

Three former Skadden fellows illustrate the types of projects supported by the Skadden Fellowship Foundation and the level of commitment displayed by its fellows:

- *Rebecca Heller (2010 Fellow)*. Heller is the director and a co-founder of the International Refugee Assistance Project (IRAP), a nonprofit organization that provides legal aid to displaced people. She began working full-time for IRAP after law school graduation and her selection as a Skadden Foundation Fellow. IRAP started with one chapter and five law students working with three pro bono attorneys.[14] It now engages 2,100 students at 29 law schools and 800 lawyers at 75 international law firms and corporations. More than 41,000 displaced persons from 100 countries have received legal aid from IRAP.

  Heller describes IRAP's work as two-fold: "First, we provide legal aid to refugees, displaced persons and visa applicants—whatever is needed to navigate the resettlement process and get them to safety. We also . . . advocate for systemic improvements. Our policy team, working with members of Congress and their staff, has produced memos, research and draft language for a series of major bills—we've passed eight different pieces of federal legislation since our founding, which have resulted in new visas or additional rights for over 160,000 refugees and displaced persons."[15]
- *Toby Merrill (2012 Fellow)*. While a Skadden Fellow, Merrill founded the Project on Predatory Student Lending (PPSL) at the Legal Services Center at Harvard Law School. PPSL has represented over one million student borrowers in litigation against for-profit colleges that allegedly defrauded students by misrepresenting programs and employment prospects. These legal actions resulted in the cancellation of student debt exceeding $10 billion. "So many people have been cheated by their schools," states Merrill. "There's so much unjust and unlawful debt being collected."[16]

  Merrill was named in the first annual TIME 100 Next list, recognizing emerging leaders who are "poised to make history."[17] In summarizing Merrill's work that led to this recognition, TIME states, "Years before student debt would be widely considered a national crisis—Americans now

14 For information regarding the history of IRAP see https://refugeerights.org/how-we-work/our-model.

15 (2017, December 20). Skadden Fellow: Rebecca Heller "providing refuge". *Skadden Foundation News and Stories*. www.skaddenfellowships.org/news-and-stories/2017/12/skadden-fellow-profile-rebecca-heller.

16 Friedrich, Michael. (2021, May 13). How a legal organization is defending defrauded student borrowers. www.arnoldventures.org/stories/how-a-legal-organization-is-defending-defrauded-student-borrowers.

17 Felsenthal, Michael. (2021, February 17). How we chose the TIME100 next. *Time*. https://time.com/5939731/how-we-chose-2021-time100-next/.

owe a combined $1.6 trillion—Toby Merrill started using litigation to fight what she calls the 'worst-of-the-worst student debt,' the kind incurred by students who enrolled in predatory for-profit colleges that burdened them with debt and provided them with worthless degrees."[18]

- *Satcha Robinson (2018 Fellow).* Robinson works at the Reentry Justice project at the Legal Aid Society of the District of Columbia, assisting clients whose housing, employment, civil rights, and medical care are jeopardized by criminal records. Her work to mitigate collateral consequences of convictions includes criminal record sealing and challenges to housing and employment denials. As she explains, "There are so many problems that people experience when they come into contact with the criminal justice system aside from just the punishment that they might receive if they're convicted."[19] Completing a jail or prison sentence, for many criminal defendants, is just the beginning of a series of sanctions that perpetuate poverty, discrimination, disease, substance abuse, and recidivism. Although they "served their time," the actual punishment inflicted by collateral consequences can last a lifetime.

  The stigma of an arrest or criminal conviction, states Robinson, "needs to end. I think there needs to be a holistic view of what happened then, what was going on in that person's life, and where are they now. Does that still reflect where they are now? Would they be a danger to the community if it's involving landlord-tenant relationships? Would they be able to perform the job if it's in the employment context? Really there needs to be a holistic view of someone and recognize that was one point in their life."

The impact of the Skadden Foundation is summarized succinctly by Jennifer Rosenbaum, the executive director of Global Labor Justice: "It brings people to the hardest edges of where we need structural change in the United States and encourages Fellows to bring challenges that will change the system, not just win cases or get people the rights that they're due, but really get to the deeper issues of why those rights weren't accessible without a lawyer."[20]

Public defenders

About 80 percent of criminal defendants cannot afford a lawyer. They are represented by public defenders, the beleaguered lawyers whom Jonathan

18 Kelley, Carolyn. (2019, November 15). Toby Merrill named to the TIME 100 next list. *Harvard Law Today*.

19 Satcha Robinson's quotations in this paragraph and the next paragraph appear in Skadden Foundation. (2019, April). *Fellow podcast: Satcha Robinson ('18).* www.skaddenfellowships.org/news-and-stories/2019/04/fellow-podcast-satcha-robinson.

20 Skadden Foundation. *Skadden Fellows share the impact of the program after 30 years.* www.skaddenfellowships.org/#section-nav-anchor.

Rapping calls "the conscience of our criminal justice system." Public defenders, Rapping adds, "are the force needed to remind us of the ideals at the heart of American democracy and to ensure we do not lose sight of the human beings the system is there to serve."[21]

The key feature of public defenders' careers is that their caseloads and the lack of funding for investigators and support professionals impair or prevent adequate legal representation. Law professor Eve Primus describes the impediments that render the constitutional right to counsel an illusion:

> A lack of sufficient funding forces public defenders to handle caseloads that no one could effectively manage. Defenders' abilities to provide quality representation are further compromised by a lack of independence from other branches of government, an absence of attorney training programs, and a failure at all levels to oversee effectively the provision of public-defense services. The result is an assembly line into prison, mostly for poor people of color, with little check on the reliability or fairness of the process.[22]

Inadequate funding is compounded by pressure from judges to expedite case resolutions, clear dockets for other cases, or meet case management goals. As Rapping relates, "As I began studying criminal justice more broadly, I learned that it is common for judges to tolerate, or even encourage, substandard lawyering in an effort to keep their dockets moving without the healthy friction zealous counsel introduces into the process."[23] These concerns are corroborated by a Nebraska judge who acknowledged that judges "have 'paid attorneys back' for too many trials or other offenses" by not appointing them as counsel for indigent defendants.[24]

The American Bar Association (ABA) has established guidelines for public defenders' caseloads. The disparities between these guidelines and public defenders' actual caseloads, the ABA concludes, make "a mockery of the constitutional right to counsel."[25] In Louisiana, for example, the ABA found

21 Rapping, *supra* note 8 at 207.
22 Primus, Eve Brensike. (2017). Defense counsel and public defense. In Luna, Erik (Ed.). *Reforming criminal justice: Pretrial and trial processes* (vol. 3, p. 121). Phoenix, AZ: Academy for Justice.
23 Rapping, *supra* note 8 at 173.
24 National Right to Counsel Committee. (2009). *Justice denied: America's continued neglect of our constitutional right to counsel* (p. 84). Washington, DC: The Constitution Project.
25 Oppel, Jr., Richard A., & Patel, Jugal K. (2019, January 31). One lawyer, 194 felony cases, and no time. *The New York Times*. The ABA, in conjunction with the RAND Corporation, The National Center for State Courts, and The Law Office of Stephen Hanlon, is proposing new standards for the maximum number of cases that public defenders should handle. Those standards increase the recommended number of hours for both felonies and misdemeanors. See Poggio, Marco. (2023, September 12). Public defenders are 'dangerously' overworked, report finds. *Law 360*.

that the public defense system employs 363 full-time equivalent [FTE] public defenders, and it needs 1,769 FTE public defenders "to provide reasonably effective assistance of counsel pursuant to prevailing professional norms in Louisiana, resulting in a deficit of 1,406 FTE attorneys."[26] The Louisiana public defense system "now only has capacity to handle 21 percent of the annual workload in compliance with workload standards."[27]

The ABA found similar problems in other states. In Missouri, for instance, the ABA concluded that "public defenders have insufficient time to spend on all aspects of their cases."[28] The public defenders, the ABA reported, should spend about 48 hours on serious felonies, but "actually spend an average of about nine hours." On misdemeanors, "they should spend nearly 12 hours but actually spend about two hours."[29] In Oregon, the ABA determined that each public defender would have to work 26.6 hours per day to effectively represent their clients, and the current number of public defenders (592) should be increased to 1,888 to meet basic standards of representation in criminal cases.[30] Unable to spend the minimum amount of time necessary to adequately defend their clients, some public defenders in high-volume jurisdictions see themselves as their clients' "pallbearers," and their clients sometimes call them "public pretenders."[31]

Public defenders describe the stress they experience daily, caused by excessive caseloads and the severe threats facing their clients[32]:

- "I literally, for the first time in my life, had the responsibility of so many people's lives in my hands. It was really draining. I think the first year of this job, I would work seven days a week, I had no life. I would work from 7 am until 11 pm every single day. I didn't feel like I could do anything else, because if I didn't get everything done, someone's life could fall apart."

26 (2017, February 17). New study spotlights extremely heavy workload in Louisiana's public defender system. *ABA News*.

27 Weiss, Debra Cassens. (2017, February 1). Louisiana's public defender system is understaffed by about 1,400 lawyers, ABA study finds. *ABA Journal*. See Peng, Tina. (2015, September 3). I'm a public defender. It's impossible for me to do a good job of representing my clients. *The Washington Post*.

28 (2014, July 31). ABA report on Missouri public defender caseloads provides blueprint for national reform. *ABA News*.

29 Weiss, Debra Cassens. (2014, July 31). Study is evidence of 'crisis in public defense systems,' ABA president says. *ABA Journal*.

30 American Bar Association & Moss Adams LLP. (2022, January). *The Oregon project*.

31 Smith, Abbe. (2004). Too much heart and not enough heat: The short life and fractured ego of the empathic, heroic public defender. *U.C. Davis Law Review*, *37*(5), 1203, 1256.

32 The quotations in this paragraph and the next paragraph appear in Bacak, Valerio, et al. (2022). *The stress of injustice: Public defenders and the frontline of American inequality*. https://papers.ssrn.com/sol3/papers.cfm?abstract_id=3765714.

- "We've had some success in stopping some of the executions. It's not like it's never possible, so that creates some tensions where we need to exhaust all efforts and exert super-human efforts on behalf of every single client. That has proven to be a very stressful, exhausting task without any kind of a—it's been fairly unrelenting, I should say."
- "As of now, if I go to trial, they would face mandatory minimum of 10 to 15 years. That's rough. I'm 30. Fifteen years is half of my life. I can't imagine somebody younger than me doing 15 years of a full sentence. That would be difficult for me to live with. Like everybody else, you just find a way because you're going to lose that case one day and you're just going to have to deal with it."

The impact of public defenders' work extends far beyond incarceration and includes the collateral consequences (denial of health care, housing, food assistance, and employment) discussed in the previous section. As a public defender explains, losing a single motion on behalf of a client could result in a felony conviction instead of a misdemeanor conviction: "then they're going to get kicked out of public housing, then they're going to be homeless. If you let yourself think about the consequences of the work too much, it's just overwhelming. To a certain extent, I suspend disbelief about the work that I'm doing."

Why do public defenders endure these daily pressures and an intractable system that makes it nearly impossible for them to fulfill their professional duties to clients? And why do they report relatively high levels of career satisfaction despite chronically low salaries? Law professors have a few observations and theories about these subjects, but studies about indigent defense "remain few and far between."[33] One of the early and most influential theories emerged from law professor Charles Ogletree's article, "Beyond Justifications: Seeking Motivations to Sustain Public Defenders." Ogletree, a former public defender, identified empathy ("understanding the experiences, behavior and feelings of others, as they experience them") and heroism ("the one who fights against all odds") as the primary motivations for public defenders.[34]

Abbe Smith, a law professor and criminal defense attorney, contends that empathy and heroism cannot sustain public defenders throughout their careers. She presents a three-part model of public defenders' motivation[35]:

- *Respect*—"respecting and embracing the client's dignity, autonomy and humanity."

33 Bacak, Valerio, et al. (2022). *The stress of injustice: Public Defenders and the frontline of American inequality*. https://papers.ssrn.com/sol3/papers.cfm?abstract_id=3765714.

34 Ogletree, Charles J., Jr. (1993). Beyond justifications: Seeking motivations to sustain public defenders. *Harvard Law Review*, *106*, 1272, 1275,

35 Smith, *supra* note 31 at 1244, 1251, 1259, and 1265.

- *Craft*—a professional craft that blends knowledge, skill, experience, creativity, tenacity, passion, attention to detail, sound judgment, and an ability to communicate. "There is craft in every aspect of defense work: interviewing and counseling, investigation, pretrial litigation, plea negotiation, trial, sentencing, and appellate advocacy."
- *Outrage*—"A sense of moral outrage, the sort of outrage that accompanies conviction. I mean outrage as a kind of principled resistance."

Smith contends that "there is nothing like defender work. There is nothing more absorbing, challenging or meaningful."

Ogletree and Smith's perspectives on public defenders' motivations are refined by criminal justice professor Valerio Bacak's empirical research. In structured interviews with public defenders, Bacak and his colleagues identified six primary reasons for remaining in public defense: fighting social inequality; defending the U.S. Constitution; interacting with clients; pursuing personal values; appreciating camaraderie with colleagues; and earning government benefits.[36] Bacak finds that "being a public defender entails meaningful work that helps disadvantaged populations," but that sense of meaning is challenged by a lack of financial and political support from legislators and a public "skeptical of the value of defending potentially guilty people."

Many of the possible motivations for public defenders are embodied in Alex Clavering's thoughts. He is a public defender and works at the Legal Aid Society of Suffolk County, New York. "I went in to the legal profession for the same reason that everybody does, or a lot of people do," Clavering muses, "and that is hoping to make the world better—and also being mildly psychotic."[37] During law school, he participated in a clinic program with the Neighborhood Defender Service of Harlem, which was "probably the best experience I had in law school." Describing his public defender role, Clavering states, "I really do love what I do. I wish we got paid more, and I wish the system wasn't horrible, but I like the job and I like trying to help people navigate these impossible situations and the systems that are constantly crushing people."

Death penalty lawyers

Defense counsel in death penalty cases are a small, exclusive subset of criminal defense lawyers. They usually are appointed by judges to represent indigent defendants, who comprise nearly all of the people sentenced to death.

36 Bacak, Valerio, et al. (2019). "Fighting the good fight": Why do public defenders remain on the job? *Criminal Justice Policy Review*, *31*, 939, 940.

37 Quotations in this paragraph appear in Pagan, McCord. (2022, February 24). Suffolk County public defender talks work, TikTok fame. *Law 360*.

If they were not indigent before trial, "the cost of a capital defense would bankrupt most of them. As a result, almost all of the defendants charged with a capital crime are defended by attorneys provided by the state."[38] The maximum hourly rate for capital defense in federal cases is $220, and many states pay $55–$145 per hour.[39] For reputable, experienced criminal defense lawyers, these hourly rates may range from one-tenth to one-third of their regular hourly rate.

The consequences of defense errors and inadequate legal representation in death penalty cases are catastrophic and under *Shinn v. Ramirez* likely to be irreversible. For that reason, some death penalty lawyers may prefer to represent people who are guilty.[40] A death sentence imposed on a guilty client has a sense of inevitability that buffers defense counsel's conscience, while the conviction and execution of an innocent client may feel like an unshakeable personal and professional failure. That sense of failure is haunting and, for some death penalty lawyers, unbearable.

Defense strategies in death penalty cases are different from other criminal cases. The goal of death penalty lawyers in most trials is to avoid death row, not to obtain an acquittal. As a capital defense lawyer explains, "There's only so much you can have your client deny responsibility during the guilt phase before jurors see him as cold-hearted and unrepentant. You don't want them to take that out on him in sentencing."[41]

Are the motivations of capital defense lawyers similar to those of public defenders representing defendants in non-capital cases? Law professor Jon Gould and criminology professor Maya Barak found answers to this question in their interviews of 60 capital defense lawyers. Gould and Barak identify six interlocking motives:

> Some attorneys are inspired by moral conviction, including religious devotion. Some move to capital work as a natural, although perhaps unintentional, professional progression from traditional criminal defense. Some seek the excitement of capital litigation with its high stakes, stark deadlines, and pressure-packed court proceedings. Some lawyers are motivated by prestige and ambition, not unlike their law school classmates who

38 The quotations in this section appear in Gould, Jon B., & Barak, Maya Pagni. (2019). *Capital defense* (p. 20). New York: New York University Press.

39 Guide to judiciary policy, Vol. 7, defender services, part A, guidelines for administering the CJA and related statutes, chapter 6: federal death penalty and capital habeas corpus representations, §630.10.10.

40 See Lyon, Andrea D. (2010). *Angel of death row*. Fort Lauderdale, FL: Kaplan Publishing. O'Brien, Sean D. (2007). Capital defense lawyers: The good, the bad, and the ugly. *Michigan Law Review*, *106*(6), 1067. White, Welsh S. (2006). *Litigating in the shadow of death: Defense attorneys in capital cases*. Ann Arbor: University of Michigan Press.

41 Gould & Barak, *supra* note 38 at 40.

> gravitate to the bright lights of Wall Street litigation or deal making. Some defense attorneys exhibit oppositional personalities and tackle cases trying to remaster their own psychological trauma. And some lawyers—usually the less talented and committed—are attracted by the higher compensation that capital cases offer over "garden variety" criminal defense.[42]

Most of the interviewed attorneys expressed multiple motives, and Gould and Barak heard each of the six motives "so often in fact that we're not prepared to say which are most common."[43] Discerning their motives, though, was difficult because the capital defenders were, in Gould and Barak's phrase, "minimally introspective."

Legal aid attorneys

The Legal Services Corporation (LSC) is the nation's largest funder of civil legal aid for low-income individuals.[44] About 50 million Americans are in the low-income population, and 15 million children—one in every five children—live in a low-income household. About 1.6 million military veterans also live in low-income households. These Americans have low expectations of the legal system; only 28 percent of low-income individuals believe that "people like me are treated fairly in the system."[45]

LSC distributes about $450 million annually to 132 independent legal aid programs in 852 offices. This funding is roughly $9 per low-income American, or, as LSC President Emeritus Jim Sandman notes, the total amount that consumers spend every year on Halloween costumes for their pets.[46] In inflation-adjusted dollars, the total congressional appropriation for LSC has ranged from a high of $990 million in 1980 to a low of $411 million in 2013.

The types of cases typically handled by those offices include evictions, foreclosures, wage theft, public benefit denials, consumer disputes, wills, child custody and support, and domestic violence. The two most common legal problems experienced by low-income households are consumer issues and

42 Ibid at 241.

43 This quotation and the following quotation appear in Gould & Barak, *supra* note 38 at 14, 65.

44 For information regarding the Legal Services Corporation see Legal Services Corporation. (2023). *By the numbers 2022: The data underlying legal aid programs*. Washington, DC: Legal Services Corporation. Legal Services Corporation. (2022). *The justice gap: The unmet civil legal needs of low-income Americans*. Washington, DC: Legal Services Corporation. Sandman, James J. (2019, March). The role of the Legal Services Corporation in improving access to justice. *Daedalus*, *148*(1), 113.

45 Legal Services Corporation (2022), *supra* note 44 at 62.

46 Sandman, Jim. (2019, September 10). *LSC President Emeritus, Jim Sandman answers the question, "What is legal aid?"* (Remarks delivered at American Bar Association Annual Meeting, August 9, 2019). www.youtube.com/watch?v=caAZcpU_XM4.

health care problems. LSC-funded organizations receive about 2 million requests for legal services every year, and they turn away 49 percent of those requests due to insufficient resources.

Many legal aid offices receive funding from sources other than LSC. The American Bar Association estimates that LSC funding constitutes 22 percent of all funding for legal aid programs, and other public funds comprise 26 percent of their funding.[47] The balance of funding is attributable to state appropriations, court fees, grants, interest from attorney trust accounts, and other sources. Despite multiple sources of funding, legal aid programs are chronically understaffed, and legal aid attorneys are chronically underpaid. As one legal aid attorney comments, "One of the more frustrating parts of the job is that we want to take more cases so we wouldn't have to turn people that need help away."[48] Another legal aid attorney, who had recently left his job, said that fair compensation "would have allowed me to provide and care for my family. I was constantly stressed about being able to provide for my family—and it added to the day to day stress from the work."[49] That attorney's comment corroborates survey results showing that the primary reason attorneys leave legal aid organizations is "financial pressure due to low salary."[50]

Legal aid attorneys, as discussed in Chapters 2 and 5, report relatively high levels of well-being and career satisfaction. In a recent survey of legal aid attorneys in Illinois, the work factors ranked highest were (in this order) meaningful work, coworker relationships, work-life flexibility, paid time off, and supervision/mentoring. The lowest ranked factors were loan repayment assistance, pay, networking opportunities, retirement benefits, and recognition. The following remarks by legal aid attorneys who graduated from Harvard Law School convey some of the advantages and disadvantages of their careers[51]:

- "My work matters, and I have a life outside of work. What more could I ask for? Well, I guess I could ask for a copier that doesn't regularly jam, and a pest-free office, and a salary that keeps pace with inflation—but I

47 ABA Resource Center for Access to Justice Initiatives. (2021). *U.S. funding for legal aid.* https://public.tableau.com/app/profile/abarray/viz/ABArrayNationalData/NationalLegalAidFunding.

48 Schroer, Kim, & Shabecoff, Alexa. (2013). Legal services guide: A guide to pursuing work in legal services/legal aid. Cambridge, MA: Harvard Law School Bernard Koteen Office of Public Interest Advising.

49 Coe, Aebra. (2022, July 22). Pay is a pain point in retention for Ill. [Illinois] Legal Aid orgs. *Law 360.*

50 The State Bar of California. (2019). *2019 California justice gap study executive report* (p. 18). https://www.calbar.ca.gov/Portals/0/documents/accessJustice/Justice-Gap-Study-Executive-Summary.pdf.

51 Schroer & Shabecoff, *supra* note 48.

can live without those. I cannot live without a job that matters, or with a job that denies me an outside life. Every day I get up and go to work knowing I am making a difference in the lives of our society's most vulnerable citizens. At LAF [Legal Assistance Foundation], we fight to keep people from losing life's most precious goods: a home, a car, a job, a child, and residency."

- "I also found that creative lawyering could use fairly mundane legal disputes to establish legal precedents that literally transformed the working conditions for millions of low-wage workers across the nation. I had the privilege of representing the finest group of clients any lawyer could ever have, and to become a far better lawyer than I ever anticipated when I left HLS. I am often asked if I regret having attended HLS, given that I have devoted my entire career to providing free legal services to poor migrant workers. I answer with an emphatic 'No!'"
- "I love my job because it lets me form professional and personal relationships with people who are very different than me in so many ways: income, race, education, age, geography, and everything in between. Many of them have serious disabilities, struggling with mental illness or physical limitations. When our relationships work well, we become partners trying to solve problems together. I empathize but I know that I cannot care too much—I cannot absorb all of my clients' struggles. They reward me with hugs, tears, and ultimately their trust. Sometimes we win, sometimes we lose, but always my job is to center my work around them, empower them, and fight for them."

These comments embody Jim Sandman's belief that legal aid "is about respecting human dignity. It's about asserting and protecting legal rights for people who can't afford to pay for assistance. It gives people hope that they can get a fair shake in our justice system."[52]

A critical question for legal aid organizations and society is, "What makes attorneys start and stay in public interest careers?" For decades, academics and practitioners have opined about the effects of salaries, student debt burdens, gender, race, class, income, religion, and political orientation. Fortunately, some of those opinions are being superseded by empirical research. A National Science Foundation-funded survey of graduates from six law schools, conducted by professors Catherine Albiston, Scott Cummings, and

52 Sandman, *supra* note 46.

Richard Abel, finds that many assumptions about public interest lawyers are incorrect. Their research provides these insights[53]:

- *Early career preference*. "[R]espondents' stated career preference for a public interest career upon entering law school had the largest significant relationship to both a first and a current job in a public interest setting."
- *Debt*. "Debt had a significant but small negative relationship to first and current jobs in a public interest setting."
- *Gender*. Identifying as female "is predictive of public interest work at later stages of one's career but not at the beginning."
- *Race, LGBTQ, international birth*. "With respect to *race*, we find that identifying as non-white was significantly positively related to both first and current public interest job. Identifying as LGBTQ was significantly positively related to both first and current jobs in public interest settings. . . . [I]n most of the models being foreign born or having at least one foreign-born parent was significantly *negatively* related to first job in a public interest setting."
- *Class*. "Interestingly, proxies for respondents' class, such as parental education or experiences of financial hardship while growing up, were *not* related to careers in public interest jobs."
- *Adversity*. "Experiencing challenges growing up (either personally or in one's family)—such as mental illness, domestic violence, or substance abuse—had a positive significant relationship to first job in a public interest setting. However, these same challenges were not robustly related to current public interest job."
- *Religion*. "Our data about religion also diverge from earlier studies that found that legal aid lawyers were more likely to be Jewish or Catholic rather than Protestant. We detected no relationship between religion and public interest careers."
- *Attrition*. "A critical finding is that *attrition is relatively small*: three-fourths of graduates who began in public interest work were still working in the public interest sector at the time of our survey, which was at least seven years later."
- *In-flow*. "[T]here is significant public interest *attraction*: flow from the private to the public interest sector. Indeed, 528 of our respondents (14 percent) moved from private firm practice to public interest settings."

53 Albiston, Catherine, et al. (2021). Making public interest lawyers in a time of crisis: An evidence-based approach. *Georgetown Journal of Legal Ethics*, *34*, 259, 264–265, 271–272, and 275–276.

The study authors conclude with a comprehensive perspective on public interest lawyers: "Although public interest lawyers confront challenges from political opponents, funding limitations, and shifts in political culture, those lawyers have succeeded in forging a distinctive field of practice that lifts up the voices and builds the power of groups pushed to the margins of our society. In so doing, they have contributed meaningfully to the broader struggle to protect our vibrant democracy—a struggle that is particularly salient and essential in this pivotal moment."[54]

Other non-profit legal organizations

When people think of nonprofit legal organizations, they frequently envision LSC-funded legal aid programs in urban areas like Legal Aid Chicago, Legal Services NYC, and Legal Aid Foundation of Los Angeles. The number and type of nonprofit legal organizations, however, extends far beyond LSC-funded programs. These non-LSC affiliated organizations include influential advocates like Earthjustice, Equal Justice Initiative, Human Rights Watch, Pacific Legal Foundation, The Innocence Project, Public Counsel, American Civil Liberties Foundation, Electronic Frontier Foundation, Asian Americans Advancing Justice, and the Mexican American Legal Defense and Educational Fund. Some of these organizations rival major law firms in their size and income. Earthjustice, for instance, employs 200 attorneys in 15 U.S. offices and reports annual revenue of $151 million. Human Rights Watch employs 550 people in 33 offices worldwide and reports annual revenue of $93 million. Revenue in these ranges approximates that of some law firms ranked among the 200 highest grossing firms by *The American Lawyer*.[55]

Attorneys practicing in nonprofit legal organizations display a broad range of political ideologies and generally seek to advance those ideologies through the organizations' causes. Although their ideologies may differ, their motivations tend to be similar. Law professors Alan Chen and Scott Cummings identify three common motivations:

Altruism—seeking to use legal skills to benefit clients and society at large, "in contrast to more conventional views of lawyering, which center on the advancement of client interests."[56] Public interest lawyers may not be entirely altruistic, Chen and Cummings caution, because they "may also be motivated by important intrinsic benefits or 'psychic income' that

54 Ibid at 286.

55 ALM Staff. (2023, May 23). The 2023 Am Law 200: Ranked by gross revenue. *The American Lawyer*.

56 Unless otherwise noted, quotations in this paragraph appear in Chen, Alan K., & Cummings, Scott L. (2012). *Public interest lawyering*. Frederick, MD: Aspen.

brings great satisfaction to them. These benefits may include enhanced feelings of social worth, as well as feelings of greater control over both the substance of one's work and one's lifestyle."

Moral or political commitment—a conscious moral or political commitment to a particular cause that extends beyond the conventional duty of "simply representing clients in a professionally competent manner." This commitment results in action that "seeks to use law-related means or seeks to change laws or regulations to achieve greater social justice."[57]

Seeking to change the status quo—lawyering that is "directed at altering some aspect of the social, economic, and political status quo."[58] Instead of accommodating or benefiting a single client trying to enforce a right or obtain an advantage within the existing legal framework, the lawyers "apply their professional skills in the service of a cause other than—or greater than—the interest of the client in order to transform some aspect of the status quo."[59]

Some of these motivations are crystallized in comments by two attorneys who left large firms to practice public interest law. Looking back on his large firm experience, one attorney says, "I woke up realizing that one day I was going to kick it, and on my tombstone, it was going to say: defended The Man in discrimination lawsuits. That just wasn't me. I wanted to make the switch to public interest to manage a nonprofit."[60] Another attorney says he left because "I can't spend that many hours on things I care that little about."

The Innocence Project illustrates the critical importance of nonprofit legal organizations and shows how altruism, moral or political commitment, and a desire to change the status quo can coalesce to serve the public interest. The Innocence Project started as a legal clinic at Cardozo School of Law at Yeshiva University in 1992 and became an independent nonprofit organization in 2004.[61] Its mission is to obtain—through DNA testing—the release

57 Menkel-Meadow, Carrie. (1998). The causes of cause lawyering: Toward an understanding of the motivation and commitment of social justice lawyers. In Sarat, Austin, & Scheingold, Stuart (Eds.). *Cause lawyering* (p. 37). New York: Oxford University Press.

58 Sarat, Austin, & Scheingold, Stuart. (1998). *Cause lawyering and the reproduction of professional authority: An introduction*. In Sarat & Scheingold, *supra* note 57 at 3–4.

59 Hajjar, Lisa. (2001). From the fight for legal rights to the promotion of human rights: Israeli and Palestinian cause lawyers in the trenches of globalization. In Sarat, Austin, & Scheingold, Stuart (Eds.). *Cause lawyering and the state in a global era* (p. 68). New York: Oxford University Press.

60 The two quotations in this paragraph appear in Adediran, Atinuke O. (2022). Negotiating status: Pro bono partners and counsels in large law firms. *Law & Social Inquiry*, 47(2), 635, 645.

61 Information in this paragraph appears in the Internal Revenue Service Form 990 filed by The Innocence Project, Inc. and the organization's website, https://innocenceproject.org/dna-exonerations-in-the-united-states/.

of innocent people who have been wrongfully convicted and imprisoned. Through 2020, the last year it tracked DNA exonerations, its efforts resulted in the exoneration of 375 defendants, 21 of whom served time on death row. The average age at which the exonerees started their prison sentence was 27; their average age upon release was 43. Reflecting the inherently coercive effects of police interrogations and plea bargaining, 44 of the 375 exonerees confessed to crimes that DNA evidence proved they could not have committed.

Although The Innocence Project's achievements are impressive, they address only a small fraction of wrongful convictions. The National Registry of Exonerations has recorded 3,484 exonerations between 1989 and 2024.[62] The exonerees in those cases served more than 27,000 years in prison. In 2022 alone, 233 exonerations were recorded; the average time served by those exonerees was 9.6 years, and the total time served was 2,245 years. Official misconduct—usually witness tampering, misconduct in interrogations, fabricating evidence, concealing exculpatory evidence, and misconduct at trial—occurred in 84 percent of those cases.[63]

Organizations dedicated to securing exonerations of wrongfully convicted defendants were responsible for 74 percent of the exonerations in 2022. The fact that the other exonerations—one in four—were idiosyncratic, case-dependent suggests that more organizations are necessary to eliminate the official misconduct, mistaken witness identifications, false confessions, perjury, and false or misleading forensic evidence that lead to wrongful convictions. The need to scrutinize law enforcement and prosecutorial behavior is especially acute in death penalty cases because those cases evince "an appallingly and unacceptably high rate of error."[64] A "conservative estimate" of the proportion of erroneous convictions of defendants sentenced to death between 1973 and 2004 is 4.1 percent; and "for every 8.3 executions carried out in the United States, a wrongfully condemned death-row prisoner is exonerated."

62 Information reported in this paragraph and the next paragraph appears in The National Registry of Exonerations. (2022, April 12). *2021 annual report*. https://www.law.umich.edu/special/exoneration/Documents/NRE%20Annual%20Report%202021.pdf. The National Registry of Exonerations. (2023, May 8). *2022 annual report*. https://www.law.umich.edu/special/exoneration/Documents/NRE%20Annual%20Report%202022.pdf.

63 See Gross, Samuel R., et al. (2020, September 1). *Government misconduct and convicting the innocent*. Ann Arbor, MI: National Registry of Exonerations.

64 Data and quotes in this paragraph appear in Death Penalty Information Center. (2021, February 18). DPIC special report: The innocence epidemic. https://deathpenaltyinfo.org/facts-and-research/dpic-reports/dpic-special-reports/dpic-special-report-the-innocence-epidemic. Gross, Samuel, et al. (2014, May 20). Rate of false conviction of criminal defendants who are sentenced to death. *Proceedings of the National Academy of Sciences*, *111*(2), 7230.

Pro bono services

Juxtaposed between private law firms maximizing their profits and nonprofit legal organizations expanding their impact is pro bono work. This voluntary contribution of time and skills by lawyers in law firms and legal departments increases ordinary citizens' access to justice while improving lawyers' sense of well-being. For many attorneys, notes the eminent trial lawyer John Tucker, "the cases a lawyer accepts to fill an unmet need or lend support to a cause the lawyer believes in will be the most interesting and personally gratifying experiences of that person's career."[65]

Tucker's belief that pro bono work is engaging and gratifying is affirmed by other attorneys' experiences[66]:

- "My pro bono experience taught me how crucial it is to understand and empathize with clients."—Brian Druchniak, Jenner & Block
- "In addition to being able to give back, by virtue of my pro bono practice, I am able to gain periodic exposure to a new area of law and sharpen my legal and advocacy skills in that area. Thus, my pro bono work really helps me feel more complete as a human being and as a legal practitioner."—Usman Khan, Fish & Richardson
- "My clients have taught me to be resilient. I leave the office every day inspired and encouraged. I am a better attorney because of the work I do every day representing individuals who have overcome so many adversities."—Elsy M. Ramos Velasquez, Clark Hill
- "My experiences in pro bono have taught me that we as lawyers do have an ability to make a difference, in ways big and small, and it has also left me with a sense of responsibility to take action on the causes I care about."—Andrea Maddox, Kramer Levin
- "Pro bono work is the thing that taps me on the shoulder from time to time in order to remind me that one of the reasons I went to law school in the first place is to leave the world just a little bit better than I found it."—Geoffrey M. Pipoly, Mayer Brown

As indicated in these comments, pro bono work is regenerative altruism—enhancing attorneys' well-being through individual action to improve the legal system and ensure that everyone can enforce their legal rights.

The American Bar Association urges all attorneys to devote at least 50 hours every year to pro bono services. Most of these services should be provided to "(1) persons of limited means or (2) charitable, religious, civic,

65 Tucker, John C. (2003). *Trial and error* (p. 342). New York: Carroll & Graf.
66 Coe, Aebra. (2022, October 26). In their words: Associates' lessons from pro bono work. *Law 360*.

community, governmental and educational organizations in matters that are designed primarily to address the needs of persons of limited means."[67] Despite the ABA's strong admonition, only one-half of attorneys perform any pro bono services in a given year, and only 20 percent of attorneys provide at least 50 hours per year.[68] One out of five attorneys has never provided pro bono services.

Although 81 percent of attorneys believe that pro bono services are important, less than one-half of them intend to provide those services in the current year. When attorneys do provide pro bono services, the typical case involves services to an individual and takes 16 hours—less than 1.5 hours per month averaged over a year. Total pro bono hours provided by large law firms decreased by 15 percent in 2021.[69] Pro bono services, as a percentage of total client hours, also declined in 2021 from 4.2 percent to 3.3 percent. "These lower pro bono hours," writes legal journalist Andrew Maloney, "came in the same year that Am Law 100 firms' revenues rose on average by 14.8% and profits per equity partner shot up 19.4%, partly driven by a glut of M&A [mergers and acquisitions] and corporate work."[70] Total pro bono hours increased in 2022 but remained below 2020 levels.

The overall trends in pro bono service are alarming, as indicated by two key measures of pro bono service.[71] First, attorney participation rates were lower in 2022 (73.1 percent) than in 2021 (75.0 percent) and 2020 (77.7 percent). In 2022, associate participation rates were the lowest they have been since 2014, and partner participation rates were the lowest they have been since 2011. Second, the number of pro bono hours per attorney declined in 2022, reaching a 20-year low. The drop in pro bono hours in 2022 was particularly acute at the largest firms, decreasing more than 27 percent from 2020. These declines in pro bono service are accompanied by similar declines in law firms' charitable donations to legal services organizations. Total donations peaked in 2007, and the average amount of donations per firm decreased 14 percent

67 A.B.A. Model Rules of Prof'l Conduct R. 6.1.

68 Data in this paragraph and the next paragraph appears in ABA Standing Committee on Pro Bono & Public Service and the Center for Pro Bono. (2018). *Supporting justice*.

69 Maloney, Andrew. (2022, June 17). Amid heavy profits, Big Law's pro bono time saw 'significant' drop in 2021. *The American Lawyer*.

70 Ibid. For 2022 hours, see Jeffreys, Brenda Sapino. (2023, July 11). 'Post-pandemic reset' affects pro bono hours in 2022. *The American Lawyer*.

71 Data in this paragraph is reported in Pro Bono Institute. (2023). *2023 report on the law firm Pro Bono challenge initiative* (pp. 15, 17). https://www.probonoinst.org/wp-content/uploads/2023_PBI_Challenge-Report_Final.pdf. Standing Committee on Delivery of Legal Services. Illinois attorney contributions to pro bono legal services are declining. www.isba.org/probono. See Beck, Susan. (2015, June 29). The justice gap: How Big Law is failing legal aid. *The American Lawyer*. ("At best, the nation's biggest and wealthiest firms donate 0.1 percent of revenue to legal aid").

between 2021 and 2022. Individual attorney donations to legal aid and pro bono organizations, on average, are meager. In 2022, for instance, the average amount contributed by a registered Illinois attorney was $189.18.

What motivates attorneys to provide pro bono services? The five most frequently cited reasons are helping people in need; ethical obligation; professional duty; participating in reducing social inequalities; and feeling like a good person.[72] Daniel Tishman, a principal at Fish & Richardson, describes some of these motives in his pro bono representation of a discharged employee:

> This case was such a great experience. It was an honor to represent the client and get to know her, especially as we got closer to the trial. We were able to meet with her and her family and see throughout the trial how much of an impact this case had on her life. One of the most rewarding parts of the case was seeing how happy she was to finally have closure and the good result at the end of the case. This was one of the most rewarding things I've done in my career. Just sitting next to her when the verdict was read was very meaningful. . . .
>
> In the past year or so, I've done about 200 hours of pro bono. That's a fraction of my overall year, but the impact on the satisfaction with my job is much greater than what I put into it. It doesn't take a huge time commitment to have a big impact on a client and a big impact on your own professional satisfaction. There's plenty of work and it's very rewarding.[73]

Tishman's representation of the discharged employee resulted in a favorable jury verdict of $725,000 in compensatory and punitive damages and set a precedent in employment law.

Despite the altruistic, seemingly gender-neutral intentions underpinning pro bono work, some differences between male and female attorneys in pro bono attitudes and practices have been documented. In the early stages of their careers, female attorneys are considerably more likely than male attorneys to consider a firm's pro bono opportunities in deciding whether to join a firm.[74] At the partner level, female lawyers are more likely than male lawyers to report that their pro bono work was more satisfying than their regular assignments. Female attorneys who serve as pro bono partners and counsels in law firms focus their pro bono practices on family law, human rights/

72 ABA Standing Committee on Pro Bono & Public Service and the Center for Pro Bono, *supra* note 68.

73 American Bar Association. (2021, December 22). Pro bono spotlight: Daniel Tishman of Fish & Richardson. *ABA Center for Pro Bono, Pro Bono Exchange.*

74 Data in this sentence and the next sentence appears in Cartusciello, Yolanda, et al. (2020, March). *Multiple generations in law firms* (pp. 94, 105). Washington, DC: NALP and PP&C Consulting.

trafficking, immigration, and nonprofit corporations, while male attorneys in those roles are more likely to emphasize criminal law, prisoner's rights, impact litigation, and corporate law.[75] Law professor Atinuke Adediran finds that male pro bono partners and counsels are "more likely to practice in areas that are traditionally considered high profile by large law firms."[76] Male pro bono partners and counsels also report higher levels of autonomy than female pro bono partners and counsels in approving pro bono matters.

"The reproduction of inequality in the role of pro bono partners and counsels," states Adediran, "has implications not only for the professionals in those roles but also for the social justice goals that law firms and the legal profession seek to advance." Since pro bono work has been the nation's largest source of free civil legal assistance and many law firms contribute more than 35,000 attorney hours per year to pro bono services, "it is important to mitigate inequality in the role of pro bono partners and counsels as part of the social justice goals law firms advance."[77]

Altruistic judges

Altruism is the essential feature of judicial wisdom. Judges who have been identified as exceptionally wise judges by their peers exhibit distinct values, attitudes, and practices that embody altruism and correlated traits. At least five altruistic qualities distinguish wise judges in action[78]:

- *Understanding and fairness*. Wise judges believe that personal intelligence and knowledge of the law contribute to wisdom, but they are not sufficient to constitute wisdom. They recognize that "having the patience to listen carefully to litigants' experiences, the desire to be fair, and a real curiosity to understand would lead to both wise decisions and the ability to convey decisions wisely."

75 Adediran, *supra* note 60 at 659–660.

76 The quotations in this paragraph and the next paragraph appear in Adediran, *supra* note 60 at 663, 664.

77 Lever, Emily. (2022, June 17). Attorneys worked fewer pro bono hours in 2021. *Law 360*. (2022, July 18). The 2022 pro bono scorecard: Average hours and breadth of commitment. *The American Lawyer*.

78 The traits of wise judges and the quotations in the first two paragraphs of this section appear in Levitt, Heidi M., & Dunnavant, Bridget R. (2015). Judicial wisdom: The process of constructing wise decisions. *Journal of Constructivist Psychology*, *28*(3), 243. See Dunnavant, Bridget R., & Levitt, Heidi M. (2015). The development of wisdom in judicial decision-making. *The Humanistic Psychologist*, *43*, 9. IAALS. (2024). *JPE 2.0: National perspectives on judicial performance evaluation*. Denver: IAALS. (Surveyed judges ranked "compassion" and "temperament" above "decisiveness" and "legal analysis and ability" among the qualities that "make a good judge.")

- *Personal attention to litigants.* Ordinary judges often succumb to the pressure to expedite decision making to clear their caseloads. Wise judges, however, realize that sound decisions require a thorough understanding of litigants' experiences. "You need to treat every single case like it's the most important case that you are ever going to have because at that moment, at that time, it is the most important case," explains one judge nominated by his peers as exemplifying wisdom.
- *Respect and compassion.* Wise judges acknowledge that all litigants should be treated with respect and compassion even when they have made bad choices. They strive "to see the humanity within all litigants," researchers observe, and they enforce the law "while conveying respect and maintaining compassion for how an offender's family and community could be influenced by a sentence."
- *Perspective-taking.* Wise judges elicit and consider multiple perspectives and attempt to understand the long-term impact of their decisions on litigants and their families and communities. As one judge honored for wisdom notes, "If we have 10 different people with 10 different cultural backgrounds around the table, we can make sure that our decisions have more integrity because we're gonna have better input and we're gonna make sure that people who are currently disenfranchised will not feel . . . alienated from the system." That judge cites studies that ask citizens, "Are judges ethical and fair-minded?" Noting that "you get a 50% 'no' response rate from people of color," the judge implores, "Oh my God, what are we doing here?"
- *Responsibility for healing.* Wise judges know that promoting healing is an institutional responsibility for the courts and a professional responsibility for judges. As one judge explains, "Well look, if at the end of the day the judge doesn't bring any healing to this process, then the judge has failed. But, you know, if you think about why courts exist, courts exist to do a couple of things. One is to protect the public and maintain order in society, right? But the second thing really is to bring healing and in that process of bringing healing kind of ending this sort of cycle of violence, um, you know eliminate retribution from outside the system, to give people a sense that justice has been accomplished."

Many of the judges recognized as wise have supported diversion and alternative disposition programs like drug courts, mental health courts, veterans' treatment courts, and domestic violence programs. Some of the judges—pointing to an increase in mediation, collaborative law, and problem-solving courts for people with addiction or mental health problems—see a shift in the legal system from adversarial models to therapeutic methods. As one judge observed, "What drug courts I think have shown us nationally is if you take time with people and you help them develop . . .[we] are much more successful than what we've done traditionally, which is simply lock people up."

Although many judges integrate their altruistic values into their hearings and rulings, some judges find that legislative restrictions on their sentencing decisions present an intolerable moral conflict. They challenge mandatory minimum sentences and enhanced sentencing laws by refusing to impose the statutory sentences or resigning from the bench. Judge Gene Franchini, a New Mexico district judge who resigned and was later elected to the New Mexico Supreme Court, exemplifies their dilemma in his sentencing of a first-time offender:

> My specific oath of office is to uphold and apply the law. My conscience and sense of justice on the other hand will not allow me to sentence to the New Mexico State Penitentiary, a 26-year-old man who has no prior record, has been honorably discharged from the U.S. Navy after three years active duty and three more years Naval Reserve duty, and at the time of this offense was supporting his 41-year-old widowed mother, and who acted on the spur of the moment. To do that is to fly in the face of every thought I have had about justice and the right thing to do. Therefore, I personally and as this Court refuse to be a party to this injustice. . . .
>
> So much for the concept of due process. So much for the duty to consider all circumstances surrounding the offense and all circumstances surrounding the offender before imposing a prison sentence. So much, finally, for a judge's duty, obligation, and responsibility to judge. The law and administration of justice has always been one of the great loves of my life. I cannot and therefore will not now prostitute it or myself.[79]

For similar reasons federal district court judge J. Lawrence Irving resigned, stating, "If I remain on the bench, I have no choice but to follow the law. I just can't, in good conscience, continue to do this."[80] Although altruistic judges can justify their sentencing decisions by citing their oaths to uphold the laws, a chronic sense of moral culpability may still haunt them. Judge Jack Weinstein, for instance, refused to hear any more drug cases in his federal district court, acknowledging "a sense of depression about much of the cruelty I have been a party to in connection with the 'war on drugs.'"[81] Sentencing laws have stripped many judges of the discretion they previously exercised, and historians may eventually question the morality of judges who enforced sentencing laws that were legitimately enacted but discriminately enforced, facially valid but practically malevolent.

79 Franchini, Gene E. (2000, Winter). Conscience, judging, and conscientious judging. *The Journal of Appellate Practice and Process*, 2(1), 20–21.

80 Alexander, Michelle. (2020). *The new Jim Crow* (p. 116). New York: The New Press.

81 Ibid. See Bellin, Jeffrey. (2023). *Mass incarceration nation* (p. 128). New York: Cambridge University Press.

8

ACCELERATING WELL-BEING, ALTRUISM, AND REFORM

The mental health and altruism crises are endemic. They will not improve with the minor, incremental steps that lawyers, judges, and their professional organizations have considered during the last 40 years. If legal professionals' perspectives and ideas had been accurate and ameliorative, we already would have seen major improvements in both their psychological well-being and the legal system they operate. This public experiment in professional self-regulation, premised on the dubious assertion that lawyers will voluntarily serve the public interest while advancing their private interests, has failed. Like many other self-regulated professionals, lawyers did not adapt as the concept of competence evolved from expertise to efficiency, access, affordability, innovation, responsiveness, reliability, and fairness.[1]

Although lawyers and judges can point to some helpful innovations in recent decades, the overall effect of allowing them to evaluate and treat their own mental health, while enjoying an exclusive franchise to provide legal services and adjudicate legal rights, has been unfortunate for citizens. The net effect of lawyers' self-treatment and self-regulation, for the vast majority of citizens, is an increasingly expensive and decreasingly accessible legal system. The net effect of judges' independence in diagnosing and handling their stress, depression, trauma, boredom, and isolation has been a disconnect with society and an alarming loss of public trust and confidence in the

1 See Adams, Tracey L. (2016). Professional self-regulation and the public interest in Canada. *Professions & Professionalism*, 6(2), 1. Adams, Tracey L. (2016). Self-regulating professions: Past, present, future. *Journal of Professions and Organization*, 4(1), 70. Hadfield, Gillian. (2000). The price of law: How the market for lawyers distorts the legal system. *Michigan Law Review*, 98, 953.

DOI: 10.4324/9781003514848-8

courts. This loss has been accompanied by the "bureaucratization of our courts, which has transformed the ancient art of judging into a species of office management whose main virtue is efficiency rather than wisdom."[2]

Substantial improvements in well-being and the legal system have not occurred because the current models deliver large financial and personal returns, without commensurate accountability, to influential segments of society. The current models preserve hierarchies, privileges, and conventions within the legal profession and enable a profession notoriously change-resistant to delay technological advances and stymie civil and criminal justice reforms. These models also protect millions of jobs in law schools, law enforcement, court administration, state bar organizations, dispute resolution services, probation agencies, prison guards' unions, court fine collection agencies, bail bonds, and prison construction, maintenance, and operations. The standard of living for millions of Americans is dependent on a legal system that has proven to be an international embarrassment.

It will take decades to correct our lawyer-centric legal system because the values underpinning that system have misled multiple generations of currently practicing lawyers. As legal historian Robert Gordon explains, lawyers have grown accustomed to espousing public service while neglecting it:

> Law is a service profession; but it is also a public profession. Lawyers are supposed to serve their clients faithfully and zealously; but they also are supposed to work, both on and off the job of representing clients, as counselors, citizens, reformers, community activists, and public servants, to maintain the integrity of the framework of laws, institutions, and procedures that constrain their clients' practices and their own—and not just to maintain that framework, but to help transform it so that it more nearly will approach the conditions of justice and civic community. . . .
>
> This is an inspiring ideal for a profession and, so long as its expression stays on this plane of comfortable vagueness, not a controversial one. At the bar association dinner, those lawyers who have not fallen asleep during the speech can be seen nodding their heads and applauding afterwards. . . .
>
> Yet if after the rhetoric you ask what the ideal demands in practice, the standard answers may seem a bit anticlimactic. Lawyers, we are told, should avoid vulgar advertising, volunteer some pro bono time, and support the bar's efforts to strengthen lawyer discipline, curb litigation abuse, promote legal-services programs for the poor, and improve public relations with its outside critics. Nothing wrong with this, to be sure, but as a program it seems rather a comedown from the much richer and more

2 Kronman, Anthony T. (1993). *The lost lawyer* (p. 4). Cambridge, MA: The Belknap Press of Harvard University Press.

ambitious conceptions of their public obligations that lawyers have historically entertained and occasionally, though infrequently, acted upon. Even in its modest forms, the program has to struggle hard for survival in the current conditions of practice.[3]

This compressed, highly scripted version of public service is central to the public service theatre performed by many bar associations after their formation in the late 1800s. It presumes that a perpetual license to promote clients' self-interests in lawyers' practices should be issued if they propose—but do not commit to—spending about two percent of their time serving, through pro bono services, the society that grants the license. In its extreme form, according to law professor Ann Juergens and attorney Diane Galatowitsch, "lawyers may swing between an amoral pursuit of clients' self-interests and then salve their consciences by helping—for free!—a small number of those seeking to avoid being crushed by injustice."[4] The primary driver of public service then becomes expiation rather than social responsibility, *noblesse oblige* rather than genuine altruism. Small wonder, then, that most Gen Z law students and lawyers are skeptical of law firms' social responsibility programs and, when surveyed, *dis*agree with the statement, "Law firm corporate social responsibility programs are authentic and valued."[5]

Although it may take decades to eliminate conditions that harm lawyers' mental health and impair the legal system, many helpful steps can be taken immediately. This chapter outlines reforms that would quickly upgrade values, attitudes, behavior, and outcomes within the legal system and can be implemented now. These changes incorporate data and findings discussed in previous chapters and are categorized by constituencies: state bar associations, law firms, judges, district attorneys, public defenders, and law schools.

State bar associations

State bar associations are at least 20 years behind the medical profession in identifying altruism as an element of professionalism. While state bar organizations have been preoccupied with protecting lawyers from competitors and disciplining unethical attorneys for conduct largely related to alcohol and

3 Gordon, Robert W. (1990). Corporate law practice as a public calling. *Maryland Law Review*, *49*(2), 255–256.

4 Juergens, Ann, & Galatowitsch, Diane. (2018). Fostering client altruism and the common good in the practice of law: Learning from emerging movements in business and economics. *Mitchell Hamline Law Review*, *44*(1), 4.

5 Major, Lindsey, & Africa. (2023). *Gen-Z: Now influencing today's law firm culture* (p. 11). Hanover, MD: Major, Lindsey & Africa.

drug abuse, the medical profession has promoted altruism.[6] Medical school professor Laura Verrier describes this movement:

> Over the last twenty years, medicine as a profession has attempted to renew its dedication to altruism as part of the professionalism movement. In the Physician Charter, altruism is declared the fundamental principle that is necessary for fostering trust in the physician-patient relationship. The Medical Schools Objectives Project, sponsored by the Association of American Medical Colleges, states in bold text "Physicians must be altruistic." The beginning of medical school has been considered to be a crossing of a threshold and a transition in one's social role in society defined by professionalism. In the American Board of Internal Medicine's Project Professionalism, it states "altruism is the essence of professionalism."[7]

Altruism, declares Verrier, is a "fundamental, defining value of the profession"; and it has been linked to the profession "throughout the history of medicine."[8]

Unlike the medical profession, the legal profession has an aversion to explicit altruism. It does not require attorneys to act altruistically in improving the administration of justice, increasing access to the legal system, upgrading legal education, or volunteering for public service. Although the American Bar Association states that attorneys "should aspire to render at least (50) hours of pro bono publico legal services per year," no mechanism exists for requiring it.[9] As a result, only 20 percent of attorneys satisfy the 50-hour aspiration. Most attorneys report that their employers neither encourage nor discourage pro bono work, and only 9 percent of employers allow billable hour credit for pro bono work.[10] Roughly one-half of all attorneys do not perform pro bono services in any given year, and only 14 percent of employers have adopted a policy supporting pro bono work. If discretionary pro bono work was successful in animating attorneys' latent altruistic

6 See Krill, Patrick R. (2014, Fall). If there is one bar a lawyer cannot seem to pass: Alcoholism in the legal profession. *The Brief*, *44*(1). ("Notably, at least 25 percent of attorneys who face formal disciplinary charges from their state bar are identified as suffering from addiction or other mental illness, with substance abuse playing at least some role in 60 percent of all disciplinary cases.")

7 Vearrier, Laura. (2020, April 16). Enlightened self-interest in altruism (ESIA). *HEC Forum*, *32*, 149. (citations omitted).

8 Ibid at 147, 148.

9 A.B.A. Model Rules of Prof'l Conduct R. 6.1.

10 Data in this paragraph is reported in Standing Committee on Pro Bono & Public Service. (2018). *Supporting justice: A report on the pro bono work of America's lawyers*. Chicago: American Bar Association.

propensities and increasing access to justice, we would see considerably more evidence of its effectiveness.

The American Bar Association has considered making pro bono work mandatory but ultimately places a higher priority on preserving lawyer autonomy than requiring public service. The chair of the association's Standing Committee on Pro Bono and Public Service, Henry Su, emphasizes "respect for autonomy in the profession" and contends that pro bono requirements are "inconsistent with treating lawyers as professionals."[11] As he explains, "As a lawyer, you're a professional. We're not going to tell you what to do. You do it because you want to do it." This view of professionalism is perplexing since the essence of professionalism is "decision making in the public interest" and "subjecting rampant individualism to the needs of the community."[12]

To accelerate lawyers' professionalism and altruism, state bar associations should follow the medical profession's lead and incorporate altruism into their principles, standards, policies, and rules. They also should require minimum pro bono hours as a condition of attorney license renewal, and the number of required hours should quickly increase from 50 to 80. Fifty hours represent only 2.2 percent of the total time that partners spend on billable and non-billable work in an average year; 80 hours would represent 3.5 percent of their total annual hours.[13] That is a small contribution to society for the exclusive right to provide legal services, as Aric Press, former editor-in-chief of *The American Lawyer* asserts: "I think it's work that lawyers do because they belong to a profession, and professions have obligations to the broader society in which they operate. Otherwise they don't deserve the privilege of self-regulation and the honor of a special status in our courts. Part of the price for that status is serving those who can't afford legal services."[14]

Some attorneys presumably would refuse to perform mandated pro bono services, citing philosophical objections or the demands of other business. State bar associations should allow those non-compliant attorneys to continue rendering legal services as "legal technicians," but they would not be licensed as attorneys under the new criteria for professionalism. Altruism and public service are essential elements of professionalism, and those attorneys who decline the responsibilities of professionalism should have the option

11 Poggio, Marco. (2023, October 27). Local lawyers step up for national pro bono week. *Law 360*.

12 Evetts, Julia, et al. (2006). Professionalization, scientific expertise, and elitism: A sociological perspective. In Ericsson, K. Anders, et al. (Eds.). *The Cambridge handbook of expertise and expert performance* (pp. 107, 112). New York: Cambridge University Press.

13 Major, Lindsey & Africa. (2020). *2020 partner compensation survey*. Hanover, MD: Major, Lindsey & Africa. (Morgan Lewis, for example, integrates pro bono work into its compensation policies by requiring a minimum of 20 hours for bonus eligibility.)

14 Press, Aric. (2015, January). Big Law and me. *The American Lawyer*, 69.

of employment as legal technicians. Changing the position of recalcitrant attorneys to the non-professional category of legal technicians would have the additional advantage of lowering overall legal costs since clients would object to paying attorney rates for non-attorneys' time.

In the long term, state bar associations must take responsibility for providing legal services to indigent citizens. Bar associations have obtained for lawyers an exclusive right to practice law, and that right, in turn, requires them to serve the entire range of citizens dependent on them. Law firms' current practice of providing legal services to the most lucrative segment of the legal services market—while withholding those essential services from citizens who are less affluent but more dependent—is avaricious and indefensible in a nation that espouses the rule of law. As law professor Deborah Rhode observes, "It's a shameful irony that the nation with the highest concentration of lawyers fails so miserably to make their services available to those who need them most."[15]

In addition to their responsibility to promote altruism and ensure that all citizens have access to legal services, state bar associations must revamp their lawyer assistance programs. These programs provide assessments, education, counseling, and referrals for lawyers experiencing substance abuse, addiction, and other mental health problems.[16] Their principal shortcoming is that they are woefully underutilized by lawyers. In Illinois, for example, only 445 new client cases were opened by the Lawyers' Assistance Program during the last fiscal year, an abjectly small number in a state with 96,440 lawyers. In California, only 172 lawyers—among 190,000 lawyers on active status—enrolled in the program during the most recent annual reporting period. Considering the extent of mental illness in the legal profession and the fact that substance abuse is implicated in about 50 percent of state bar disciplinary actions, this underutilization of lawyer assistance programs merits an immediate, comprehensive response by state bar associations.

Law firms

Law firms engage in three practices correlated with attorneys' mental distress: billable hour requirements; billable hour-based compensation and promotion systems; and loose oversight of abusive partners. Each of these practices

15 Engstrom, Nora Freeman. (2023). She stood up: The life and legacy of Deborah L. Rhode. In *Remembering Deborah Rhode: Her life and legacy* (p. 25). https://law.stanford.edu/wp-content/uploads/2023/02/Remembering-Deborah-Rhode.pdf,

16 Data in this paragraph appears in Krill, Patrick R. (2014). If there is one bar a lawyer cannot seem to pass: Alcoholism in the legal profession. *The Brief*, *44*(1), 48. Lawyers' Assistance Program. Annual report 2022–2023: Together we shine brighter. State Bar of California. (2023, March 1). Lawyer assistance program report 2022 annual report. https://www.calbar.ca.gov/Portals/0/documents/reports/2022-Lawyer-Assistance-Program-Annual-Report.pdf.

could be halted by law firm management committees within 30 days, resulting in dramatic improvements in attorney well-being.

Billable hour requirements are unhealthy and unprofessional. As demonstrated in Krieger and Sheldon's survey of 7,805 attorneys and the regression analysis of their responses,

> the specific practice factor that had the strongest negative relationship with well-being was required billable hours. This practice was associated with increasing income but decreasing autonomy, relatedness, and internal motivation, an apparent example of managers undermining workers' self-determined motivation and well-being by promoting a focus on external rewards. Thus, as billable hours go up, income goes up and happiness goes down.[17]

Alcohol consumption among the attorneys in Krieger and Sheldon's study also increased as billable hours increased. In other surveys, attorneys have identified "no work-life balance" as the main reason for being unhappy and ranked "number of hours" as the second most dislikable aspect of their job, following "lack of control over my work schedule."[18]

Billable hour requirements indicate that law firms lack better methods of evaluating their attorneys' performance and cannot trust their own attorneys to make judgments about the appropriate amount of time required to fulfill their obligations to clients and the firm itself. These requirements are inherently demeaning to attorneys and antithetical to their exercise of professional judgment. They also corrupt the attorney-client relationship by injecting a revenue quota into a fiduciary relationship. As Daniel Pink, a bestselling author and law school graduate, explains, billable hours shift lawyers' focus from "the output of their work (solving a client's problems) to its input (piling up as many hours as possible). If the rewards come from time, then time is what firms will get."[19] Although law firm leaders contend that billable

17 Krieger, Lawrence S., & Sheldon, Kennon M. (2015). What makes lawyers happy?: A data-driven prescription to redefine professional success. *The George Washington Law Review*, *83*, 615.

18 Cartusciello, Yolanda, et al. (2020, March). *Multiple generations in law firms* (p. 120). Washington, DC: NALP and PP&C Consulting. The Mosaic Collective. (2020). *The Mosaic Mood Index* (p. 4). In the 2024 *American Lawyer* Mental Health Survey of the Legal Profession, 42 percent of lawyers reported that billable hours had a "major effect" on their stress level, and 62 percent said that billable hour pressures negatively impacted their mental well-being. Choudhury, Rashmita. (2024, May 17). Mental health by the numbers: The 2024 survey infographic. *The American Lawyer*.

19 Pink, Daniel. (2009). *Drive* (p. 97). New York: Riverhead Books. Billable hour requirements also are a good illustration of "Goodhart's Law," a central concept in economics. That law states, "When a measure becomes a target, it ceases to be a good measure." See Yates, Kit. (2023). *How to expect the unexpected* (p. 321). New York: Basic Books.

hour requirements do not influence the number of hours that attorneys bill to clients, that argument, if true, would also demonstrate that billable hour requirements have no actual effect on attorneys' behavior and should be eliminated as purposeless.

Law firms' preoccupation with billable hours permeates attorneys' promotion and compensation systems. Economists find that this fixation on billable hours produces a "rat-race equilibrium" in which associates work "inefficiently long work hours," and support for their promotion to partner "falls as work hours fall."[20] When long-hour associates are promoted to partnership, the incentives for overwork persist. Total billable hours, total working attorney receipts, and client origination are the most important factors in determining partner compensation. In some firms, they are the only actual factors, overriding ostensible factors like work product quality, mentoring, training, leadership, and public service.[21] Sixty-nine percent of surveyed partners, for instance, state that non-billable hours are "not at all important" or "not very important" in determining compensation.[22] It is remarkable that, in a profession outwardly dedicated to "the ideals of public service," two-thirds of its most successful members—those elevated to partner status—view non-billable work as being insignificant in their firms' compensation decisions.[23]

Apart from the mischief generated by billable hour requirements and a myopic focus on billed hours, law firms need to protect their attorneys from bullying and harassment. Roughly one-half of female attorneys and one-third of male attorneys are subjected to bullying and harassment, as discussed in Chapter 3. Many law firms sanction this misconduct for two major reasons. First, the offending partner generates outsized revenue for the firm. As an attorney subjected to harassment remarks, "Law firms say they have a 'no jerks' policy, but this policy doesn't apply when that partner brings in a lot of money."[24] Second, the firm rationalizes the misbehavior as an indignity necessarily absorbed by overpaid associate attorneys. Psychologist and law firm consultant Larry Richard describes this phenomenon: "What I've been

20 Landers, Renee M., et al. (1996, June). Rat race redux: Adverse selection in the determination of work hours in law firms. *The American Economic Review*, *86*(3), 329.

21 See Kiser, Randall. (2019). *American law firms in transition: Trends, threats and strategies* (pp. 209–213). Chicago: American Bar Association. Roberts, Peter. (2020, September 1). Parsing the dollars: Thoughtful approaches to compensation. *Law Practice Magazine*.

22 Major, Lindsey, & Africa. (2018). *2018 Partner compensation survey* (p. 39). Hanover, MD: Major, Lindsey & Africa.

23 "A lawyer should strive to attain the highest level of skill, to improve the law and the legal profession and to exemplify the legal profession's ideals of public service." A.B.A. Model Rules of Prof'l Conduct, Preamble and Scope.

24 Smith, Patrick. (2022, September 1). 'No consequences': Sexual harassment persists in law firm culture. *The American Lawyer*.

told by some senior partners at some big firms is that there's a dire need for high-quality corporate associates and they're paying to get them, so they're not worried about the issue of whether the partners are too harsh with them. If they're paying you a $100,000 signing bonus, firm leaders think that that should cover the harshness. That's not the answer I'd like to hear or how I would counsel them, but that's what I'm hearing from them."[25]

Law firms' excuses for overlooking abusive behavior give associate attorneys the impression that revenue is paramount and their well-being is secondary. Four associates relate their experiences with difficult partners at major law firms[26]:

- "We preach 'Be Cooley' but that only applies when times are good. When work slows, partners turn from being these 'cool, fun' people into rude, dismissive, cruel people." (Cooley associate)
- "When I am staffed with good managers I genuinely like my firm; it's not perfect but the good people are amazing. When you get a bad manager, it poisons everything. I was not prepared for the extent that a manager's whims can dictate your life." (Weil, Gotshal & Manges associate)
- "Ropes & Gray is fantastic as an institution; however, the culture does not encourage partners to invest in associates and, as a consequence, we feel fungible and like we have no future at the firm, particularly when we don't get timely, constructive feedback. When we have no chance of becoming partner and are not getting good, informal training and professional development, it can be hard to justify staying." (Ropes & Gray associate)
- "The excellent partners and other attorneys who are role models, mentors, and decent human beings do not cancel out or compensate for the partners who are terrible to work with. The rotten few ruin what would otherwise be a great place to work." (Morgan Lewis associate)

Law firm partners and HR personnel know who consistently mistreats associates and degrades their emotional health. The annual associate attrition rate of 18–26 percent also confirms that the working environment in many law firms is intensely stressful; the higher attrition rate of 26–34 percent for associates of color suggests that many law firms are not just stressful but may be discriminatory as well.[27] If law firm leaders were advising their own clients reporting similar conditions, they presumably would urge

25 Roe, Dan (2022, August 31). In-demand midlevels can't escape Big Law's bad partner problem. *The American Lawyer*.

26 Ibid. Roe, Dan. (2023, August 22). How to kill your culture in a minor recession, according to midlevels. *The American Lawyer*.

27 NALP Foundation. (2022, April 26). Update on associate attrition. NALP Foundation. (2024, April 10). Update on associate attrition.

them to take prompt, concrete action to change the workplace and terminate caustic managers who are not amenable to coaching or counseling. Law firm leaders should demonstrate the same objectivity and scrupulousness in protecting their own attorneys from abusive partners.

Judges

Roughly one-half of judges report that they experience secondary trauma, and about one quarter of judges meet criteria for debilitating stress. More than 25 percent of judges said that they missed ten days or more of work during the past year "due to feeling stressed or unable to perform as well as [they] would like."[28] Seven percent of judges said that they had missed 15–19 days of work during the past year specifically due to stress.

Judges' stress-induced absenteeism, states criminal justice professor Monica Miller, "suggests that court administrators should take note of sick days—while preserving confidentiality and not singling out judges—to identify judges who might be experiencing stress-related outcomes that prompt sick days. Interventions should be offered in such situations to prevent escalation." Miller also recommends that "judges should be educated about the causes of stress and the effects stress might have on their ability to perform their jobs. Additionally, stress-relieving measures could be implemented by the courts, such as providing counseling for judges, creating peer support groups, or allowing judges to go on sabbatical."

Twenty-percent of judges also meet at least one criterion for depressive disorder, and ten percent report problematic alcohol use, as discussed in Chapter 4. Their scores on a clinical measure of depression are "nearly double that of the general population." Assessing their own performance, judges report that they are "only moderately able to perform their jobs to the best of their abilities." A significant minority of judges acknowledge that they have "feelings of failure," are concerned about "not achieving goals," and experience difficulties separating "work and personal life."

The risks associated with judges' mental health impairments are too high to allow them to self-diagnose their conditions and self-manage their care. These risks are compounded by the advanced age of many judges and the accelerated onset of dementia symptoms in elderly adults. The average age of federal court judges, for instance, is 68, and a plurality of U.S. circuit court judges is at least 70 years old. People in this cohort age have a serious incidence of cognitive impairment. If federal court

28 The data sources for this section are cited in Chapter 4 or are reported in Miller, Monica K., et al. (2018, Winter/Fall). Judges and stress: An examination of outcomes predicted by the model of judicial stress. *Judicature*, *102*(3), 50. All quotations appear in the Miller article.

judges' incidence of cognitive impairment is similar to the general population's incidence, roughly 100 federal court judges could be adjudicating cases this week while being cognitively impaired. Considering that the number of state court judges is about 34 times the number of federal court judges, the extent of mental impairment in the judiciary might be alarming.

To reduce the risks attendant to mental health impairments, courts should implement mandatory, confidential mental health assessments for all judges. These assessments should be conducted annually, and the results would be provided only to the individual judge participating in the assessment. The courts also should facilitate judges' confidential access to counselors and psychologists for assessment and treatment.

In an ideal system, all judges' mental health assessments would be provided to a presiding judge or a judge in a similar administrative capacity to assure treatment or other appropriate responses. The judiciary, however, is unlikely to permit this intrusion into their autonomy. It is remarkable that people in other occupations responsible for human safety—like pilots and commercial vehicle drivers—have to undergo medical examinations to protect society, but judges can endanger citizens' physical and mental well-being through prison sentences, injunctions, fines, forfeitures, and monetary judgments issued during an entire career devoid of clinical scrutiny.

In addition to monitoring, evaluating, and improving their mental health, judges need to break their allegiance to lawyers and become more accountable to the public. The entire society is judges' true constituency, not the lawyers who provide a steady source of accolades and approbation. Reflecting judges' current alienation from the general society, 60 percent of surveyed citizens believe that judges "don't understand the challenges facing people who appear in their courtrooms and need to do a better job of getting out into the community and listening to people."[29] Since judges' service is owed to the public, not lawyers, most of their professional time outside the courtroom should be spent with the people, organizations, and communities that bear the consequences of their decisions.

The close relationship between judges and lawyers has been harmful to society and diverts judges' attention away from broad social responsibilities to attorneys' narrow concerns and interests. Rebecca Love Kourlis, a former justice of the Colorado Supreme Court and the founding executive director of the Institute for the Advancement of the American Legal System, calls

29 GBA Strategies. (2017, November 15). 2017 state of the state courts—survey analysis. (An annual survey conducted at the direction of the National Center for State Courts.) https://www.ncsc.org/__data/assets/pdf_file/0012/16131/sosc-2017-survey-analysis.pdf.

the unwholesome relationship between judges and lawyers the "lawyer/judge protectorate" and urges its demise:

> The era of the lawyer/judge protectorate must come to an end—either gracefully or not so gracefully. To build public trust, we must recreate a system that is truly trustworthy. And, to do that, I believe we must put everyday people at the system's center, not the lawyers and judges. Access to justice means access to understandable, accessible, and affordable legal and court services—for everyone.[30]

"Lawyers and judges have failed the public," Kourlis declares, and they have to earn public trust by rebuilding the system "in a far more open, transparent, accessible way."

District attorneys and public defenders

In its report to the United Nations, The Sentencing Project describes two distinct criminal justice systems in the United States: "one for wealthy people and another for poor people and people of color."[31] In this dual system, wealthy citizens "can access a vigorous adversary system replete with constitutional protections for defendants." For indigent and minority defendants, however, constitutional rights are largely theoretical, and in practice, as law professor David Cole explains, "the rules assure that law enforcement prerogatives will generally prevail over the rights of minorities and the poor." The operation and funding of the criminal justice system typically perpetuate these disparities between wealthy citizens, represented by private attorneys, and poor and minority defendants, usually represented by public defenders.

Although lawyers and judges characterize the legal system as adversarial, that depiction is farcical in most criminal cases. District attorneys and police departments usually are funded generously while public defender offices are funded sparsely and reluctantly. In San Diego County, for instance, the amount of the district attorney's budget is more than twice that of the public defender's office—although 80 percent of the defendants are represented by

30 Kourlis, Rebecca Love. (2019, September 13). Public trust and confidence in the legal system: The way forward. https://iaals.du.edu/blog/public-trust-and-confidence-legal-system-way-forward.

31 Quotations in this paragraph appear in The Sentencing Project. (2018, March). Report of the sentencing project to the United Nations special rapporteur on contemporary forms of racism, racial discrimination, xenophobia, and related intolerance, p. 1. https://www.sentencingproject.org/reports/report-to-the-united-nations-on-racial-disparities-in-the-u-s-criminal-justice-system/.

the public defender.[32] Nominal funding of public defenders' offices achieves ostensible compliance with the constitutional right to counsel while assuring that, once arrested, most defendants will never experience the robust defense promised by an adversarial system.

Overworked public defenders simply do not have the resources to conduct a thorough investigation and mount a vigorous defense, as former public defender and MacArthur Fellow Jonathan Rapping explains:

> Overwhelmed and under-resourced public defenders frequently make decisions based solely on the universe of facts as given to them by the prosecution. When there is limited time to investigate and litigate, evidence helpful to the client remains unknown, constitutional violations go uncovered, and the protections at the heart of our system of justice are unrealized. Roughly 95 percent of cases result in pleas because the lawyers are ill-prepared to challenge the allegations.[33]

The American Bar Association, as discussed in Chapter 7, has determined that funding and staffing of public defender offices would have to be doubled, and in some cases quintupled, to provide reasonably effective assistance of counsel.

Pitting deliberately under-funded public defenders against well-funded district attorneys makes a mockery of the constitutional right to effective assistance of counsel. Public entities should end this prejudicial practice and adopt policies that effectuate parity between public defenders and district attorneys, including investigative services for public defenders that are equivalent to the law enforcement investigators assisting district attorneys.

Two additional measures would help to correct biases and inequities in criminal justice. First, to open the mindsets that have fostered the debacle widely known as "incarceration nation," district attorneys should serve as public defenders for one year every three to five years. The ideological rigidity and polarization that develop among many career prosecutors are anathema to any civil society simultaneously attempting to enforce laws, protect citizens, respect constitutional rights, achieve justice, and rehabilitate and reintegrate people convicted of a crime. These goals require objective analyses and intelligent polices that may be hindered by lifelong roles as prosecutors surrounded by like-minded careerists. By periodically serving as public defenders, district attorneys might better understand the acute deficiencies in the criminal law system and their dehumanizing, socially catastrophic

32 Doll, Dina Sayegh. (2021, October 26). Criminal justice reform requires bolstering the public defender. *Bloomberg Law*.

33 Rapping, Jonathan. (2020). *Gideon's promise* (p. 98). Boston: Beacon Press.

consequences. These role-reversal programs, which would require intensive training and a sophisticated form of job shadowing initially, could be started on a pilot, voluntary basis.

The benefits of switching from the prosecutor role to the defense role are illustrated in David Dischley's career. In his *New York Times* article, Dischley acknowledges that as a prosecutor "I thought people who committed crimes should have considered the consequences of their actions beforehand."[34] But in his role as a defense lawyer, he is driven by the insight that some people "just made a mistake." As he explains, "good people can find themselves in bad situations, and we need to consider how to help them." He finds that "working in a job so diametrically opposed to my previous work has helped me to grow."

Second, district attorneys and public defenders have to relinquish their adversarial roles in the treatment of the mentally ill defendants who now constitute 30–50 percent of arrestees. The National Judicial Task Force to Examine State Court's Responses to Mental Illness spent two years studying state court systems and has issued recommendations including "diverting individuals with mental illnesses to treatment, reforming the competency to stand trial system, changing civil commitment laws, training judges and court professionals on trauma and behavioral health and collecting data on cases involving individuals with mental illnesses."[35] Prosecutors and public defenders should move rapidly to adopt and implement the task force's recommendations. The current practice of incarcerating mentally ill defendants is a ghoulish enterprise that will eventually be ranked among the nation's most extensive and least defensible tragedies.

Law schools

Law schools play a large role in maintaining our dysfunctional legal system. They have a distressing record of undervaluing altruism in the admissions process, minimizing public service and access to justice in their learning outcomes, and downplaying public service throughout three years of instruction. That record is extensive: students graduating from the most prestigious law schools are as unlikely to be employed in public interest jobs as students

34 Dischley, David. (2011, December 24). First a prosecutor, now a defense lawyer. *The New York Times*. For an introduction to the benefits of role reversal see Johnson, David. (1971). Effectiveness of role reversal: Actor or listener. *Psychological Reports*, *28*(1), 275. Stark, James H., & Frenkel, Douglas N. (2013). Changing minds: The work of mediators and empirical studies of persuasion. *Ohio State Journal on Dispute Resolution*, *28*, 263.

35 Martinson, Sarah. (2022, October 26). Courts urged to work with states to address mental illness. *Law 360*.

graduating from the least prestigious schools.[36] Law schools seem to be disconnected from the principle that, as expressed by D.C. Circuit Judge David Tatel, "the legal profession has a special obligation here because we have a monopoly on the practice of law, and I think with that monopoly, we have an obligation to make sure the legal system works for everyone."[37]

While overlooking or minimizing the importance of altruism and public service, many law schools may be contributing to their students' mental distress. Fifty percent of law students report that they have experienced depression "because of law school."[38] Seventy-five percent "reported increased anxiety because of law school-related issues," and 23 percent believe that law school caused them to increase their alcohol usage. Most law students feel that their well-being has "slightly worsened" or "significantly worsened." The percentage of law students reporting that their well-being has "significantly worsened" is higher among female, nonbinary, and Black students.

Law schools generally give nominal weight to altruism in the admissions process, preferring to emphasize factors like LSAT scores and GPAs that directly affect their U.S. News and World Report law school rankings. The law school admissions process differs from that of medical school admissions committees, which "seek out applicants who they believe will choose altruism as a guiding principle in their careers."[39] Dr. Mikel Snow, associate dean for admissions and students at the University of Wisconsin Medical School, describes the importance of altruism in medical school applicants:

> The admission committee . . . is trying to project whether the applicant will always and foremost put the patients' and community's needs above his or her own when he or she becomes a physician. This selflessness manifests itself in the practicing physician in many different ways, from business relationships with referral partners, conflicts of interest from investments, responses to incentives provided by drug and equipment manufacturers,

36 For law schools ranked in the upper 20 percent by *U.S. News & World Report*, the percentage of graduating law students reporting employment in the public interest sector is, on average, 8.23 percent. For law schools ranked in the lower 20 percent, the percentage of graduating law students reporting employment in the public interest sector is, on average, 7.27 percent. The average student debt load for these two cohorts is $120,694 and $124,466, respectively. See charts included in Charnosky, Christine. (2023, December 15). 2023 go-to law schools: For judicial clerkships, government and public interest jobs, small schools reign. *The American Lawyer*. For student debt loads, see data reported by law schools and summarized at lawschooltransparency.com.

37 Knezevich, Alison. (2023, July 21). Judge Tatel on returning to his pro bono roots. *Law 360*.

38 The data in this paragraph appears in Blaemire, Jessica R. (2023, February 3). Analysis: Well-being in law school—law students aren't OK. *Bloomberg Law*. See Jaffe, David. (2023, May 17). Law schools should take on students' mental health and substance use from day one. *ABA Journal*.

39 Vearrier, *supra* note 7 at 149.

> willingness to volunteer for free medical clinics, etc. The list is endless and the potential for conflicts of interest is similarly pervasive. In the admission process, the interest is not just in whether the applicant will succumb to one specific temptation, but whether he or she will choose altruism as a guiding principle in most situations, if not all.[40]

Medical schools conduct interviews to determine whether applicants are sincerely and consistently altruistic. They have been innovative in developing Multiple Mini Interviews (MMIs) to assess applicants' judgment, self-awareness, empathy, maturity, and other traits in scenarios replicating clinical conditions. MMIs typically last two hours and consist of eight to twelve stations with problem-based prompts and different interviewers/assessors at each station. Law schools, in contrast, infrequently invest resources in conducting interviews and generally limit their evaluations to test scores, GPAs, letters of recommendation, and other materials submitted by the applicants. If an interview occurs, it is likely to be conducted by phone or video and lacks the sophistication, comprehensiveness, and reliability of MMIs. Not surprisingly, these different processes for selecting who will enter a profession yield different types of professionals.

Since medical school admissions committees prioritize altruism, the medical profession is comprised of physicians scoring relatively high on altruism assessments. In one study, for instance, physicians were twice as likely as the general population and elite groups (people with graduate degrees and +$100,000 annual household income) to place others' interests above their own. The finding that "physicians are on average more altruistic than others suggests that physician professionalism is not merely a self-serving myth," the researchers concluded. "Rather, it suggests that many physicians will likely put patients first in the many important areas of care in which their performance is not rewarded financially and likely cannot be measured."[41]

Physicians' altruistic propensities contrast sharply with attorneys in large law firms whose lowest score, relative to a comparison sample of professionals and managers, was on altruism.[42] Diminished altruism also was demonstrated in a study of Yale Law School students. They "were less likely to be classified as fair-minded and more likely to be classified as selfish"

40 Albanese, Mark A., et al. (2003, March). Assessing personal qualities in medical school admissions. *Academic Medicine*, *78*(3), 317.

41 Li, Jing, et al. (2022). Experimental evidence of physician social preference. *Proceedings of the National Academy of Sciences*, *119*(208), e2112726119.

42 Foster, Jeff, et al. (2010). Understanding lawyers: Why we do the things we do. *Hildebrandt Baker Robbins*.

than the general population.[43] The researchers also discovered that students' preference for efficiency (maximizing personal financial outcomes) or equality (reducing disparities in financial outcomes among individuals) predicted their career choices. "More efficiency-focused behavior in the laboratory was associated with a greater likelihood of choosing private sector employment after graduation," the researchers state, "whereas more equality-focused behavior was associated with a greater likelihood of choosing nonprofit sector employment."

Consistent with the low weight accorded to altruism in their admissions criteria, law schools disregard or minimize the importance of altruism in their learning outcomes. Although 187 law schools have posted learning outcomes, only 23 schools include "public service," and only 21 cite "access to justice."[44] Fewer than one in five law schools identify "pro bono" service or work as a learning objective or performance criteria. "Client service," "community service," and "fiduciary duties" are specified as learning objectives by two percent of the law schools, and "public interest" merits inclusion by one percent. Absent a serious effort to incorporate the legal profession's "ideals of public service" into their curricula and learning objectives, most law schools are sending a defeatist message to altruistic students: public service is neither important nor encouraged.

Law students do lose their interest in public service between their first day of classes and graduation. An early study found that most first year law students identified altruistic goals among their three major reasons for entering law school; but in their third year "only 2 percent indicated a preference for legal aid jobs and only 5 percent were still considering public interest jobs."[45] A recent study indicates that 49 percent of the law students who start law school intending to practice public interest law change their career goals by the third year of law school.[46] This "public interest drift" is consistent with Krieger and Sheldon's studies of law schools' detrimental

43 Quotations in this paragraph appear in Fisman, Raymond, et al. (2015, September 25). The distributional preferences of an elite. *Science*.

44 Data in this paragraph is derived from the University of St. Thomas' database of United States Law School Learning Outcomes, as updated in November 2023. https://law.stthomas.edu/about/centers-institutes/holloran-center/learning-outcomes-database/index.html.

45 Granfield, Robert. (1992). *Making elite lawyers: Visions of law at Harvard and beyond* (p. 48). New York: Routledge, Chapman and Hall. (Quoted in Albiston, Catherine, et al. (2020). Making public interest lawyers in a time of crisis: An evidence-based approach. *Georgetown Journal of Legal Ethics*, *34*(2), 235).

46 The State Bar of California. (2019). Public interest drift: Findings from the 2019 California law student survey, p. 4.

effects and the transformation of students' values, ethics, and interests. Their study revealed

> shifts from helping and community-oriented values to extrinsic, rewards-based values in the first year; similar shifts in motivation for becoming lawyers, from salutary internal purposes (for interest, enjoyment, and meaning) to more superficial and external reasons (such as for financial rewards, recognition, or to impress or please others); and decreases in values of all kinds after the first year, suggesting generalized demoralization or loss of personal purpose. . . . As expected, the data also showed that students beginning law school with the most internal motivations and intrinsic values earned higher grades, but we also found that those students then shifted to more external (money-oriented) job preferences.[47]

The personal devolution documented by Krieger and Sheldon is in stark contrast to the medical school curriculum's emphasis on altruism and correlated personality characteristics. As medical school professor Mark Albanese explains, "With a culture that values altruism and faculty who demonstrate altruism always and foremost, it is conceivable that students might be nurtured into becoming altruistic physicians. Further, if people mature at different rates, those at earlier stages of development may be even more likely to be affected by an altruistic culture."[48] The concept of law professors demonstrating altruism "always and foremost" is so far removed from contemporary pedagogy that law students probably would be perplexed and disoriented by the abrupt change.

The denigration of altruism in law schools is a serious breach of their obligation to inculcate professionalism in law students. It also disregards attorneys' responsibilities for public service in a democratic society. The overall effect, critics conclude, is to pull law students "away from altruistic, public interest goals" and shift their values from a "justice-oriented consciousness" to a "game-oriented consciousness."[49] In the short-term, law schools can start to correct these deficiencies and biases by explicitly including altruism in the criteria for law school admissions; adopting systems to identify and promote altruistic applicants in the admissions process; incorporating

47 Krieger & Sheldon, *supra* note 17 at 566. Their study is described in Sheldon, Kennon M., & Krieger, Lawrence S. (2004). Does legal education have undermining effects on law students? Evaluating changes in motivation, values, and well-Being. *Behavioral Sciences and the Law*, 22, 261.

48 Albanese, *supra* note 40 at 318.

49 Mertz, Elizabeth. (2007). *The language of law school* (p. 98). New York: Oxford University Press.

altruism in learning outcomes and performance criteria; integrating altruism into the curriculum; and employing a method of instruction that consistently encourages public service careers, pro bono work, and client service.

Law schools are pivotal in elevating altruistic values and encouraging public service careers among law students. As economist Raymond Fisman noted in his study of the Yale Law School students who were more selfish and less fair-minded than the general population, they will "exert considerable influence over public and private policy in the United States today" and "will have a large and highly disproportionate impact on the future of the country as a whole."[50] Unless the power eventually exercised by law students is tempered with altruism engendered throughout law schools, both the legal profession's mental health crisis and society's dysfunctional legal system will continue to intensify.

Perspective

Historians may well conclude that the U.S. legal profession—lawyers, judges, law firms, state bar associations, and law schools—has been sleepwalking through the last 50 years. The profession seems largely unaffected by the chronic inequities of the civil and criminal legal systems and the abysmal ranking of those systems among other industrialized countries. Like sleepwalkers, many legal professionals are performing complex, directed tasks but cannot be fully aroused. Although their eyes are open, they exhibit reduced levels of consciousness and lack awareness of their surroundings. In this state of "disassociated arousal," partly asleep and partly awake, sleepwalkers can describe their motivations and the reasons for their activities. But as sleepwalking expert Antonio Zadra notes, their behaviors "make little sense," and their explanations have "neither the logic nor the judgment typical of wakefulness."[51]

50 Fisman, *supra* note 43.

51 (2018, September 7). Sleepwalking brains. *Science Update*. www.scienceupdate.com/2018/09/sleepwalking-brains-3/. American Association for the Advancement of Science. (2013, March 14). Sleepwalkers sometimes remember what they've done. *EurekAlert!* www.eurekalert.org/news-releases/805489. See Zadra, Antonio, et al. (2013, March). Somnambulism: Clinical aspects and pathophysiological hypotheses. *The Lancet Neurology*, *12*(3), 285.

9

CONCLUSION

The story of American lawyers and law firms is sordid and inspirational, egregious and heroic. At times, it mirrors the expediency and greed of an elite class of professionals obsessed with wealth and disenfranchised from ordinary citizens. At other times, it mirrors the aspirations and achievements of magnanimous, principled attorneys dedicated to the rule of law and the vindication of human rights. Since the legal profession lacks a unifying concept of achievement and professionalism, lawyers' attitudes, values, and actions range from idiosyncratic to antagonistic. The profession pits defenders of status against advocates of equality, adherents of precedent against advocates of reform, masters of procedural advantage against protectors of substantive rights, and instruments of harassment against models of civility. In this legal system driven by avarice, altruism, sophistry, and integrity, lawyers' roles and motivations are kinetic, and clients' freedoms, reputations, and assets are saved and forfeited every minute.

In their darker moments, lawyers like William Cromwell—the "silver-tongued business lawyer from Brooklyn" who co-founded the esteemed Sullivan & Cromwell law firm in 1879—have "taught the robber barons how to rob."[1] In their more enlightened moments, lawyers like Jim Sandman, President Emeritus of the Legal Services Corporation, have advocated for equal justice and access to the courts. "We can't afford to tolerate the continued degradation of justice to the detriment of the disadvantaged," argues Sandman. "We can't afford to default on the vision of our founders and on the foundational and

1 Oller, John. (2019). *White shoe* (pp. 4, 25). New York: Dutton.

DOI: 10.4324/9781003514848-9

foremost of their values."[2] As these divergent models of lawyers' role indicate, the American legal system, like its entire society, rests on fractured views of justice, fairness, propriety, and privilege.

A deep cynicism and despair pervade the legal system and lawyers' thoughts. Anthony Kronman, the former dean of Yale Law School, describes this as a "crisis of morale," undermining lawyers' belief that their work has meaning and threatening their sense of fulfillment. This crisis, Kronman explains, "is the product of growing doubts about the capacity of a lawyer's life to offer fulfillment to the person who takes it up. Disguised by the material well-being of lawyers, it is a spiritual crisis that strikes at the heart of their professional pride."[3] This crisis, caused largely by the loss of meaning and the substitution of cynicism, has thrown many lawyers into a cycle of ever-increasing extrinsic rewards followed by a debilitating sense of disappointment and disillusionment when those extrinsic rewards fail to provide personal fulfillment. As one lawyer described his feelings after being promoted to partnership, "It's like wading through treacle [thick, sticky liquid] to get to the promised land and finding that in the promised land there is just more treacle. . . . I was expecting a huge change but actually when you get there, it's much of a muchness and I'm paid more money, but nothing has changed."[4]

Altruism could overcome lawyers' cynicism, lack of meaning, and inability to achieve intrinsic fulfillment. But, despite the proven mental health and societal benefits from altruism, many lawyers do not believe that altruism exists. Since they deny the existence of altruism and altruistic motives, they neither see others' altruistic actions nor act pro-socially themselves.[5] In their minds, others' actions are always driven by extrinsic motives like money, status, and publicity. This deep cynicism leads to a dispiriting passivity and amorality, gutting motivation and corroding well-being. It encourages attorneys to denigrate or neglect altruistic behavior that would simultaneously aid society and enhance their own well-being. The risk of falling into this conundrum of denying altruistic motives and not seeing altruism when it is evident

2 Sandman, Jim. (2019, September 10). LSC President Emeritus, Jim Sandman answers the question, "What is Legal Aid?" *American Bar Association Annual Meeting*, August 9, 2019. www.youtube.com/watch?v=caAZcpU_XM4.

3 Kronman, Anthony T. (1993). *The lost lawyer* (p. 2). Cambridge, MA: The Belknap Press of Harvard University Press.

4 Gustafsson, Stefanie, & Karreman, Dan. (2023). Emotions careers: The interplay between careers and emotions in professional organizations. *Human Resource Management Journal*, *2023*, 1.

5 Carlson, Ryan W., & Zaki, Jamil. (2022, August). Belief in altruistic motives predicts prosocial actions and inferences. *Psychological Reports*, *125*(4), 291.

to others might be particularly troublesome for large law firm lawyers who scored above average on cynicism and below average on altruism.[6]

The recognition and practice of altruism are also threatened by heightened status, power, and affluence—a phenomenon that usually accompanies attorneys' career successes. Although more prestige and money, in theory, could make people more attentive, generous, and kind, these extrinsic rewards generally result in lower levels of empathy, concern, perspective-taking, benevolence, and altruism.[7] As psychology professor Dacher Keltner explains, "when we are feeling powerful, we are moved more by our own experiences than by those of other people. The shift in attention brought about by power—from others to ourselves—costs us in terms of being moved by others' inspiring acts."[8] Power inevitably undermines our well-being, Keltner concludes, because "it diminishes perhaps the strongest, most reliable source of meaning and happiness in life: empathy, compassion, gratitude, and elevation and the acts of altruism they inspire."

If we open ourselves to being moved by "others' inspiring acts," as Keltner urges, we might spend a few moments looking at judge Harry Pregerson's life. He was born in unincorporated East Los Angeles in 1923. The son of Ukrainian Jewish immigrants, Pregerson grew up in a Depression-era community of Japanese, Italian, Irish, Eastern European, and Mexican-American residents. "I remember going to school with kids who didn't have shoes," Pregerson recalled. "I thought, 'Somebody needs to help them.'"[9]

Pregerson served as a U.S. Marine Lieutenant in World War II, sustaining severe gunshot wounds to both legs in the Battle of Okinawa in 1945.[10] He received a Purple Heart, the nation's oldest active military award, for those injuries. After the war ended, he completed his undergraduate education at the University of California, Los Angeles; graduated from Berkeley Law in 1950; and worked as an attorney in private practice until his appointment as

6 Foster, Jeff, et al. (2010). Understanding lawyers: Why we do the things we do. *Hildebrandt Baker Robbins.*

7 See Hogeveen, Jeremy, et al. (2014). Power changes how the brain responds to others. *Journal of Experimental Psychology: General*, *143*(2), 755. Huber, Giedre Lideikyte, & Pittavino, Marta. (2022). Who donates and how? New evidence on the tax incentives in the canton of Geneva, Switzerland. *Journal of Empirical Legal Studies*, *19*, 758. Useem, Jerry. (2017, July/August). Power causes brain damage. *The Atlantic*.

8 Dacher Keltner's quotations appear in Keltner, Dacher. (2016). *The power paradox* (pp. 215, 216). New York: Penguin Press.

9 Southwestern Law School. *Judge Harry Pregerson public service legal programs; more about the late Judge Harry Pregerson*. www.swlaw.edu/experiential-learning/public-service-programs/judge-harry-pregerson-public-service-legacy-programs.

10 Doyan, Kristen, & Wast, Gabrielle. (2021, January 26). 9th Circuit cowboy: The story of a true public servant. *Juris*.

a state court judge in 1965. He was appointed to the federal bench in 1967 and to the U.S. Court of Appeals in 1979.

During the confirmation hearing for the appeals court, Senator Alan Simpson asked him, "If a decision in a particular case was required by case law or statute, and yet that offended your own conscience, what might you do in that situation?"[11] Pregerson replied, "I would try and find a way to follow my conscience and do what I perceived to be right and just." He elaborated on his answer later in the hearing: "My conscience is a product of the Ten Commandments, the Bill of Rights, the Boy Scout Oath, and the Marine Corps Hymn. If I had to follow my conscience or the law, I would follow my conscience."

Throughout his judicial career, Pregerson was an advocate for veterans and a "protector of those on the margins of American society, including racial minorities, immigrants, and the poor."[12] Unlike other judges, he visited every defendant he had sentenced to prison. While serving on the appeals court, he established day care centers for federal employees' children and supervised four shelters that provided housing, food, medical care, legal assistance, job counseling, and computer training for about 3,300 homeless citizens every year.[13] These shelters were administered in conjunction with the Salvation Army, Department of Veterans Affairs, and General Services Administration. "I get so charged up coming out here," Pregerson remarked during one of his shelter visits. "I meet some of the best people I've met in my life this way."

For Pregerson, this work on behalf of veterans, parolees, and other homeless citizens was an extension of his judicial philosophy. "I looked upon being a judge as a chance to help as many people as I could through the law," Pregerson stated. "And it has given me that opportunity, no doubt about it."[14] Pregerson's daughter nicknamed him "the rescue machine," and even his detractors begrudgingly dubbed him a "thug for the Lord."

Pregerson's life crystallizes many of the concepts, values, and benefits embodied in altruism. He was, in the words of two law students who reviewed a film about his life, the definition of a public servant, "a wildly empathetic person."[15] His actions demonstrate that altruism is a host of positive emotions, convictions, and bonds that convert empathy into action. Altruistic action then

11 Quotations in this paragraph appear in Roberts, Sam. (2017, November 29). Harry Pregerson, judge guided by conscience, dies at 94. *The New York Times*.
12 (2017, November 30). Harry Pregerson, Ninth Circuit judge and friend to King Hall, dies at 94. *UC Davis School of Law News*. https://law.ucdavis.edu/news/harry-pregerson-ninth-circuit-judge-and-friend-king-hall-dies-94.
13 This description of the projects and the next quotation appear in Deutsch, Linda. (2000, March 5). Federal judge finds an extra calling as angel for the homeless. *Los Angeles Times*.
14 Quotations in this paragraph appear in Dolan, Maura. (2017, November 26). Harry Pregerson, one of the most liberal federal appeals court judges in the nation, dies at 94. *Los Angeles Times*.
15 Doyan & Wast, *supra* note 10.

becomes the ultimate expression of our moral and ethical commitments, separating in real-life dilemmas the courageous from the conforming, the principled from the pernicious, and the reliable from the rapacious.

Pregerson did not have the benefit of contemporary psychological research proving the value of altruism. His life, however, was a vibrant example of how people achieve meaningfulness through altruism. Nearly every day was, for Pregerson, an opportunity to enhance meaningfulness in the six ways modern psychologists have identified: "make people happy, connect people and contribute to others, help others identify goals and feel motivated, help others develop a sense of coherence and structure in their lives, provide financial resources that can support meaningful pursuits, and explore religious and philosophical beliefs and values that foster purpose and meaning."[16] If psychologists had built a prototype for meaningfulness and altruism, they could have modeled it after Pregerson.

Pregerson's altruism never waned. His fellow Ninth Circuit judge Marsha Berzon describes him as "a man of principle, enormous compassion, and indefatigable energy."[17] In the later years of his life, Pregerson's war injuries hampered his mobility, and he balanced himself with walking poles to visit the homeless shelters. A few days before his death in 2017, he told his son, U.S. District Court Judge Dean Pregerson, that he regretted his failing health because "the hard thing is that I don't have strength anymore to help people."[18]

Unlike Pregerson in his final days, the vast majority of attorneys and judges do have the strength to help people and change how the legal system affects their lives. For those attorneys and judges, the only serious barrier to altruism is their own inertia and a reluctance to acknowledge that public service is both a pathway to well-being and a professional imperative. Their choices are epitomized in class action litigator Elizabeth Cabraser's thoughts on justice: "I think what's compelling to judges and lawyers and everyone who does the law for a living is that justice is an unfinished project. It won't be finished in our lifetime. You can look at it in two ways. One is: Why bother? The other is: This is fabulous—I have a life's work."[19] As we have seen throughout this book, the choice between those two options is largely determinative of well-being and social value. If attorneys and judges lack wisdom in making those choices, the autonomy that society grants to them will be retracted because democratic societies cannot entrust their legal systems to emotionally unhealthy, socially neglectful legal professionals.

16 Swenson, David, et al. (2020). Stress and resiliency in the U.S. judiciary (p. 32). *Journal of the Professional Lawyer*.

17 Cohen, Andrew. (2017, November 30). Longtime federal appeals court judge Harry Pregerson '50 dies at 94. *Berkeley Law Alumni News*.

18 Dolan, *supra* note 14.

19 (2017, June 14). Top plaintiff lawyers. *Daily Journal Supplement*, 11.

APPENDIX A

Additional studies of lawyer well-being

This Appendix summarizes studies, not reviewed in Chapter 2, regarding lawyers' well-being. These studies concern lawyers in Australia, Canada, England, France, Germany, Guernsey, Isle of Man, Jersey, New Zealand, Republic of Ireland, the United States, and Wales.

French lawyers survey (2023)

Psychologists Marion Nickum and Pascale Desrumaux analyzed questionnaire responses received from 181 French lawyers.[1] Their average age was 40 years, and most estimated that their average work week was 50 hours. Their mean burnout score was 4.07; a score between 3.5 and 4.4 signals the presence of burnout. Higher workloads were positively linked to burnout. Autonomy, as evidenced by control over workload and decision latitude, was negatively correlated with burnout.

Massachusetts lawyers well-being study (2023)

In this comprehensive survey of 4,450 registered and active lawyers in Massachusetts, 66 percent of respondents reported satisfaction with their lives.[2] But 77 percent reported burnout; 40 percent said they had considered leaving

1 Nickum, Marion, & Desrumaux, Pascale. (2023). Burnout among lawyers: Effects of workload, latitude and mediation via engagement and over-engagement. *Psychiatry, Psychology and Law*, *30*(3), 329.

2 The survey results appear in NORC at the University of Chicago. (2023, February 1). Lawyer well-being in Massachusetts.

the legal profession due to burnout or stress during the last three years; 26 percent reported anxiety; 21 percent reported depression; and 7 percent reported suicidal ideation. About one-half of the attorneys reporting anxiety, depression, and suicidal ideation did not seek professional assistance.

Forty-two percent of respondents met the criteria for hazardous or unhealthy alcohol use. Alcohol abuse was more prevalent among "lawyers who identify as White, do not have a disability, are earning more than $150,000 annually, or are younger, aged 24–44 compared to 45–64. Moreover, such use was more common among lawyers who identify as female than lawyers who identify as male—the reverse of the trend commonly found among the general population." Only 2 percent of the lawyers who screened for hazardous or unhealthy alcohol use sought substance use treatment.

Sixty percent of respondents had experienced vicarious trauma from their legal work. Factors correlated with vicarious trauma include annual income below $150,000; working in a litigation practice; and being female, non-White, non-heterosexual, or young (age 24–44).

New Jersey State Bar Association survey (2023)

Like the Massachusetts attorneys described previously, most of the New Jersey attorneys were satisfied with their careers.[3] Fifty-one percent of the 1,643 surveyed attorneys said that they were enthusiastic about being a lawyer. But 68 percent had experienced anxiety within the last two weeks; 23 percent displayed depressive symptoms; 10 percent reported suicidal ideation within the last two weeks; 49 percent showed moderate to high levels of burnout; and 56 percent exhibited problematic alcohol consumption. The attorneys whose firms had billable hour requirements in the 1,850–2,000 hour range were twice as likely to be problematic drinkers as the attorneys in firms with lower billable hour requirements. Twenty-eight percent of the surveyed attorneys were considering leaving the legal profession as a result of mental health problems.

The incidence of mental illness among the New Jersey lawyers was substantially higher than the incidence found in the general population:

> These lawyers reported burnout at nearly two times the level of any other working population, suicidal ideations at three times the rate of other working populations, problem drinking at six times the rate of working populations, anxiety at five times the rate of normal working populations and depression at three-and-a-half times the rate reported for other working populations.

3 The survey results appear in New Jersey State Bar Association. (2023). Putting Lawyers First Task Force: An excerpt of the report and recommendations on improving the legal profession for lawyers. New Brunswick, NJ: New Jersey State Bar Association.

Summarizing the survey results, Jeralyn Lawrence, the president of the New Jersey State Bar Association, states, "What that survey found was astonishing, scary and sad and the alarm bells are sounding."

Unmind study of U.S. large law firms (2023)

Unmind assessed well-being in six large U.S. law firms, collecting data from 3,814 participants (18 percent partners; 29 percent associates; and 53 percent professional staff).[4] It determined that associates' stress levels exceeded those of the general population, and associates were more at risk of burnout than partners and professional staff. One in four associates *dis*agreed with the statement, "I trust the senior leaders in my firm to make decisions that are in the best interests of employee mental health and wellbeing." The five factors most strongly correlated with an employee's intention to leave a law firm were low scores on "fulfillment," "psychological safety," "social wellbeing," "supervisor support," and "stress."

German lawyers study (2022)

The Liquid Legal Institute, in collaboration with Bundesverband der Unternehmensjuristen (BUJ e.V.), the largest association of German in-house counsel, and EUPD Research, a market research and consulting services company, surveyed 152 German lawyers.[5] Fifteen percent of the surveyed lawyers were "flexible lawyers," defined as lawyers working on a free-lance basis on fixed-term projects for companies or law firms.

The flexible lawyers generally reported fewer mental health problems than the non-flexible lawyers employed in conventional, salaried positions. Thirty-six percent of the flexible lawyers and 70 percent of the non-flexible lawyers, for instance, reported that they had "experienced work-related mental health problems once or several times in my professional life." Seventy-two percent of flexible lawyers and 82 percent of non-flexible lawyers believe that lawyers' mental health issues result in lower job performance.

When asked to identify the causes of mental health problems, the surveyed lawyers emphasized "long work weeks," "uncontrollable high work loads," "billing by the hour," "traditional hierarchical structures," "individualistic and competitive working style common amongst lawyers," and "lawyers are perfectionists and tend to be afraid that things go wrong." About one in four flexible lawyers and one in three non-flexible lawyers also agree that

4 Croft, Jazz, et al. (2023). *The state of wellbeing in law*. London: Unmind.
5 Jacob, Kai, et al. (2022). *Lawyer well-being: Personal health of legal professionals in times of disruption*. Ottobrunn, Germany: Liquid Legal Institute.

"occasionally having to act against one's personal moral compass in order to deliver good legal services leads to depression."

England and Wales solicitors survey (2021)

Psychologist Lucinda Soon and her colleagues surveyed 340 solicitors in England and Wales to assess their psychological health and test the validity of Self-determination Theory (SDT) in predicting lawyer well-being.[6] A plurality of respondents worked in large law firms. Soon found that, on average, the lawyers' psychological well-being was significantly below that of the general population in England. She also determined that the three basic needs identified in SDT (autonomy, competence, and relatedness) "each showed a moderate to strong, positive and significant relationship with psychological well-being." Lawyers' satisfaction of those three needs, moreover, was correlated with higher levels of mindfulness, "which in turn contributes to their well-being."

UK, Republic of Ireland, Jersey, Guernsey, and Isle of Man legal professionals study (2021)

This survey of 1,700 legal professionals in the United Kingdom, Republic of Ireland, Jersey, Guernsey and Isle of Man—most of whom worked in large law firms—reveals a high level of burnout, depression, anxiety, sleeplessness, and hazardous drinking.[7] Their average burnout score on the Oldenburg Burnout Inventory was 42.2; a score above 34.8 denotes a "high risk of burnout." The highest levels of burnout were exhibited by legal professionals between 26 and 35 years old. These professionals also reported the lowest levels of autonomy, in accord with Self-Determination Theory (SDT).

Sixty-one percent of respondents said they "had experienced anxiety either often, very often, or all of the time, over the last 12 months"; and 29 percent said they had experienced depression often, very often, or all of the time. Twenty-two percent of respondents said they were "unable to cope" with work-related stress. One in eight legal professionals had slept five hours or less, on average, each night during the last two weeks. Among the legal professionals who had consumed alcohol within the last two weeks, 35 percent consumed, on average, three or more drinks per night.

The high levels of anxiety and hazardous drinking reported in this study are generally consistent with a survey of law students at an undisclosed United

6 Soon, Lucinda, et al. (2021). The effects of basic psychological needs satisfaction and mindfulness on solicitors' well-being. *International Journal of the Legal Profession*, 29(2), 143.
7 Lawcare. (2021). Life in the law 2020/21.

Kingdom university.[8] About one-half of the law students "had a Hospital Anxiety and Depression Scale anxiety score suggestive of a possible anxiety disorder." More than two-thirds of the first- and second-year law students "had an Alcohol Use Disorders Identification Test (AUDIT) score suggestive of an alcohol use disorder." Over one-third of the first- and second-year law students "reported other substance use within the past year." On all three measures—anxiety, alcohol abuse, and other substance use—law students' average scores were considerably higher than medical students' average scores at the same university.

U.S. asylum attorney burnout and vicarious trauma study (2021)

Using well-regarded psychological assessment tools, law professor Lindsay Harris and criminology professor Hillary Mellinger evaluated the well-being of 718 asylum attorneys. They found that the attorneys' average work burnout score (63.6) on the Copenhagen Burnout Inventory was at least 18 points higher than the work burnout scores for professionals in 15 other helping professions.[9] Hospital doctors, for example, have a work burnout score of 39.8, nearly 24 points below the asylum attorneys' burnout scores.[10] The asylum attorneys also displayed exceptionally high scores on the Secondary Traumatic Stress Scale (STSS). Their average overall STSS score was 2.95, considerably higher than the mid-point of 2.5 for the STSS. Their average STSS scores also were substantially higher than those of male immigration judges (1.84) and female immigration judges (2.5).

The regression analysis reveals some factors correlated with higher and lower levels of burnout and vicarious trauma. Female attorneys and attorneys of color had higher burnout and secondary trauma scores. Factors correlated with lower burnout and secondary trauma scores included more support staff, lower caseloads, working fewer weekly hours, and being employed by an academic institution or nonprofit organization.

The extreme burnout and secondary trauma experienced by the asylum attorneys, Harris and Mellinger explain, compel many attorneys to leave the profession or at least express an intent to leave. As one attorney exclaimed,

8 Bogowicz, Paul, et al. (2018, March). Alcohol and other substance use among medical and law students at a UK university: A cross-sectional questionnaire survey. *Postgraduate Medical Journal*, *94*(1109), 131.

9 Harris, Lindsay M., & Mellinger, Hillary. (2021). Asylum attorney burnout and secondary trauma. *Wake Forest Law Review*, *56*, 733, 768. For an earlier study of asylum practitioners in England and the Republic of Ireland, see Graffin, Neil. (2019). The emotional impacts of working as an asylum lawyer. *Refugee Survey Quarterly*, *38*(1), 30.

10 Harris & Mellinger, *supra* note 9 at 768. The spread is even wider when prison wardens' average work burnout scores (32.6) are compared with the asylum attorneys' scores (63.6).

"I've lost my appetite for the law altogether after this shit show area of law. I have no faith in justice or the law anymore."[11]

Utah lawyers well-being study (2020)

Matthew Thiese, an occupational epidemiologist at the University of Utah School of Medicine, heads a research team studying lawyer well-being. Building upon seven peer-reviewed studies that indicate "some level of serious concern," his team surveyed a representative sample of Utah lawyers to assess symptoms of depression, anxiety, stress, and substance abuse.[12] The survey results show that "an alarming percentage of lawyers experience chronic stress, burnout, depression, substance abuse, and a lack of connection with peers."[13] Specific findings, as summarized in *Living Well in Law*, include:

- "48.7% reporting some level of burnout.
- 44.4% of responding lawyers report symptoms of depression.
- Utah lawyers report higher alcohol use concerns than the general working population. Criminal litigators report the highest amount.
- Utah lawyers are 5 times more likely to report thoughts of being 'better off dead or hurting themselves' as compared to the general working population.
- Lawyers in Utah are 8.5 times more likely than the general working population to report suicidal ideation."[14]

The lawyers experiencing high levels of burnout were five times more likely than other lawyers to acknowledge a problem with drug abuse.

Perhaps the most intriguing finding is that the surveyed attorneys were quite satisfied with their jobs. When asked, "All in all, how satisfied are you with your job?" 46 percent of attorneys said they were "very satisfied," and another 46 percent said they were "somewhat satisfied."[15] Considering that nearly one-half of the attorneys reported depression and burnout and their

11 Ibid at 736.

12 Thiese, Matthew S. (2020, March/April). The Utah lawyer well-being study: Preliminary results show Utah lawyers at risk. *Utah Bar Journal*, 29–30. Thiese states that the "data analysis shows an adequate distribution among gender, age, years of practice, type of practice, and geographic location. This means that the study results can be comfortably and accurately generalized to the larger Utah lawyer population."

13 Utah Community Builders & Salt Lake Chamber. (2022, April). *Living well in law* (p. 7). https://slchamber.com/living-well-in-law/. (A report published in partnership with Utah State Bar, Well-being Committee for the Legal Profession, and Utah Suicide Prevention Coalition.)

14 Ibid.

15 Thiese (2020), *supra* note 12 at 30.

incidence of suicidal ideation was 8.5 times higher than the general population, the attorneys' high job satisfaction levels are paradoxical.

The Utah lawyers' satisfaction levels suggest that many attorneys are unaware of their mental states and the effects of poor mental health on their performance. The satisfaction levels also suggest that many lawyers have distanced themselves from their mental health to meet the demands and obtain the benefits of a stressful profession. Although Thiese describes the high satisfaction levels as "areas where lawyers are doing well," another possible interpretation is that lawyers' stated satisfaction levels are so inconsistent with their self-reported mental disorders as to constitute a coping mechanism.[16]

Australian and New Zealand lawyers wellness survey (2019)

In this survey of 200 lawyers practicing in Australian and New Zealand law firms, 63 percent reported that they or someone close to them at work had experienced depression, and 85 percent had personally experienced anxiety or were close to someone at work who had experienced anxiety.[17] About one in three lawyers worked more than 45 hours per week on average.

In a later study, researchers attempted to identify the principal factors in Australian lawyers' high rates of depression, anxiety, burnout, and secondary traumatic stress.[18] After conducting structured interviews, they identified two major factors. First, lawyers are immersed in a culture of stress and overwork early in their careers. As the researchers explain, "Negative early career experiences were very common, with half of the respondents recounting experiences such as bullying and being forced to work very long hours, often for bosses described as bullies." The effects of stress and overwork were intensified because these lawyers "had not been trained in the interpersonal and personal coping skills they would need to manage relationships with clients and exposure to vicarious trauma." Second, "the culture in law" undermines lawyer well-being. The interviewed lawyers specifically referenced racism, sexual harassment, bullying, hypercriticism, poor managerial

16 Ibid.

17 Meritas. (2019). Australia and New Zealand wellness survey. An earlier study of 384 Australian lawyers found that "37% of participants displayed Moderate to Extremely Severe depressive symptoms, and 35% were a positive screen for hazardous or harmful drinking." That study also differentiated among nonbillers, lower-to-moderate billers, and high billers, finding that high billers experienced "greater demands, fewer resources and poorer psychological outcomes." Bergin, Adele J., & Jimmieson, Nerina L. (2013). Australian lawyer well-being: Workplace demands, resources, and the impact of time-billing targets. *Psychiatry, Psychology and Law*, *21*(3), 427.

18 Brady, Michelle. (2021). *Report: VLSB+C Lawyer wellbeing project*. https://lsbc.vic.gov.au/sites/default/files/2020-07/Lawyer%20Wellbeing%20report.pdf.

training, lack of support to assist with vicarious trauma, and "the cultural valuing of prestige and income generation over wellbeing."

Canadian lawyers surveys (2012), (2019)

In a survey of 1,180 members of the Canadian Bar Association, 58 percent of law lawyers said they have "personally confronted" stress/burnout; 48% have confronted anxiety; and 26% have confronted depression.[19] Thirty-nine percent of the lawyers reported working more than 50 hours in a typical week, and 61 percent said they "always" or "often" spend time working in the evenings. Thirty-five percent of the lawyers identified alcoholism as "one of the most prevalent health and wellness issues facing lawyers today."[20]

In a later survey of 2,086 lawyers practicing in Quebec, 43 percent reported a "significant" or "very significant" level of psychological distress (the two highest levels on a five-point scale).[21] Fourteen percent reported a lower ("moderate") level of psychological distress; the moderate level is "associated with a high probability of an individual experiencing an anxiety disorder or major depression in the preceding 12 months." Using the Copenhagen Burnout Inventory scale, the researchers also found that one in five lawyers qualified "as being in a burnout situation" and the primary contributors to burnout were clients and work.

U.S. attorney mental health and substance abuse survey (2016)

In the largest survey regarding attorneys' mental health and substance abuse, researchers discovered "a concerning amount of behavioral health problems among attorneys in the United States."[22] After surveying 12,825 attorneys,

19 Ipsos Reid. (2012). *Survey of lawyers on wellness issues* (p. 20). https://www.cba.org/CBAMediaLibrary/cba_na/PDFs/CBA%20Wellness%20PDFs/FINAL-Report-on-Survey-of-Lawyers-on-Wellness-Issues.pdf.

20 Ibid at 6, 8, and 18.

21 Cadieux, Nathalie, et al. (2020). *Research report: A study of the determinants of mental health in the workplace among Quebec lawyers, Phase II—2017–2019*. Research Report, Université de Sherbrooke, Business School.

22 Krill, Patrick R., et al. (2016). The prevalence of substance use and other mental health concerns among American attorneys. *Addiction Medicine*, *10*(1), 46. Yair Listokin and Raymond Noonan criticize the survey methodology in this study and other studies because "the data were not collected from a random sample of lawyers." Listokin, Yair, & Noonan, Raymond. (2021, March). Measuring lawyer well-being systematically: Evidence from the National Health Interview Survey. *Journal of Empirical Legal Studies*, *18*(1), 4, 5. Listokin & Noonan rely on the Center for Disease Control's National Health Interview Survey (NHIS), which collected data on about 1,000 lawyers between 2010 and 2017 (an average of 125 lawyers per year). The NHIS data, Listokin and Noonan report at p. 32, shows that "lawyers drink excessively at much higher rates than other groups of highly educated professionals," but

the researchers found high rates of depression and anxiety symptoms. Twenty-eight percent of the attorneys said they were experiencing depression; 19 percent were experiencing anxiety, and 23 percent were experiencing stress. Forty-six percent of the attorneys said they had concerns with depression "at some point in their career."[23] Consistent with these high rates of depression, 11 percent of the attorneys said they had experienced suicidal thoughts, and 3 percent reported self-harm behaviors.

Substance abuse among the surveyed attorneys was common. Thirty-six percent of the lawyers had scores "consistent with hazardous drinking or possible alcohol abuse or dependence."[24] Sixteen percent of the lawyers had used sedatives within the last 12 months; 6 percent had used opioids; and 5 percent had used stimulants.

The researchers noted that attorneys were fortunate in having "the greatest access to, and resources for, therapy, treatment, and other support."[25] But the attorneys' fear of damaging their reputation, the researchers caution, might prevent them from using "the resources at their disposal while working in the competitive, high-stakes environment found in many private firms."[26]

---

their "mental health resembles mental health in professions with similarly educated workers." This finding is perplexing since depressive, mood, and anxiety disorders are comorbid with alcohol abuse and dependence. See Petrakis, Ismene L., et al., (2002), "Comorbidity of alcoholism and psychiatric disorders: An overview," and other articles published in the Alcohol and Comorbid Mental Health Disorders issue of *Alcohol Research and Health*, 26(2).

23 Krill (2016), *supra* note 22 at 51.

24 Ibid at 48.

25 Ibid at 51.

26 Ibid.

APPENDIX B

Additional studies of practice setting effects

This Appendix summarizes studies, not included in Chapter 2, regarding practice setting effects.

California Lawyers Association and Washington, D.C. Bar study (2022)

In this study of 1,959 randomly selected lawyers, researchers found that (1) "lawyers working in private firms were significantly less likely to feel valued for their skill or human worth and far more likely to report feeling most valued for their productivity;" and (2) "private firm lawyers experience the worst mental and physical health."[1] Examining the effects of private firm size, they concluded that "the larger the firm, the less likely lawyers are to feel valued for their professional or human worth, and the more likely they are to feel most valued for their financial and productivity contributions and, consequently, report worse health."

University of Virginia Law School study (2019)

Law professor John Monahan and psychiatry professor Jeffrey Swanson conducted a 30-year longitudinal study of law students who graduated from the University of Virginia School of Law in 1987. As reported in their previous 20-year study ("working conditions at large private law firms emerged as a

1 Krill, Patrick R., et al. (2022). People, professionals, and profit centers: The connection between lawyer well-being and employer values. *Behavioral Sciences*, *12*, 177.

significant problem for many respondents"), they found that "working conditions at large private law firms stayed problematic."[2] Specifically, "76.7 percent of respondents working in large private law firms were either 'moderately negatively' or 'very negatively' affected by changes due to stronger stress on economic sustainability compared with 38.4 percent of respondents working in other settings [small private law firms, government, business/ financial, and other organizations]."[3]

Sheffield Legal Assessment report (2014)

Bruce MacEwen, founder of the legal consulting firm Adam Smith, Esq., and Mark Levin, co-founder of The Right Profile, LLC, a talent assessment company, studied the careers, personalities, and satisfaction levels of 973 attorneys practicing attorneys in 505 different law firms.[4] The law firms represented 96 percent of the AmLaw 50 firms and 83 percent of the AmLaw 100 firms. MacEwen and Levin found that attorneys in the largest law firms (501+ attorneys) reported the lowest levels of career satisfaction in intellectual challenge, social impact, work/life balance, and overall satisfaction. Attorneys in the smallest firms (1–25 attorneys) reported the highest levels of satisfaction in all four categories.

2 Monahan, John, & Swanson, Jeffrey. (2009). Lawyers at mid-career: A 20-year longitudinal study of job and life satisfaction. *Journal of Empirical Legal Studies*, *6*(3), 451. Monahan, John, & Swanson, Jeffrey. (2019, March). Lawyers at the peak of their careers: A 30-year longitudinal study of job and life satisfaction. *Journal of Empirical Legal Studies*, *16*(1), 4.

3 Monahan & Swanson (2019), *supra* note 2 at 18–19.

4 Levin, Mark, & MacEwen, Bruce. (2014). Assessing lawyer traits & finding a fit for success: Introducing the Sheffield Legal Assessment. https://attorneyassessment.com/wp-content/uploads/2020/04/Attorney-Trait-Assessment-Study-Whitepaper.pdf.

INDEX

Note: Page numbers in *italics* indicate figures